God's Word and the Church's Council:

Vatican II and Divine Revelation

Edited by

Mark O'Brien OP

Christopher Monaghan CP

Vatican II Series

Vatican II Series

1. *Openings to Renewal: letters to the Church*, Peter Cullinane, 2011.

2. *My Journal of the Council*, Yves Congar OP, translated by Mary John Ronayne OP and Mary Cecily Boulding OP. English translation Editor, Denis Minns OP, 2012

3. *Vatican Council II: Reforming Liturgy*, edited by Carmel Piltcher, David Orr and Elizabeth Harrington, 2013.

God's Word and the Church's Council:

Vatican II and Divine Revelation

Edited by

Mark O'Brien OP

Christopher Monaghan CP

ATF Theology
Adelaide

2014

Text copyright © 2014 remains with the individual authors for all papers in this collection.

All rights reserved. Except for any fair dealing permitted under the Copyright Act, no part of this book may be reproduced by any means without prior permission. Inquiries should be made to the publisher.

National Library of Australia Cataloguing-in-Publication entry (pbk)

Title: God's word and the church's council : Vatican II and divine revelation / Mark Alan O'Brien, Christopher John Monaghan, editors.

ISBN: 9781922239723 (paperback)
9781922239754 (hardback)
9781922239730 (ebook : pdf)
9781922239747 (ebook : kindle)

Series: Vatican II.

Notes: Includes index.

Subjects: Catholic Church--Liturgy.
Vatican Council (2nd : 1962-1965 : Basilica di San Pietro in Vaticano)

Other Authors/Contributors:
Monaghan, Christopher J., editor.
O'Brian, Mark, editor.

Dewey Number: 262.5

Cover design by Astrid Sengkey
Layout/Artwork by Anna Dimasi

Text Minion Pro Size 11

Published by:

An imprint of the ATF Ltd.
PO Box 504
Hindmarsh, SA 5007
ABN 90 116 359 963
www.atfpress.com

CONTENTS

Foreword
  Mark Coleridge vii

Introduction
  Mark O'Brien OP and Christopher Monaghan CP

1. *Dei Verbum* and Revelation
   Gerald O'Collins SJ, AC 1

2. Vatican II and 'The Study of the Sacred Page' as
   'The Soul of Theology' (*Dei Verbum* 24)
   Francis J Moloney SDB 19

3. Scripture and Tradition in the Patristic Age
   Denis P Minns OP 41

4. 'I handed on to you what I also received' (1 Cor 15:3)
   The Scripture-Tradition Connection/Controversy
   Dianne Bergant CSA 55

5. 'The Unity of the Whole of Scripture'
   Justin Taylor SM 69

6. *Dei Verbum*: Literary Forms and Vatican II—
   An Old Testament Perspective
   Antony F Campbell SJ 87

7. *Dei Verbum* and the Witness of Creation:
   Reading Ecclesiastes 3:9–22 Ecologically
   Marie Turner 101

8. A Review and Assessment of the Church's
   Engagement with Historical Critical Analysis
   of the New Testament as outlined in *Dei Verbum*
   Jerome Murphy-O'Connor OP 113

9.	Breaking Open the Word: The Legacy of *Dei Verbum* *Elizabeth Dowling RSM*	135
10.	Translating Biblical Texts Within an Ecclesial Context *Dale Launderville OSB*	149
11.	*Dei Verbum*, Communication and Media *Peter Malone MSC*	163
12.	*Dei Verbum* and the Philosophy of Hans-Georg Gadamer *John F Owens SM*	179
13.	Where do we Go From Here? The Future of Catholic Biblical Studies in the Wake of Vatican II *Donald Senior CP*	193
14.	History as Bulwark, Bridge and Bulldozer: *Dei Verbum* and Ecumenical, Biblical Endeavour *Alan Cadwallader*	207

List of Contributors	225
Biblical Index	231
Citations from *Dei Verbum*	234
Index of Names and Subjects	235

Foreword

Christians are sometimes included among the People of the Book. This is not quite true, or at least it is not true of Christians in the way it is of Jews and Muslims. Christianity takes the Bible very seriously, but that does not make it a religion of the Book. However important the Bible may be for Christians, it does not have the same status for them as the Tanak does for Judaism or the Koran for Islam. This is because Christianity is a religion of the Word rather than the Book. The figure of Jesus crucified and risen occupies the wholly central place that the Tanak does for Judaism and the Koran for Islam. Jesus is the Word made flesh, and that is the mystery which lies at the heart of Christianity. This was never clearer than when the Fathers of the Second Vatican Council voted overwhelmingly in favour of *Dei Verbum*, the Dogmatic Constitution on Divine Revelation, one of the four great Constitutions which underpin the teaching and legacy of the Council.

The Constitution had a rocky road towards the final approval fifty years ago. In introducing the schema on Revelation, Cardinal Ottaviani admitted that it was open to criticism and that there was room for improvement. What he did not countenance, however, was outright rejection of the schema. But that is what he got. It was Cardinal Liénart of Lille who led the charge, declaring that the schema was 'a cold scholastic formula, while revelation is a supreme gift of God—God speaking directly to us'. Cardinal Frings of Cologne followed suit, complaining that 'what is even worse than the presentation is the doctrine itself'. By this he meant the schema's presentation of two sources of revelation, Scripture and Tradition. Cardinal Ruffini of Palermo disagreed with Liénart and Frings, but he did concede that the Council was 'faced with a question of extreme importance', indeed, he said, 'the heart and centre of the Council'. It was the French Bishop Schmitt who insisted that 'all revelation comes in the person of Christ, for he is the author, the Word of God' and that was the view which carried the day. There were not two sources of revelation but only one, and that was Jesus Christ himself. 'Let us not', Schmitt went on, 'reduce Christian revelation and Christianity itself to a kind of ideology ... something purely intellectual': to which most of the Fathers said, 'Hear, hear!' At that point, the original schema was dead in the water and we were on the way to *Dei Verbum*.

The Constitution also had a considerable pre-history. Its immediate antecedent was Pope Pius XII's Encyclical Letter, *Divino Afflante Spiritu* (1943). The Encyclical came against the background of the Modernist crisis which had seen the Catholic Church question and at times condemn approaches to biblical study that had emerged in the nineteenth century in the wake of the Enlightenment. Now the Pope opened to approaches which would come to be known as the historical-critical method, and this gave fresh impetus to Catholic biblical studies in the years leading up to the Council. In other words, *Dei Verbum* did not come out of nowhere. It had a quite particular past and, as the last fifty years have shown, it would have a future unforeseeable when the final vote was taken in St Peter's.

Since the Council, *Dei Verbum* has worked powerfully to ensure that Catholic biblical studies have flourished in every way, with Catholic scholars leading the charge as the long-regnant historical-critical method has given way to a range of other approaches without ever disappearing from the field. Perhaps the best known and most acute critic of the historical-critical method has been Pope Benedict XVI, who for many years has insisted on the essentially theological character of biblical interpretation and the essentially biblical character of theological investigation. This was never more evident than when he intervened personally in the Synod of Bishops on the Word of God in the Life and Mission of the Church (2008), with strong traces of those interventions found in the Post-Synodal Exhortation, *Verbum Domini*. That Synod marked the definitive reception of *Dei Verbum* in the Catholic Church. It also made clear that the Church, as it looks to a new season of mission, must become a more biblical Church if it is to become a more missionary Church.

In the end, the purpose of the Second Vatican Council was to equip and empower the Church to become not only more missionary but missionary in new ways at a time when we could no longer simply put up a sign saying 'Business as Usual'. The Church would become more missionary and missionary in new ways only if it encountered in new and deeper ways the Word of God, the Word made flesh, not just in the Scripture but certainly there.

It is important that Catholics see the encounter with the Word of God not just as one among many elements of the Christian life but as the matrix of all elements. It is within this context that the Bible is to be read, studied and prayed. Not just individuals or individual communities within the Church but the whole Church has to allow the Bible to become a place of privileged encounter with the Word made flesh. This means an experience of the Bible not just as a document from the past but as a living voice here and now, the voice of Christ himself who is never 'once upon a time' but always presence and power here and now as the Lord risen from the dead. In hearing that living voice as we read, study and pray the Bible is to allow all the elements of Scripture—stories and metaphors above all—to shape our heart and mind and soul. It is to allow those elements to open our eye to see the world, the Church and ourselves with the eye of God. At that point, we are properly equipped for mission.

That was what the Council and its Constitution on Divine Revelation were all about; and it is, I hope, what this volume is all about. It is the work of different people, all of whom are children of the Council in ways both personal and professional; and we owe them a deep debt of gratitude. In its own way, may this book too be a text which has power in the Church to lead us beyond a seductive introversion to the new kind of engagement to which the Bible, like the Council, is calling us now.

+ Mark Coleridge
Archbishop of Brisbane
April 2014

Introduction

Mark O'Brien OP and Christopher Monaghan CP

The fiftieth anniversary of the Second Vatican Council's Dogmatic Constitution on Divine Revelation (*Dei Verbum*) is an opportune time to look back and to look forward: to see what it achieved and how it has contributed to the life of the post-conciliar Church. This volume provides critical reflections on these aspects of *Dei Verbum* by authors from around the world. In inviting their contributions a primary aim has been to see how the Council took up the challenge of the interpretation and use of the Bible in the modern world and the course it chartered for the future. The authors write from the perspective of their respective disciplines: while the majority are biblical scholars, others comment on the document and its impact in relation to theology, liturgy, philosophy, in particular hermeneutics, and communications media.

One of the major developments in modern study of the Bible has been historical-critical analysis, the examination of biblical texts within their historical contexts (the world behind the text). The Council sought to forge a relationship between this approach and more traditional forms of analysis. Readers will find reflections on this endeavour in several of the book's chapters.

A number of other chapters are devoted to questions that arise from critical study of the Bible and its relationship to Church Tradition. The book's contributors have singled out in particular the question of the unity and diversity of Scripture, the hermeneutical principles that operate in the interpretation of texts in general, the need to make accurate translations available to the wider Church, and ecumenical cooperation in the study of the Scriptures.

Dei Verbum could not of course resolve all issues and a number of these continue to be debated, for example the nature of inspiration, the inerrancy of the inspired Word, and the relationship of the historical-critical method to other methods that have emerged since the Second Vatican Council and that focus more on the context of the reader (the world in front of the text).

As part of the living tradition of the Church *Dei Verbum* is a work-in-progress. In recognition of this there are chapters that consider the ways the Church has continued to address questions concerning the interpretation of the Bible, as is evident in the ongoing work of the Pontifical Biblical Commission, as well as a number of official Church Documents, in particular Benedict XVI's *Verbum Domini*.

The remainder of the Introduction provides a concise, but we hope informative, summary of the contribution of each author.

Chapter 1:
Gerald O'Collins,
'*Dei Verbum* and Revelation'

O'Collins begins with the principle for interpreting conciliar texts that was articulated in 1985 at the Extraordinary Synod of Bishops, namely, that each of the documents needs to be interpreted in the light of all the others. The second principle enunciated at the Synod was that the four major Constitutions of the Council provide the hermeneutical key for all the other Conciliar degrees and declarations. It is suggested that of the major Constitutions promulgated at the Second Vatican Council *Dei Verbum* takes primacy of place, and that the self-revelation of God in Christ provides the primary key for understanding all the documents of the Council. *Dei Verbum* is not examined in isolation and the chapter makes a significant contribution by indicating how themes undeveloped in *Dei Verbum* were treated in other conciliar documents. As an eminent theologian who has studied these documents for some decades O'Collins is ideally placed to evaluate the document and identify its strengths and deficiencies.

The first section of the chapter examines six clear themes about God's revelation that are developed within the document. The next section explores the category of 'experience' that is argued to be 'introduced sparingly' in *Dei Verbum*. O'Collins suggests that the suspicion that had crept into the Church regarding human experience was cautiously addressed in *Dei Verbum* and further developed in the decades that followed.

In the last section O'Collins treats four themes left untouched by *Dei Verbum*, namely, (1) who are the human beings addressed by God's self-disclosure, (2) why human beings should accept this revelation of God, (3) the relationship of revelation to the 'other' who has not heard the Christian message and (4) the call for the Council to heed the signs of the times.

This chapter is a thoughtful engagement with the strengths and weaknesses of *Dei Verbum* and it undoubtedly makes its own valuable contribution from a theological perspective.

Chapter 2:
Francis J Moloney,
'Scripture as the Soul of Theology'

This chapter explores the relationship between Scripture and theology that *Provindentissimus Deus* (On the Study of Holy Scripture) and *Divino Afflante Spirito* (Inspired by the Holy Spirit) anticipated and was subsequently treated in *Dei Verbum*. Moloney argues that the Biblical text can nourish theological reflection, indeed it must, as theology and Scripture relate restlessly to the 'Great Story' that has the potential to generate energy for on-going study. An unresolved tension in *Dei Verbum* was the relationship of Scripture and Tradition and Moloney rightly notes that studying the sacred page and developing a relevant theology in a time of change is a significant challenge.

The chapters of Dowling and Moloney both draw attention to the ways in which the search for objectivity in biblical interpretation is now somewhat moderated and how it is customary to pay attention to the worlds behind, within, and in front of the text. A consequence of this is that exegetes must work together with theologians providing interpretations focussing on both the subjective and culturally conditioned elements of a given text.

Moloney suggests that the focus on the world in front of the text runs the danger of detaching the text from its original context and setting. While it is true that no single interpretation can claim ultimate truth Moloney explores what it might mean to read the text from within a tradition, and in particular, from the point of view of faith. The Bible has shaped the modern reader, at the same time our present context also shapes the modern interpreter of biblical texts. This chapter suggests that the task of the interpreter of the Bible is to be a place where worlds meet and horizons merge.

For the Catholic tradition the Bible is our 'Great Story', the house we live in. Moloney suggests that Scripture is always founding the house and that the theologian is constructing and watching over the house. There is a tension, and there should be, since neither the theologian nor the exegete should resolve the restlessness and the tension that is part and parcel of the messiness of the incarnation.

Chapter 3:
Denis P Minns,
'Scripture and Tradition in the Patristic Age'

The relationship between Scripture and Tradition was an intensely debated issue at the Council. Factors fueling it were the Reformation doctrine of '*Sola Scriptura*' (Scripture alone), modern scientific analysis of Scripture and its critique of 'traditional' readings, and debates within the Catholic tradition itself. To reassess their relationship the Council advocated a 'return to the sources', namely the early church and its teaching. As Minns notes in his introduction, such a well-intentioned recourse was likely to be coloured by 'polemical pressures' (42) driving the debate. Fifty years on these pressures have eased considerably and he judges that we should be able to examine on their own terms some of the key debates of the patristic period about Scripture and Tradition.

Minns traces the earliest appeal to tradition to a letter by a Christian teacher, Ptolemy, to a disciple, Flora. Ptolemy was however drawing on the practice of contemporary philosophical schools to ensure consistency between a founder's views and what was handed on. Paul himself seems to do the same with his claim that 'I received from the Lord what I also handed on to you' (1 Cor 11:23). Subsequently, Irenaeus of Lyons (second century) drew a distinction between tradition as process and as product. His understanding of product as something unchangeable came under pressure during the debates of the fourth and fifth centuries, especially over the divinity of Christ. Minns's essay identifies the various factors that fueled the debates and the difficulties each side had in grounding its own position and refuting the other. It is testimony to the limited ability, even of powerful minds, to cover all bases satisfactorily. A particularly striking example is Basil the Great's debate with opponents who rejected his appeal to traditional liturgical formulas and customs, arguing that they went beyond the strict datum of Scripture (an early version of *Sola Scriptura*). Minns's selection of particular periods, the major debates and the key figures involved provides an informative insight into the patristic contribution to our understanding of the relationship between Scripture and Tradition.

Chapter 4:
Dianne Bergant,
'"I handed on to you . . . what I also received" (1 Cor 15:3)
The Scripture-Tradition Connection/Controversy'

As Dianne Bergant notes, tradition is essential for enabling people to 'identify who they are and how they are to live' (56). In time elements of a tradition assume authoritative forms that are written down—in the case of Israel as its Scripture. But while this stabilises a tradition the process continues; tradition is a dynamic reality. The believing community plays a crucial role in determining what elements of the tradition are 'canonical' and what elements are not, even though they may continue to be treasured. It is not so much the existence of Scripture and Tradition that is in dispute but the relationship between the two and their relative authority in the community.

Whereas Minns's essay focuses on key figures in the Patristic period, Bergant leads the reader through later debates between the eastern and western churches, the crisis of the Reformation, and into the modern era. The church's claims to have the backing of tradition for an increasing repository of teachings and practices eventually sparked the reformers' call to hear again the true 'Word of God', free of 'mediaeval piety and ecclesiastical bias' (59). In reply the Council of Trent affirmed that Scripture and Tradition comprise two sources of revelation, but without articulating the relation between them.

The Second Vatican Council sought to clarify matters by asserting that Scripture and Tradition flow from the one divine 'well-spring' so that both 'form one sacred deposit of the word of God, committed to the Church'. God is affirmed as the one source of revelation while the Magisterium, the teaching office of the church, is not a source of revelation as such but its servant.

Bergant makes the important observation that even though *Dei Verbum* emphasises the close relationship between Scripture and Tradition, its approval of historical critical study of Scripture has led to a rather unfortunate divide between study of the text and the Tradition of biblical interpretation. Biblical scholars tend to focus on the former and church authorities on the latter. But there are signs of change and Bergant sees a key example of this in Benedict XVI's recent three volume work *Jesus of Nazareth*.

Chapter 5:
Justin Taylor,
'The Unity of the Whole of Scripture'

According to Justin Taylor, a key paragraph on this topic in *Dei Verbum* 12, in particular, is the statement that 'God speaks in Sacred Scripture through men in human fashion'. The document first deals with the second part of this sentence, emphasising the importance of studying Israel's literary and thought forms within their ancient Near Eastern context. This reveals the rich diversity of the Bible. The document then takes up the first part of the sentence, drawing attention to the unity of Scripture, the one Word of God conveyed in human words under the inspiration of the one Spirit. In discerning this unity the reader is aided by church tradition and the 'harmony which exists between elements of the faith (*analogiae fidei*)'.

Taylor next compares the contribution of *Dei Verbum* with Benedict XVI's 2010 Exhortation *Verbum Domini*. He shows that while the Exhortation, as one would expect, endorses *Dei Verbum* it also revises, clarifies and expands on it in certain areas. This is another example of diversity within unity and the dynamic nature of the tradition. As previous generations sought to discern the meaning of biblical texts and relate it to their world, we are called to do the same in our day. Taylor also discusses Benedict's criteria in support of the unity of Scripture. The unity of Scripture is ultimately grounded in its claim to be the Word of God, and for Christians that Word is 'a Person, incarnate in Jesus Christ'. The final part of the essay considers Benedict's understanding of the relationship between the Testaments and the implications of the New Testament's claim that Jesus is the fulfillment of the Old. Taylor also notes a perceptive parallel that Joseph Ratzinger drew in his 1968 *Commentary on the Documents* of *Vatican II* between the production of the Bible and that of *Dei Verbum* itself. In both cases there was at times intense debate and diversity of opinions yet the final product in both cases is recognised as embracing their respective diversities within a 'deeper unity'.

Chapter 6:
Antony F Campbell,
'*Dei Verbum:* Literary Forms and Vatican II— an Old Testament Perspective'

As a general observation Antony Campbell notes that '*Dei Verbum* intends to affirm an overall image of the past and encourage a sure march into the future'. At the more specific level of the text he finds that *Dei Verbum* strives to give due weight both to modern critical analysis, as exemplified in the historical-critical method, and to traditional biblical interpretation, as exemplified in the Fathers. He discerns a connection here with the *sensus plenior* (fuller sense) proposed by some recent Catholic scholars: while this is distinguished from the literary sense as probing the 'deeper meaning' of the text, it also seeks to maintain 'reasonable homogeneity' with the literary sense. In Campbell's assessment *Dei Verbum* 'quietly insists on the reverence owed to tradition and equally quietly insists on the openness to the future owed to biblical studies' (92).

Campbell notes the document's emphasis on paying attention to the literary forms of the biblical text as a key to their understanding and provides a perceptive comment, or perhaps interpretation, of the document's reference to discerning the 'intention of the sacred writers' who composed these literary forms. For him, this phrase is best interpreted as 'the meaning of the text' (96). One only has access to the intention of the author via his/her text. The document's attention to literary forms reflects the impact of modern critical analysis of the Bible, in particular, form criticism. According to Campbell, form criticism's aim of recapturing the *Sitz-im-Leben* or 'life setting' of a text has proved to be elusive. Nevertheless, he identifies two questions of the form critical agenda that endure and apply to each text; namely, what sort of text is it, and why is it preserved in this form in the Bible? Attempts to answer these questions within the contexts both of Christian and Jewish faith should make readers appreciate the richness and complexity of the biblical text and that at times this will be a disturbing encounter. As a final comment Campbell suggests the general term 'mystery' to describe the Word of God, and mystery is always unfolding its meaning.

Chapter 7:
Marie Turner,
Dei Verbum and the Witness of Creation: Reading Ecclesiastes 3:9–22 Ecologically'

Dei Verbum 12 states that Scripture should 'be read and interpreted in the sacred spirit in which it was written', but done in a way that nourishes the Christian community. In light of this, Turner asks how the book of Ecclesiastes (or Qoheleth) can be read as illuminating the economy of salvation in some way, given the refrain 'vanity of vanities (or 'absolute absurdity') that recurs throughout it. One response is the so-called supersessionist reading of the Old Testament which claims that it has effectively been 'replaced' by the New. Against this *Dei Verbum* 14 asserts that the books of the Old Testament 'remain permanently valuable'.

Turner sees an important and permanently valuable (and so Christian) element in Qoheleth's theology of creation. In order to demonstrate this, she examines the discourse on creation in 3:9-22 in relation to contemporary focus on ecology. At the more specific level of terminology she questions the customary rendering of the Hebrew term *habel* as 'vanity'. This overlooks another sense of the term as 'breath', or what is elusive. Qoheleth asserts that genuine enjoyment derives from the gifts of the earth, which are also the gifts of God as creator; however they are not under our control, but elude our grasp like breath. The negative sense of *habel* relates more to Qoheleth's experience of the economic uncertainties of his day. Human life and its endeavours stand in sharp contrast to the enduring life cycles of earth that Qoheleth describes as *'olam* or eternal, a word that is only used otherwise of God.

Qoheleth also asserts that everything in creation has its 'time' (cf 3:11) and that we are able to enjoy the 'seasons' of the earth within our allotted time. But our inability to control these seasons or our own time teaches us that God 'has done this, so that all should stand in awe before him' (3:14). In short, creation plays a key role in revealing the nature of God and the appropriate response of human beings to this. But the book of Ecclesiastes plays an integral role in teaching us how to see creation properly.

Chapter 8:
Jerome Murphy O'Connor,
'A Review and Assessment of the Church's Engagement with Historical Critical Analysis of the New Testament as outlined in *Dei Verbum*'

This chapter by the late Jerome Murphy-O'Connor provides an incisive and telling reflection on the ways in which the Catholic Church has engaged with historical critical analysis over the last century. The chapter gives valuable and detailed historical background, as well as the kind of forthright evaluation that has been a trademark of Murphy-O'Connor's academic career. The basic argument proposed is that while official Church teaching has supported and continued to advance *Dei Verbum* and its teaching there has been an on-going wave of discontent and criticism of historical-critical scholarship. Murphy-O'Connor traces the origins of this opposition by examining the background to Vatican II in section one, moving to an examination of the production of Vatican II in section two. The final section traces what has happened after Vatican II stressing the consistent support provided by the highest authority in the Church for the historical-critical method.

One of Murphy-O'Connor's initial observations is that it was most unfortunate that the advent of form-criticism coincided with the end of the Modernist crisis. The Church was already wary and the presuppositions of the form critics only served to exacerbate matters by their scepticism regarding the historicity of the Gospels. One consequence of the heightened wariness that resulted was a culture of self-censorship among Catholic biblical scholars in an environment of denunciation and accusation. *Divino Afflante Spiritu* made an invaluable contribution to discussion highlighting the need to pay attention to literary forms when making judgments about the historicity of biblical texts. Despite this strong statement debate, claims, and counterclaims continued up to the beginning of the Second Vatican Council.

The second section dealing with the production of *Dei Verbum* notes the important role played by *The Historical Truth of the Gospels* written in 1964. Murphy-O'Connor explores how *Dei Verbum* treated the question of historicity. In the light of modern research into oral history and tradition he concludes that *Dei Verbum* might have been too circumspect when it came to judgments about the historicity of the Gospels.

The final section looks at developments after *Dei Verbum* noting the on-going work of the Pontifical Biblical Commission. While the culture of self-censorship of biblical scholars finally came to an end opposition to a critical treatment of the Scriptures has continued.

Chapter 9:
Elizabeth Dowling,
'Breaking Open the Word: The Legacy of *Dei Verbum*'

Dowling contributes a chapter that is both a personal reflection and a helpful outline of developments in critical methodologies since the time of Vatican II. The chapter is personal to the extent that her own work as an exegete was indirectly enabled by *Dei Verbum* with its call to make the Scriptures accessible to as wide a readership as possible.

Dowling highlights three ways in which *Dei Verbum* influenced Catholic biblical scholarship: (1) stressing that access to the Scriptures is for all God's faithful; (2) biblical scholars are called to constantly renew their methods and approaches; and (3) placing the Scriptures in the life of the Church with the call for the whole Church to read the Scriptures; thereby redressing the imbalance that had resulted in the Catholic Church's reaction to the reformers' focus on *Sola Scriptura*.

The chapter addresses the developments in biblical interpretation since Vatican II noting the movement from the focus on the author, to the text, and then to the reader. Until *Dei Verbum* the focus was largely the world behind the text. Since then the importance of the context of the reader in the interpretation of the text has been emphasised as the focus in hermeneutics has shifted to the world in front of the text. Accompanying the shift in focus from the world behind the text to the world in front of the text has been the recognition of a misplaced optimism regarding the possibility of any objective reading of a text.

Particular attention is paid to the development of feminist, postcolonial and ecological reader-centred approaches that make their own distinctive contribution to the interpretation of biblical texts by clearly stating their presuppositions, biases and concerns in open and exegetically responsible ways. The treatment of these approaches highlights their focus on both critique and retrieval.

The chapter concludes noting how contemporary biblical interpreters use a variety of methodologies, and combinations of methodologies and stances. These endeavours are viewed positively as being open to new methods that *Dei Verbum* encouraged.

Chapter 10:
Dale Launderville,
'Translating Biblical Texts Within an Ecclesial Context'

Dei Verbum 22 states that 'Easy access to the Sacred Scriptures should be available to the Christian faithful' and that the church's concern is to provide 'suitable and accurate translations' from the originals. The essay by Dale Launderville is therefore of particular interest in relation to the new English translation of liturgical texts and the principles employed in it. It has clear implications for the translation that will be adopted in the proposed new Catholic Lectionary.

As Launderville notes, a standardised translation of the Bible is necessary for a community activity such as the liturgy. The question of course is who decides on which translation? He examines the translation process under three headings: (1) standardisation as unity-in-diversity rather than uniformity, (2) the necessity of standardising a pluriform biblical text for religious use, and (3) standardising a biblical text for liturgical use versus standardising it for study.

Apropos the first heading, Launderville provides an outline of the directives and guidelines issued by the Vatican for the new translation, and the debate these triggered. A central issue was the Vatican's insistence on the Latin Vulgate as the 'standard' or 'original' for translation, which seemed to contradict *Dei Verbum*'s reference to 'the original texts of the sacred Books', which would seem to give primacy to the Hebrew and Greek versions. This debate leads to the consideration of another important factor under heading (2). The more biblical scholars search for the earliest text, the more they discover a diversity of texts rather than one original from which the others derive. This has led some to distinguish between a 'received' text within a tradition and therefore more suited for religious and liturgical use (for example the Vulgate), and an 'original' text reconstructed by scholarly endeavour.

This traditional text still needs of course to be translated in a standardised form, and this leads to Launderville's third consideration and the lively debate between two theories of translation—formal and dynamic equivalence. He outlines the two theories (the former advocated by the Vatican), and provides informative comments on their respective merits and limitations.

Chapter 11:
Peter Malone,
'Dei Verbum, communication and media'

Peter Malone, as a world recognised film critic, makes a unique contribution to this present volume on *Dei Verbum*. In his chapter in this volume Malone speaks of the living voice of the Gospel resounding in our present context, and Malone sharpens the focus, providing a survey on the Church's sometimes all too suspicious stance taken with regard to the media.

An overview is provided of Church statements regarding the media from the time of the Council to the present day. Malone notes how the Church has been often suspicious and wary of mass media—seen as enemy rather than dialogue partner. The chapter plots how this attitude gradually changed from the time of *Inter Mirifica* (Vatican II Decree on Social Communication) in 1963 through to *Communio et Progressio* (On the Means of Social Communication) in 1970, and further developed in 1975 with *Evangelii Nuntiandi* (Evangelisation in the Modern World).

Malone suggests that since that time the impact of World Communications Day and the work of the Pontifical Council for Social Communication indicate development of the understanding of the role of the media as the Church reads the signs of the times and communicates the Gospel message in ways that *Dei Verbum* encouraged and endorsed.

The contribution of Pope John Paul II in stressing that media are gifts from God is acknowledged by Malone as the Church has come to see the media as the new Areopagus. This has led to the appreciation of belonging to the Global Village where the communications media have become the principal means of guidance and inspiration for many people. The chapter concludes asking what *Dei Verbum* would look like if it was written today in the world of Google, Twitter,

Facebook, and YouTube. In a time of such change, at ever accelerating pace, one thing is certain, that making the living voice of the Gospel resound in our time is going to be an ongoing challenge.

Chapter 12:
John Owens,
'*Dei Verbum* and the Philosophy of Hans-Georg Gadamer'

John Owens notes an intriguing aspect of *Dei Verbum*. On the one hand it sought to engage and assess, positively but critically, the scientific analysis of the Bible practiced by Protestant scholars for several centuries but forbidden to their Catholic counterparts. On the other hand its insistence that practitioners of scientific methods should also pay due attention to the unity of Scripture and the living tradition of the Church anticipated an important development in philosophical hermeneutics (interpretation). The past is not just an object of scientific analysis but an active conversation partner in the search for meaning. According to Owens, a key figure in developing this hermeneutic has been Hans Georg Gadamer, whose major work *Truth and Method* appeared four years before *Dei Verbum*. According to Gadamer, all understanding develops in this manner and involves a kind of 'fusion of horizons'. This resonates well with *Dei Verbum* 2 that sees the reading of Scripture as a personal encounter in which 'readers hear the voice of God speaking'.

Nevertheless, Owens uncovers some important differences between Gadamer's understanding of tradition and that of the church. For Gadamer the truly 'experienced' person is 'radically undogmatic' and this would seem to counter the Catholic notion of dogma. Owens identifies two Catholic doctrines that stand as a direct challenge to Gadamer's view, namely that there is no further public revelation after the advent of Jesus, and *Dei Verbum*'s claim that authentic interpretation of the tradition has been entrusted 'exclusively to the living teaching office of the Church' (*DV*10).

Can the church claim to have the last word in such matters or does the hermeneutical process rule out any last word? Should the Church, and all human beings, be always ready to reassess and change their position on anything or are there some things on which we should refuse to change? Owens provides an informative discussion of the issues involved; for example, whether Gadamer's hermeneutics is descriptive or in some way prescriptive (setting norms), in which case does it 'dogmatise' a form of relativism? Readers will find plenty of material here for further reflection and debate.

Chapter 13:
Donald Senior,
'Where do we go from here? The future of Catholic Biblical Studies in the wake of Vatican II'

Don Senior has been a member of the Pontifical Biblical Commission since 2001, and brings the richness and depth of that experience to this reflection on the development of Catholic Biblical studies, and the role played by *Dei Verbum* in it. The first section places *Dei Verbum* within the context of profound biblical renewal during the twentieth century that witnessed the Catholic Church changing its attitude to the use of historical-critical methodologies.

Dei Verbum stressed that revelation was not so much a body of propositions but God's self–revelation, and as such it is inspired and inerrant. At the same time the document stressed that this divine word is also a human word. *Dei Verbum* did not resolve the inherent tension by defining the meaning of inspiration and it is an on-going task that the Pontifical Biblical Commission has been commissioned to address.

The second section explores the on-going impact of *Dei Verbum* and Senior demonstrates this by reference to a number of major statements made by the Pontifical Biblical Commission between 1993 and 2008.

Verbum Domini is the focus of the third section of the chapter. Senior concentrates on Benedict XVI's reflections on how the Scriptures need to be read within the context of a living community of faith. Benedict stresses in *Verbum Domini* the value of scientific and historical-critical study of bible while at the same time noting that for a living community of faith there are other approaches that need to be valued and utilized. Benedict XVI refused to allow a wedge to be driven between the rational and the spiritual thereby avoiding the dangers of both fundamentalism and reductionism.

Senior's concluding reflections are that there is a wide array of newer approaches to the study of the bible that can complement historically grounded methodology. Senior suggests that Catholic

Biblical scholars in the future will need to be grounded in both the Scriptures and theology. This will have consequences for lay men and women who are commencing their careers in the area of biblical interpretation.

Chapter 14:
Alan Cadwallader,
'History as bulwark, bridge and bulldozer: *Dei Verbum* and ecumenical, biblical endeavour.'

By casting the net wider than the Catholic tradition this chapter contributes to this present volume by tracing the development and acceptance of the historical-critical method. The long process by which the Catholic tradition came to terms with historical-critical approaches to biblical texts was largely paralleled in Anglican and Protestant traditions.

Cadwallader outlines how the historical-critical method came to be the accepted method for biblical interpretation across the different churches. Matters that continue to be debated regarding historicity and the Bible were clearly identified during that period. The views of Wescott, Hort, Lightfoot, Newman and Wiseman are examined providing insight into the ways in which these issues were addressed and approached from different perspectives at that time. Wescott's Lambeth Conference address on the 'Critical Study of Holy Scripture' reveals not only the acceptance of the historical-critical method, but the awareness of the difficulties that it posed from a faith perspective.

As the chapter proceeds Cadwallader tracks the gradual acceptance of the historical-critical method by means of a number of Vatican pronouncements that extend beyond *Dei Verbum* to the post-synodal Apostolic Exhortation *Verbum Domini* in 2010. From an ecumenical perspective the fact that the different churches came to use the same historical-critical methods provided a bridge for scholars from various Christian churches. The ecumenical dimensions of these Vatican documents are highlighted.

Cadwallader notes that *Dei Verbum* did not resolve all debates on the interpretation of the Bible, in particular, the relationship between Scripture and Tradition, and the charge that the historical-critical method does not allow sufficiently for reading from a faith perspective. Limitations have been identified with the historical-critical method and its claims to being value-free and objective. This is welcomed by Cadwallader since it invites the interpreter of the Bible to interpret it from a wide range of perspectives that can complement, challenge, and supplement the historical-critical method.

1

Dei Verbum and Revelation

Gerald O'Collins SJ, AC

The 1985 Extraordinary Synod of Bishops met in Rome (24 November to 8 December) to celebrate the Second Vatican Council (which had ended twenty years earlier on 8 December 1965), to evaluate the Council's role in the postconciliar Church, and to develop some principles for the further reception of its teaching.[1] The final report of the synod produced six principles for interpreting the sixteen conciliar texts.[2]

Avery Dulles paraphrased the first principle as follows: 'Each passage and document of the Council must be interpreted in the context of all the others, so that the integral meaning of the Council may be rightly grasped.'[3] Presupposing that meaning and truth are to be found in the whole, this principle recalled approaches to the Scriptures that interpret the texts in the light of the final, canonical form of the entire Bible.[4] Yet the synod's report added at once a second principle that brought to mind another scriptural approach: namely, those interpretations which in various ways presuppose a 'canon

---

1. See *Synod 1985: An Evaluation,* edited by Giuseppe Alberigo and James Provost (Edinburgh: T&T Clark, 1986).
2. *The Final Report of the 1985 Extraordinary Synod* (Washington, DC: National Conference of Catholic Bishops, 1986).
3. Avery Dulles, 'The Reception of Vatican II at the Extraordinary Synod of 1985', in Giuseppe Alberigo, in *The Reception of Vatican II,* edited by Jean-Pierre Jossua and Joseph A Komonchak (Washington, DC: Catholic University of America Press, 1987), 349–63, at 350.
4. See The Pontifical Biblical Commission, *The Interpretation of the Bible in the Church* (Vatican City State: Libreria Editrice Vaticana, 1993), 50–53, 93–94.

within the canon'.[5] 'The four major constitutions of the Council', the report states, 'are the hermeneutical key for the other decrees and declarations.'[6] These constitutions are, in chronological order of their promulgation, The Constitution on the Sacred Liturgy (*Sacrosanctum Concilium* [*SC*]), the Dogmatic Constitution on the Church (*Lumen Gentium* [*LG*]), the Dogmatic Constitution on Divine Revelation (*Dei Verbum* [*DV*]), and the Pastoral Constitution on the Church in the Modern World (*Gaudium et Spes* [*GS*]).[7]

If these four constitutions provide such a 'hermeneutical key', does one of them, as a kind of *primus inter pares* enjoy a certain 'primacy' over the other three when we set ourselves to interpret Vatican II and its teaching? Many scholars and others have assigned this primacy to *LG*, but, given the priority of divine revelation over the doctrine of the Church (which is derived from revelation), it would be preferable to name *DV* in first place. Jared Wicks rightly commented on certain editions of the conciliar documents:

> Some editions place *Lumen Gentium* at the head of the Vatican II constitutions, but would not the conciliar ecclesiology be better contextualized if it were placed *after* the council text starting with 'hearing the word of God reverently and proclaiming it confidently . . .' and ending with 'the word of God . . . stands forever,' as does *Dei Verbum*?[8]

Wicks, Christoph Theobald, and others make a persuasive case for the primacy of *DV* when interpreting the conciliar teaching.

Naming *DV* 'the Dogmatic Constitution on Divine *Revelation*' implies that the self-revelation of God, even if explicitly addressed only

---

5. *Dei Verbum* itself adopts a version of the 'canon within the canon', when it endorses the special place of the four Gospels ('they are deservedly pre-eminent') within all the books of the Bible (article 18).
6. Dulles, 'Reception of Vatican II', 350.
7. The translations from these documents are my own.
8. Jared Wicks, 'Vatican II on Revelation—From Behind the Scenes', in *Theological Studies* 71 (2010): 637–50, at 639. In various publications, Christoph Theobald has also assigned a pivotal role to *Dei Verbum* for the interpretation of the sixteen conciliar texts; for details, see Massimo Faggioli, *Vatican II: The Battle for Meaning* (Mahwah, NJ: Paulist Press, 2012), 127–28, 181.

by the first chapter, takes precedence over what follows on tradition (Chapter 2) and the inspired Scriptures (Chapters 3 to 6). All of this suggests how supremely important it is to present correctly Chapter 1 of *DV*, along with what can be gleaned about divine revelation from other passages in the conciliar documents. Let me take up this task in three stages, and glean what the constitution clearly develops about revelation, what it barely touches on, and what needs to be added from some of the other fifteen conciliar texts.

Six Clear Themes from *Dei Verbum*

At least six themes about God's revelation emerge as clearly developed by *DV*. (1) First of all, right from the beginning *DV* presents revelation as primarily being God's self-disclosure: after quoting 1 John 1:2–3 about the Word, who is divine Life and Light in person, 'appearing to us' (*DV* 1), the constitution states firmly: 'it pleased God, in his goodness and wisdom, to reveal himself and to make known the sacrament (*sacramentum*) of his will (see Eph 1:9)' (*DV* 2). The tripersonal God took the initiative to enter freely into a dialogue of love with human beings, so that through their response of integral faith they may receive salvation. Along with 1 John 1:2–3 and Ephesians 1:9, the opening chapter of *DV* 4 cites a third, classical New Testament text that also indicates the personal character of the divine self-revelation: 'after God spoke in many places and numerous ways in the Prophets, lastly in these days he has spoken to us in [his] Son' (Heb 1:1–2).

The opening chapter of *DV* makes it repeatedly clear that revelation *primarily* means the self-revelation of God or of Truth (in upper case) itself. *Secondarily*, of course, the divine revelation discloses something about God and human beings. The interpersonal 'dialogue', which is God's self-communication, says and communicates information. Through encountering the divine Truth in person, human beings know new truths.

Hence the second chapter of *DV* opens as follows: 'God most kindly (*benignissime*) arranged that *the things which he had revealed* for the salvation of all peoples should remain integrally throughout time, and be transmitted to all generations' (*DV* 7; English italics mine). Since it deals with the transmission of revelation, that same chapter naturally speaks of 'all revealed things' (*DV* 9) and uses a classic term for the content of the revelation communicated through Christ and his apostles: 'all that it [the official magisterium] proposes to be believed as being divinely revealed it draws from this one *deposit of faith*' (*DV* 10; italics mine). At the end *DV* talks of 'the treasure of revelation entrusted to the Church' (*DV* 26), which she should faithfully preserve and proclaim.

The distinction *DV* makes between the primary and secondary sense of revelation comes in an appropriate style of language. It highlights *the* mystery (singular) of the tripersonal God revealed through Christ in the history of salvation and inviting human beings to share in a new communion of love. This choice of the 'singular' follows not only the verse cited from Ephesians 1:9 (see above) but also other passages from the Pauline letters: for instance, Romans 16:25–26; Ephesians 3:4, 9; 6:19; Colossians 1:27; 4:3. Revelation primarily means meeting the Mystery of God in person and only secondarily knowing the divine mysteries (plural and in lower case). Talk of 'the mystery' forms a leitmotif in *DV*; five times the constitution speaks of 'mystery' in the singular (*DV* 2, 15, 17, 24, and 26) and never of 'the mysteries' in the plural. The same tendency shows up in other texts promulgated by Vatican II: the sixteen documents use 'mystery' in the singular 106 times and 'mysteries' in the plural only twenty two times.

Right from his first encyclical Pope John Paul II (pope 1978–2005) exemplified the same tendency. *Redemptor Hominis* (*RH*) (1979) spoke fifty nine times of 'the mystery of redemption', 'the paschal mystery', 'the mystery of Christ', 'the mystery of the divine "economy"', and so forth, without ever using the term 'mystery' in the plural.[9] The 1980 papal encyclical *Dives in Misericordia (DM)* followed suit, referring thirty nine times to 'the mystery' (of God, of Christ, and so forth) and only twice to 'mysteries'.

Over the primary and secondary sense of revelation, Vatican II differs from Vatican I. In its constitution on divine faith (*Dei Filius* of 1870 [*DF*]), the First Vatican Council, while once talking of God

---

9. On what he called '*reductio in mysterium*', see Karl Rahner, 'The Concept of Mystery in Catholic Theology', in *Theological Investigations*, volume 4, translated by Kevin Smyth (London: Darton, Longman & Todd, 1968), 36–73 (especially 60–73); also 'Reflections on Methodology in Theology', *Theological Investigations*, volume 11, translated by David Bourke (1974), 68–114 (especially 101–14).

'revealing himself' (*DzH* 3004; *ND* 113), in general understood divine revelation to be primarily God communicating the divine truths (plural), which otherwise would be inaccessible to human reason or at best known only with difficulty. This entailed presenting human faith as submitting to the divine 'authority' and believing to be true 'that which God has revealed' (*DzH* 3008; *ND* 118); it also entailed speaking of 'the mysteries' (plural) 'contained in divine revelation' (*DzH* 3041; *ND* 137; see *DzH* 3016–17; *ND* 132–33).[10] After Vatican I, a development of doctrine intervenes with Vatican II presenting divine revelation as being primarily the self-disclosure of God and not primarily the manifestation of divine truths which would otherwise not be known. There has been a shift from 'knowing about God' to 'knowing God' personally.

(2) A second theme to emphasise concerns the nature of revelation as *salvific* and *sacramental*. Right from its prologue *DV* indicates how God's self-revelation and the offer of salvation coincide. Vatican II wanted 'the whole world' to hear 'the summons to salvation' (*DV* 1). The plan or 'economy of revelation' is, more or less, synonymous with 'the history of salvation' (*DV* 2). Repeatedly and without hesitation the constitution passes from the language of revelation to that of salvation, and then back to revelation (for example, *DV* 3, 4, 6, 7, 14, 15, 17, and 21). Thus it recognises that we deal with two inseparable, if distinguishable, realities. God's revealing word necessarily offers salvation. In Johannine terms, since Jesus is *the* Truth in person, he is also *the* Life in person.

When enunciating the Easter mystery, *DV* deftly links revelation and salvation: through his life, death, and resurrection (along with the sending of the Holy Spirit), Christ revealed that 'God is with us, to deliver us from the darkness of sin and death, and to raise us up to eternal life' (*DV* 4). The self-revelation of God and redemptive deliverance of human beings go hand in hand.

As something which applies equally to the 'economy of revelation' and 'the history of salvation', *DV* puts on display sacramental language.

---

10. 'DzH' abbreviates *Enchiridion symbolorum, definitionum et declarationum*, edited by Heinrich Denzinger and Peter Hünermann, seventeenth edition (Freiburg im Breisgau: Herder, 1991). 'ND' abbreviates Josef Neuner and Jacques Dupuis, *The Christian Faith in the Doctrinal Documents of the Catholic Church*, seventh edition (Bangalore/New York: Theological Publications in India/Alba House, 2001).

When administrating the sacraments, the words and actions of persons interact to communicate God's revelation and salvation: thus 'this economy of revelation takes place (*fit*) by deeds and words, which are intrinsically connected with each other. As a result, the works performed by God in the history of salvation manifest and bear out the doctrine and realities signified by the words; while the words proclaim the works and bring to light the mystery they contain' (*DV* 2; see also 4 and 14). It is above all in the case of Jesus himself that the words and deeds of a person convey the saving self-revelation of God: 'Christ established on earth the Kingdom of God [and] revealed (*manifestavit*) his Father and himself by deeds and words' (*DV* 17). It is worth noting how a year earlier *LG* had said something very similar, using 'shines forth (*elucescit*)': 'this kingdom [of God] shines forth before human beings in the word, works, and presence of Christ' (*LG* 5).

Some have interpreted this 'sacramental' way of presenting God's saving and revealing self-communication as having an ecumenical origin. Was it a Catholic way of welcoming and joining together themes favoured by two different schools of Protestant theologians? Did *DV* combine the language of (a) such word-of-God theologians as Karl Barth and Rudolf Bultmann with (b) that favoured by Oscar Cullmann, George Ernest Wright, and Wolfhart Pannenberg about God's revealing and saving acts in history? Without discounting completely this explanation, one should recall how from November 1962 Pieter Smulders began to be involved in preparing what would become *DV*; in passages that he helped to draft one finds the language of divine revelation being mediated through 'words' and 'deeds'.[11] A world-class expert on St Hilary of Poitiers, Smulders was familiar

---

11. On Smulders's role in the preparation of *Dei Verbum*, see Gerald O'Collins, *Retrieving Fundamental Theology: Three Styles of Fundamental Theology* (Mahwah, NJ: Paulist Press, 1993), 57–62, 160–64. One should also add what Smulders communicated several months earlier to Archbishop Giuseppe Beltrami, the papal nuncio in The Hague: revelation embraces not only the '*locutio Dei*' (the revelatory word) but also the '*magnalia Dei*' (the great deeds of God). On this see Wicks, 'Vatican II on Revelation', 637–50, at 643–45; this excellent article also draws attention to (a) the role of Jean Daniélou, Karl Rahner, Joseph Ratzinger, and other *periti* elaborating the text of *DV*, as well as providing references to (b) an outstanding series of articles by Wicks on the contribution to the Council that came from Ratzinger and Smulders, and to (c) relevant dissertations on the Council produced by Wicks's doctoral students.

with his use of that language. In the opening article of *Tractatus Mysteriorum*, Hilary wrote of the biblical 'words (*dicta*)' and 'facts (*facta*)' that 'announce (*nuntiare*)' and 'express/reveal (*exprimere*)' the coming of Christ.[12] A few days before Smulders was first co-opted into his work towards elaborating the constitution on revelation, Bishop Emile Guano had proposed at a plenary session of Vatican II that the 'exordium' of the new 'schema' on revelation should state that 'God speaks to human beings through . . . his Word made flesh'. Christ 'speaks to human beings, to begin with through his words (*dicta*) but also . . . through his works (*facta*) and deeds (*gesta*), indeed through his very person'.[13] One should also recall how the language of 'words' and 'works' also turned up in a paper ('On Revelation and the Word of God') that Jean Daniélou prepared in November 1962 for Cardinal Gabriel Garrone, a member of the joint commission charged with revising the 'schema' on 'the Sources of Revelation'.[14]

In the event, the final text of *DV* four times described revelation as communicated 'by deeds and words' (*DV* 2, 4, 14, and 15). As terms which suggest somewhat better the personal nature of revelation, '*gesta*' (twice) and '*opera*' (twice) rather than '*facta*' (only once) were used in the definitive version of the constitution. Finally, one should not overlook the way in which earlier Catholic theology had already taken up the language about revelation being mediated through 'words and deeds'. Back in 1900, Herman Schell wrote of the divine revelation as follows: 'the supernatural revelation of God means the free self-communication of God *through word and deed* to a personal and real community of life with the created spirit'.[15] In short, a 'Catholic' combination of two Protestant schools of thought (the word of God and the saving divine acts in history) may have contributed to the sacramental language that *DV* used in presenting

---

12. *Traité des mystères*, 1.1 in *Sources Chrétiennes*, edited Jean-Paul Brisson (Paris: Cerf, 2005), 71.
13. *Acta Synodalia S. Concilii Oecumenici Vaticani II*, I/111 (Vatican City: Libreria Editrice Vaticana, 1971), 260. In combining word and deed, Bishop Guano did not suggest that he intended to blend two (Protestant) views about the mediation of revelation and salvation.
14. For details, see Wicks, 'Vatican II on Revelation', 647–50.
15. Herman Schell, *Katholische Dogmatik*, edited by Josef Hasenfuss, Heinrich Petri and Paul Werner Scheele, volume 1 (Munich: Schöningh, 1968), 28, note 1; translation and emphasis mine.

revelation. But there were other sources for this language—and not least, one must add, *SC*.

Promulgated in December 1963, the constitution on the liturgy spoke not only of the eucharistic 'mystery of faith' involving both 'sacred action' and 'instruction by God's word' (*SC* 48) but also of the act of 'celebration' and the 'words' that constitute the other sacraments (*SC* 59). Being what Massimo Faggioli has happily called 'a theological starting point' for Vatican II,[16] *SC* prepared the way for the sacramental language of *DV*. This liturgical constitution also encouraged holding together 'the economy of revelation' with 'the history of salvation' through rehabilitating 'the table of God's word' (*SC* 51) alongside 'the table of the Lord's Body' (*SC* 48). The revealing word belongs inseparably with the saving sacrament of the Eucharist. To sum up: *DV*'s stress on the salvific and sacramental nature of divine self-revelation applies to the broader reality of revelation what *SC* had already enunciated about the liturgy.

(3) A third major theme, perhaps better a major 'term', embodied in Chapter 1 of *DV* is that of the divine *self-communication*: 'by divine revelation God wished to manifest and *communicate himself* and the eternal decrees of his will concerning the salvation of human beings' (*DV* 6).[17] The special value of this term comes from the way in which it holds together God's self-revelation and self-giving through saving grace. The divine communication is not merely 'informative' but also constitutes a real self-communication of God, which both makes salvation known and brings it in person.

Smulders had some role in the language of divine 'self-communication' entering the final text of *DV*.[18] After the Council, this term moved further ahead in official Catholic teaching. John Paul II used it in a 1980 encyclical *Dives in Misericordia* 7 (*DM*) and then repeatedly in a 1986 encyclical on the Holy Spirit, *Dominum et Vivificantem*, (13 [twice], 14, 23, 50 [four times], 51 [twice], and 58

---

16. Massimo Faggioli, *Vatican II: The Battle for Meaning* (Mahwah, NJ: Paulist Press, 2012), 103.
17. This passage echoes Vatican I and the only passage where it spoke of revelation as God's self- revelation: 'it pleased his [God's] wisdom and goodness to reveal himself and his eternal decrees' (DzH 3004; ND 113). Where Vatican I's constitution on faith (*Dei Filius*) spoke of God 'revealing himself', *DV* doubled the verb to speak of God's 'manifesting and *communicating himself*' (*italics mine*).
18. O'Collins, *Retrieving Fundamental Theology*, 52–53.

[twice]). We saw above how Hermann Schell had written in 1900 of 'the free self-communication of God', and we find the term in the works of Karl Barth, Rudolf Bultmann, Romano Guardini, Karl Rahner, and Freidrich Daniel Ernst Schleiermacher. But that language had already enjoyed its place in the long history of theology. In the third part of his *Summa Theologiae*, St Thomas Aquinas endorsed a principle from Pseudo-Dionysius the Areopagite ('good diffuses itself') to expound the incarnation as the supreme act of God's self-communication: 'it belongs to the scheme (*rationem*) of goodness to communicate itself to others as Dionysius shows. Hence it belongs to the scheme of the highest good to communicate itself to the creature in the highest way' (3a. 1.1 resp, translation mine).

(4) In a fourth major theme *DV* recognises the paschal mystery as the highpoint of divine self-revelation:

> Jesus Christ . . . completed and perfected revelation and confirmed it with the divine witness. [He did this] by the total presence of Himself and [self-] manifestation—by words and works, signs and miracles, but especially by his death and glorious resurrection from the dead, and finally by sending the Spirit of truth (*DV* 4).

As we noted above, this paragraph at once linked the climax of revelation with its saving point and purpose: Christ revealed that 'God is with us, to deliver us from the darkness of sin and death, and to raise us up to eternal life' (*DV* 4).[19]

Once again *SC* had prepared the ground for such teaching by highlighting Easter as that 'supremely solemn' of all feasts (*SC* 102), as well as every Sunday, when the Church celebrates 'the paschal mystery' being 'the foundation and kernel of the whole liturgical year' (*SC* 106). The highpoint in liturgical celebration, the resurrection of the crucified Jesus, came to be acknowledged as the highpoint of his redemptive revelation. The liturgy indicated the priority of Easter for the doctrine of revelation.[20]

---

19. See Raúl Biord Castillo, *La Resurrección de Cristo como Revelación. Análisis del tema en la teología fundamental a partir de la Dei Verbum* (Rome: Gregorian University Press, 1998).
20. The language of *DV* about 'the total presence of Christ' enjoys a prior 'intimation'

(5) A fifth significant, and still sometimes contentious, teaching of *DV* concerns the way it sets out the divine self-disclosure as being past, present, and future. Here, once again, we will see how the constitution follows the lead of *SC*.

We have just quoted the text of *DV* about the *past* completing and perfecting of revelation at the resurrection of the crucified Jesus and the outpouring of the Spirit at the first Pentecost. Nevertheless, the constitution also portrays revelation as a *present* event that invites human faith: '"The obedience of faith" (Romans 16:26) must be shown to God as he reveals' himself (*DV* 5). *DV* associates revelation as it happened then and as it happens now in the Church: 'God, who spoke in the past, uninterruptedly speaks to the spouse of his beloved Son' (*DV* 8). In its closing chapter the constitution cites St Ambrose of Milan to picture what happens when personal prayer accompanies the reading of sacred Scripture and 'a dialogue' takes place between God and human beings: 'we address him when we pray; we listen to him when we read the divine oracles' (*DV* 25). Besides being completed in the past and repeatedly actualised in the present, revelation is also to be expected in the future at 'the glorious manifestation of our Lord, Jesus Christ' (*DV* 4).

Faced with this scheme of revelation as past, *present*, and future, some are still tempted to allege that present revelation is not revelation in the proper sense but only a growth in the collective understanding of biblical revelation completed and 'closed' once and for all with Christ and his apostles. Undoubtedly such a growth of understanding can and does take place. *DV* takes up this theme: 'the tradition that comes from the apostles makes progress in the Church, with the help of the Holy Spirit. There is growth in knowledge of the realities and words that are passed on . . . thus, as the centuries go by, the Church is constantly moving towards the fullness of divine truth' (*DV* 8). Nevertheless, we would not do justice to tradition if we credited it only with the development in understanding of a closed and past revelation, but denied that it actualises the revelation of God. *DV* offers no such 'low' version of tradition. The constitution sees in the following terms the results of tradition as guided by the Holy Spirit:

---

in what *Sacrosanctum Concilium* taught about the pluriform presence of Christ in the liturgy (*SC* # 7). See Gerald O'Collins, 'Vatican II on the Liturgical Presence of Christ', in *Irish Theological Quarterly*, 77 (2012): 3–17.

> Through the same tradition . . . the Sacred Scriptures themselves are more deeply understood and ceaselessly actualised. Thus God, who spoke in the past, speaks uninterruptedly with the spouse of his beloved Son. And the Holy Spirit, through whom the living voice of the Gospel rings out in the Church—and through her in the world—leads believers into all truth, and makes the word of Christ dwell abundantly in them (*DV* 8).

Here the Council expresses its conviction that, through the force of tradition, the divine self-revelation recorded in the Scriptures is not only 'more deeply understood' but also 'actualised'. God continues to speak, and through the Spirit 'the living voice of the Gospel' never ceases to ring out.

To deny present revelation is to doubt the active power here and now of the Holy Spirit as guiding tradition and mediating the presence of the risen Christ. In effect this also means reducing faith to the acceptance of some revealed truths coming from the past rather than taking faith in its integral sense—as the full obedience personally given to God revealed here and now through the living voice of the Gospel. In short to deny the revelation of God as happening also in the present is to *sell* short its human correlative, faith.

Of course, if one persists in thinking that revelation *primarily* means the communication of revealed truths, it becomes easier to relegate revelation to the past. As soon as the whole set of revealed truths is complete, revelation ends or is 'closed'. For this way of thinking later believers cannot immediately and directly experience divine revelation. All they can do is remember, interpret, and apply truths revealed long ago to the apostolic church.

DV and other conciliar and post-conciliar documents describe, to be sure, revelation as something which reached its full completion in the past—through 'the total presence' of Christ and his 'self-manifestation' (*DV* 4). There was content to this personal revelation, so that the constitution could refer to 'the things that he [God] revealed for the salvation of all peoples' (*DV* 7), 'the divinely revealed realities (*divinitus revelata*)' (*DV* 11), and 'the deposit of faith' entrusted to the apostolic church and to be maintained faithfully through the tradition (*DV* 10). Nevertheless, *DV* does not hesitate to speak of 'hearing the Word of God' here and now (*DV* 1), of the obedience of faith being given to God who reveals himself in the present (*DV* 5), of God 'continuing to converse' with the whole Church, and of the Holy Spirit ensuring that 'the living voice of the Gospel' rings out in the present (*DV* 8). In representing the divine self-revelation in Christ as not only a matter of the past and the future but also a present reality, *DV* once again follows the lead of the liturgical constitution.

Christ, *SC* explains, is actively present in the eucharistic celebration. 'It is he himself', for example, who 'speaks when the holy Scriptures are read' (*SC* 7). A later paragraph adds that in the sacred liturgy 'God speaks to his people and Christ is still proclaiming his Gospel' (*SC* 33); this is to recognise how the faithful encounter the living Word of God. To express the full scope of this personal encounter (through the past and the future, as well as in the present), the liturgical constitution cites the antiphon for the Second Vespers on the Feast of Corpus Christi (now the Feast of the Body and Blood of Christ) and calls the Eucharist 'a paschal banquet in which Christ is consumed, the mind is filled with grace, and a pledge of future glory is given to us' (*SC* 47). The complete antiphon reads: 'O sacred banquet in which Christ is consumed, his suffering is remembered [from the past], the mind is filled with grace [in the present], and a pledge of future glory is given to us (*O sacrum convivium, in quo Christus sumitur, recolitur memoria passionis eius; mens impletur gratia; et futurae gloriae nobis pignus datur*)'. When quoting the antiphon, *SC* does not include 'his suffering is remembered', since the same paragraph has just spoken of the Eucharist as 'a memorial of his [Christ's] Death and Resurrection'. The passage from the constitution naturally highlights salvation and, specifically, the grace and glory communicated by the Eucharist. Nevertheless, it also points to revelation as past (remembering Christ's death and resurrection), as present ('the mind' being 'filled with grace'), and as future (the vision of God in 'future glory'). One might adapt the antiphon and say:

> O sacred revelation, in which Christ is encountered: a revelation fully conveyed through his life, death, and resurrection (along with the sending of the Spirit) which we remember; a revelation which can here and now fill our minds through the grace of his self-disclosure;

and a revelation which promises us his glorious self-manifestation to come.

One could sum up *DV*'s teaching on revelation by saying that, through Christ, it has been fully communicated in the past, that it will be consummated at the future end of history, and that it happens here and now. Revelation as present actualises the living event of the divine self-manifestation but does not 'enlarge' the essential 'content' of what was completely revealed through Christ's life, death, resurrection, and sending of the Holy Spirit. Revelation continues to be an actual encounter with the self-manifesting God, but this personal dialogue adds nothing to 'the divinely revealed realities' (which essentially amount to Jesus Christ crucified, risen from the dead, and to come one day in glory, together with all that these events effect and imply). We might express the three 'moments' of revelation by distinguishing between, but not separating, 'foundational' (past) revelation, present or 'dependent' revelation (which essentially depends upon foundational revelation), and future (or eschatological) revelation.[21]

(6) A sixth and final theme on revelation to be gleaned from *DV* touches the human response to the present self-disclosure of God: the obedience of faith (*DV* 5) or submission to God of the whole human person. Revelation is a reciprocal event, and is not truly 'there' until human beings respond with faith. In the words of the constitution, 'by revelation' 'the invisible God' 'addresses human beings as his friends . . . and moves among them, in order to invite and receive them into his own company' (*DV* 2). In short, revelation reaches its goal when believing hearts and minds open themselves to the divine self-communication and share the life and 'company' of God.

At the third session of the Council, Cardinal Julius Döpfner expressed the reception of faith (in a summary offered by Jared Wicks): 'faith is primarily God's work in humans to make his word of revelation effective, so that in faith revelation's essence completes itself. Beyond a dialogue, faith is *participative* of and in what God reveals.'[22] Together with the cardinal's reflection, one should also cite

---

21. On these distinctions, see O'Collins, *Rethinking Fundamental Theology: Toward a New Fundamental Theology* (Oxford: Oxford University Press, 2011), 128–35.
22. Wicks, 'Vatican II on Revelation', 640, note 7; see also Gianluca Montaldi, *In fide ipsa essentia revelationis completur: Il tema della fede nell'evolversi del Concilio*

a similar position on revelation's essential link with faith developed by a notable Vatican II *'peritus'*, Joseph Ratzinger. Now that the complete edition of Ratzinger's *'Habilitationsschrift'* has been published, we can see how he followed St Bonaventure. Revelation is realised only when the action of God reaches its 'term' or intended outcome: namely faith.[23] Divine revelation exists in living subjects, those who respond with faith. In a lecture given in 1963, Ratzinger insisted that 'revelation always and only becomes a reality where there is faith . . . revelation to some degree includes its recipient, without whom it does not exist.'[24]

Human Experience and Divine Revelation

Thus far we have seen how *DV* has yielded six clear items of teaching on revelation: it is primarily God's self-manifestation and secondarily the disclosure of new truths; it is essentially salvific and sacramental; it can be happily expressed as God's 'self-communication'; it reached its highpoint with Christ's death and resurrection; as foundational, dependent, and eschatological, it spans past, present and future, respectively; it reaches its intended outcome in the response of human faith. The constitution has more to say (or imply) about such themes as the complex relation between revelation and tradition, and the equally complex relation between revelation and Scripture.[25] But let me limit myself to raising some pressing questions about human experience, the context in which the self-revelation of God takes place and yet a theme that barely makes an appearance in the constitution on revelation (*DV* 8, 14).

The Gospel of John, the letters of St Paul, the *Confessions* of St Augustine, and other classical works established and encouraged an experiential approach to understanding and interpreting the divine-human relationship. A long line of spiritual and mystical authorities examined this relationship in the key of experience. William of Saint-

---

Vaticano II; La genesi di DV 5–6 (Rome: Gregorian University Press, 2005), at 355–60.
23. For details see Wicks, 'Vatican II on Revelation', 642, note 12.
24. Joseph Ratzinger, 'Revelation and Tradition', in Karl Rahner and Joseph Ratzinger, *Revelation and Tradition*, translated by Willian J O'Hara (London: Burns & Oates, 1966), 26–49, at 36.
25. On this see O'Collins, *Rethinking Fundamental Theology*, 190–233.

Thierry (1085–1148) proved one of many Christian men and women who explored in depth our spiritual experience. Nevertheless, two modern documents of the Catholic magisterium, *Dei Filius* (from Vatican I in 1870) and *Pascendi* (from Pope Pius X in 1907), warned, respectively, against denying that external signs could lend credibility to divine revelation, against appealing only to the internal experience of individuals (*DzH* 3033; *ND* 127), and against making faith in God depend on the 'private experience' of individuals and maintaining that interior, immediate experience of God prevails over rational arguments (*DzH* 3484). This justified opposition to one-sided and partial versions of religious experience unfortunately encouraged the dangerous delusion that somehow we could encounter and accept the divine self-revelation 'outside' human experience.

The Second Vatican Council, in general, introduced sparingly the terminology of 'experience'. The conciliar documents reflected some unease about this language. One can ascribe that inhibition to the long shadows cast by the condemnation of 'Modernism' in the decree *Lamentabili* and the encyclical *Pascendi* (both of 1907). In condemning 'modernists', St Pius X and his collaborators showed a certain blindness to historical developments in Christianity, but were right on other scores. Some 'modernists' went astray in one-sidedly emphasising religious experience. Misuse of this category should not, however, have led to ruling it out or downplaying its centrality. Yet for much of the twentieth century that was the case in the Catholic circles of many countries. Seminarians, in particular, were trained to be suspicious of 'experience', as if it were merely private, emotional, and dangerously subjective.

In 1965, *DV* cautiously began setting the record straight at the level of official teaching. Through their special history of revelation and salvation, the Israelites 'experienced the ways of God with human beings' (*DV* 14). In the post-New Testament life of the Church, their 'experience' of 'spiritual realities' has helped believers contribute to the progress of tradition (*DV* 8). Then followed *GS*, which proved nothing less than a profound reflection on the experience of the whole human family in the light of the crucified and risen Christ. It is in the light of Christ's revelation that 'the sublime calling and profound misery, which human beings experience, find their final meaning' (*DV* 13). Here and elsewhere the constitution set itself to correlate 'the light of revelation' with human experience (for example, *DV* 33). But it was left to a pope to feed the theme of experience directly into the bloodstream of official Catholic teaching.

With his background in the phenomenology of Edmund Husserl, Max Scheler, and others of a philosophical school that aims to describing the way things, as they actually are, manifest themselves, John Paul II had no aversion to 'experience' and the language of 'experience'. In his first encyclical, *Redemptor Hominis* of 1979, he introduced the noun 'experience' four times and the verb 'experience' twice. A year later in *Dives in Misericordia* (*DM*), he appealed to collective and individual experience (*DM* 4), and went on to use 'experience' thirteen times as a noun and six times as a verb. One can readily justify the pope's choice of terminology. If the divine self-revelation does not enter our experience (to arouse faith or strengthen an existing faith), it simply does not happen as far as we are concerned. Non-experienced revelation makes no sense.[26]

Four Further Themes Left Untouched

Thus far we have examined six themes found in the teaching of *DV* on revelation and one theme (experience) that hardly comes into view in that constitution. The first principle from the final report of the 1985 Extraordinary Synod (see above) prompts me into recalling briefly what other documents of Vatican II offer, so that we might grasp the 'integral' conciliar doctrine on God's self-revelation. Four themes suggest themselves: the human condition, the credibility of revelation, divine revelation reaching those who are not Christians, and 'the signs of the times'.

(1) The brief opening chapter of *DV* did not respond to the question: who are the human beings addressed by God's self-disclosure? From the opening sentence of the Constitution, one can glean that they are (potential) hearers of the divine word (*DV* 1). They are endowed with 'reason' (*DV* 6), but need to be delivered from 'the darkness of sin and death' (*DV* 4). For a fuller account of the human condition, we must

---

26. See further Gerald O'Collins, 'John Paul II and the Development of Doctrine', in *The Legacy of John Paul II*, edited by Gerald O'Collins and Michael A Hayes (London: Continuum, 2008), 1–16. On experience and religious experience, see Gerald O'Collins, *Fundamental Theology*, second edition (Mahwah, NJ: Paulist Press, 1986) 42–55.

look elsewhere: to the Declaration on the Relation of the Church to Non-Christian Religions (*Nostra Aetate* [*NA*]) and, much more to *GS*. *NA* presents religious faith as an answer to the fundamental questions which belong to human existence and which human beings must sooner or later face (*NA* 1–2). *GS* dedicates its introduction to the human situation (*GS* 4–10) and its opening chapter to the dignity of human persons (*GS* 12–22). Here the Constitution has much to say about human beings as created in the image of God, sinful yet free, and faced with the mystery of death. It declares robustly: 'both the high calling and the deep misery which human beings experience find their final meaning in the light of this [Christ's] revelation' (*GS* 13). Elsewhere *GS* has more to say about the condition of human beings who need and receive the revealing and redemptive self-communication of God.

(2) Apropos of reasons for accepting this revelation—what we might call the 'credibility' of revelation—*DV* has little or nothing to offer, apart from the coherent clarity of its six chapters, which resulted from debates and discussions that continued through the four sessions and three intersessions of the Council. While *GS* never set itself directly to establish the credibility of God's revelation in Christ, the Constitution over and over again vividly proclaims Christ as the One who answers the deepest questions and yearnings of human beings (for instance, *GS* 22, 38, and 45). In second place, it presents attractively the Church as the community founded by Christ and offering to the whole world the light and light of his message (for instance, *GS* 40–43, 92–93). To this we should add that the unfolding story of the Council, convoked and opened by Pope John XXIII and brought to a conclusion by Pope Paul VI, caught the attention of the world and did not leave untouched many people who hungered for religious meaning and nourishment. In that sense, the whole 'event' of Vatican II provided reasons for finding a believable creed in what the Christian Church proclaims about the divine self-revelation in Christ,

(3) A third crucial issue, left untouched in *DV*, enquires about divine revelation reaching the religious 'others', those who have not heard the Christian message or have not yet found reasons for accepting it. The final paragraph of its chapter on revelation briefly repeats the teaching of Vatican I about the knowledge of God being available through the created world (*DV* 6), but does not develop

what this might mean for the many millions who follow 'other' religious faiths. Here four documents of Vatican II step in to provide new, official teaching about the possibility of responding in faith to the divine self-revelation: *LG* (16 and 17), *NA*, the Decree on the Church's Missionary Activity (*Ad Gentes*) (especially, Chapter 1), and *GS* (various paragraphs). Once again we find the first document approved by the Council, *SC,* leading the way. It initiated this concern for 'the religious others' and displayed a mindset open to the salvation of the world.[27]

(4) Finally, *GS* proposed that 'the signs of the times' (Matt 16: 3) and 'the voices of our age' (*GS* 44) can convey God's intentions. Discerning the signs of the times belongs with the call to open oneself to the full scope of the present, 'dependent' divine revelation, which also reaches us through the Church's liturgy and Scriptures, through public and private prayer, and through many other experiences, both individual and collective.[28] John XXIII had introduced the theme of 'the signs of the times' in his 1962 'bull' convoking Vatican II, *Humanae Salutis*, and a year later in the encyclical *Pacem in Terris* (126–29). *GS* picked up this theme: 'the Church carries the responsibility of scrutinising the signs of the times and interpreting them in the light of the Gospel' (*GS* 4). It is the whole 'people of God', led 'by the Spirit of the Lord who fills the whole world', who try 'to discern' 'in the events, the needs, and the longings that it shares with other human beings of our age', what 'may be true signs of the presence or of the purpose of God' (*GS* 11).

To conclude, *DV* merits its place at the head of the four constitutions promulgated by the Second Vatican Council. In particular, its doctrine of the divine self-revelation in Christ offers the primary key for understanding all the conciliar documents. Nevertheless, it is only by interpreting this Constitution in the context of the other fifteen documents that will make us grasp the integral teaching of the Council on the self-manifestation of the Word of God.

---

27. For details on what these five conciliar texts say about 'the religious others', see my *The Second Vatican Council on Other Religions* (Oxford: Oxford University Press, 2013).
28. On discerning the signs of the times, see O'Collins, *Rethinking Fundamental Theology*, 102–07.

2

Vatican II and 'The Study of the Sacred Page' as 'The Soul of Theology' (*Dei Verbum* 24)

Francis J Moloney SDB

Among the many challenging developments that emerged from the Second Vatican Council, the Dogmatic Constitution on Divine Revelation, *Dei Verbum* (henceforth *DV*), one of the last documents to be promulgated by Paul VI at the close of the Council on 18 November 1965, has an important place. The document is the result of a tortured history that ran across all sittings of the Council. It began with the rejection of the schema from the preparatory commission, *De Fontibus Revelationis*, in November 1962.[1] The subsequent discussion, sometimes bitter, at the Council and in the commissions and working parties, led to a compromise document that nevertheless issued fresh opportunities for the future of Catholic exegesis, but in a special way, for the promotion of the role of the Word of God in the life of the Church. As we focus our attention on the conciliar statement that 'the study of the sacred page is, as it were, the soul of sacred theology' (*DV* 24), we must remember that this statement is part of a larger design: a return to the use of the Scriptures to the life of the Church, so that all

---

1. See Yves Congar, *My Journal of the Council* (Adelaide: ATF Press, 2012), 151–205. For a most helpful presentation of this background, see John W O'Malley, *What Happened at Vatican II* (Cambridge and London: Harvard University Press, 2008), 36–52. All English translations of the Conciliar documents are taken from *Vatican Council II. The Conciliar and Post Conciliar Documents,* edited by Austin Flannery (Dublin: Dominican Publications, 1980). For a succinct, and first-hand account of the genesis of *Dei Verbum*, see Joseph Ratzinger, 'Dogmatic Constitution on Divine Revelation. Origin and Background', in *Commentary on the Documents of Vatican II*, edited by Herbert Vorgrimler, 5 volumes (London: Burns & Oates/Herder & Herder, 1967–9), 3:155–66.

believers might be renewed through the nourishment they receive at the tables of the Word and the Eucharist (see *DV* 21, 26).[2]

Those of us from the Roman Catholic tradition should also keep in mind that the so-called 'higher criticism' that began in earnest in the latter part of the eighteenth century and developed into a mainstream academic activity in the nineteenth century played a part in what finally emerged as *DV*. Higher criticism, nowadays more often described as historical-critical scholarship,[3] generated a response within the Catholic Church that had its formal beginnings in Leo XIII's *Providentissimus Deus (PD)*, in 1893. Pius XII's *Divino Afflante Spiritu (DAS)*, written to commemorate the fiftieth anniversary of *PD* in 1943, continued that response in a way that still makes an impact on Catholic biblical scholarship.[4] *DV* emerges from that past. These earlier encyclicals have their own contexts, and their own content. As is generally the case in Catholic teaching, *DV* did not invent the wheel, even though much that is innovative is found there.

Leo XIII (1893) and Pius XII (1943)

PD comes from an era when the negative results of emerging, and sometimes stridently anti-Christian, critical biblical scholarship had to be countered (*PD* 2, 10). Great attention is given to the long Catholic tradition of studying the Word of God (*PD* 7-8) and the need to explain the Scriptures within that tradition (*PD* 15–17). It is authentically transmitted in the Latin Vulgate (*PD* 13), and the result

---

2. *DV* 24, from which the title of this essay has been taken, emerged at Vatican II, in Chapter VI of the Constitution: 'Sacred Scripture in the Life of the Church.' This final chapter contains paragraphs 21–6.
3. Even the descriptive 'historical-critical scholarship' is very generic. The distinct scholarly areas of textual criticism, source criticism, archeological, philological and historical research, form criticism and redaction criticism belong to a historical approach to the biblical texts, and the worlds that generated them. It is to be distinguished from the increasing use of more literary methods that emerged at the end of the second Christian millennium. For a survey, see the forthcoming Francis J Moloney, 'Synchronic Interpretation', in *The Oxford Dictionary of Biblical Interpretation* (New York: Oxford University Press, 2013).
4. References to these two Encyclicals will be by means of paragraph numbers. They are available online. For *PD*, see <http://www.papalencyclicals.net/leo13/l13provi.htm.> Accessed 15 August 2013. For *DAS*, see <http://www.vatican.va/holy_father/pius_xii/encyclicals/documents/hf_p-xii_enc_30091943_divino-afflante-spiritu_en.html.> Accessed 15 August 2013.

of divine authorship (*PD* 1: 'a letter written by our heavenly Father, and transmitted by the sacred authors'), a theory that leads to a very restrictive notion of inerrancy (*PD* 21). The proper formation of Catholic teachers, and the course of studies that should be taught in the seminaries is programmed (*PD* 11–14). Everything must proceed under 'the watchful care of the Church' (*PD* 6). Despite its being produced in a hostile context with its consequent understandable defensive atmosphere, the theme of this paper is explicitly stated in 1893:

> Most desirable is it, and most essential, that the whole teaching of Theology should be pervaded and animated by the use of the divine Word of God. This is what the Fathers and the greatest theologians of all ages have desired and reduced to practice (*PD* 16).

PD is rightly regarded as a defensive text, and there were reasons for that stance at the time. However, in the midst of his careful defense of the theological agenda of the time, Leo XIII paved the way for the breakthrough of *DAS*, however tentatively, in a number of areas, especially the importance of creative biblical research,[5] and the need to know to the original languages.[6] In 1890, Leo XIII had authorised the establishment of the École Biblique et Archéologique de Jérusalem by Marie-Joseph Lagrange, OP, and the Pontifical Biblical Commission was formed in 1902, the last year of his life. In his wake, Pius X founded the Pontifical Biblical Institute in Rome in 1909.[7]

---

5. 'But he (the Catholic biblical scholar) must not on that account consider that it is forbidden, when just cause exists, to push enquiry and exposition beyond what the Fathers have done; provided he carefully observes the rule so wisely laid down by St Augustine—not to depart from the literal and obvious sense, except only where reason makes it untenable or necessity requires' (*PD* 15, referring to Augustine, *De Genesi ad litteram*, 1, viii, 7:13 [PL 34]).
6. 'Hence it is most proper that Professors of Sacred Scripture and theologians should master those tongues in which the sacred Books were originally written; and it would be well that Church students should also cultivate them, more especially those who aspire to academic degrees' (*PD* 17).
7. For a positive assessment of *PD* and Leo XIII, see William Baird, *History of New Testament Research*, 2 volumes (Minneapolis, MN: Fortress, 1992-2003), 2:163,384–85. This new openness, however, was tempered by Pius X's decree *Lamentabili sane* (1907) and his Encyclical *Pascendi dominici gregis* (1907).

Across the turn of the century there was an increasing sense of the importance of the Word of God for the life of the Church, only to be sidelined by concern over so-called 'modernism' in the Catholic communion and, more importantly, two World Wars and the arrogance, inhumanity and the slaughter that marked the first fifty years of the twentieth century (1914–19; 1940–45). Astonishingly, during a period of the widespread conflicts during the latter part of the Second World War, as the Allies struck back on all fronts, including in the Pacific, Pius XII produced *DAS* to mark the fiftieth anniversary of *PD*.[8] This remarkable document was a watershed for Catholic biblical scholarship, and its influence is ongoing. The Holy Father exhibits exquisite awareness of the importance of critical scholarship. He insisted that great advancements had taken place since 1893, and for this reason 'the biblical question' needed to be revisited fifty years later (*DAS* 11–13). He asks for a return to the ancient languages as the source for all correct interpretation (*DAS* 14–18), and also that due respect be given to the other historical sciences: archeology, philology, comparative religions and other allied sciences (*DAS* 24, 33, 36–40).[9] 'All human knowledge, even the non-sacred, has indeed its own proper dignity and excellence, being a finite participation of the infinite knowledge of God, but it acquires a new and higher dignity and, as it were, a consecration, when it is employed to cast a brighter

---

Despite its subsequent outstanding contribution to Catholic biblical studies, the Pontifical Biblical Institute (with a small sister-house in Jerusalem) was founded in 1909 partly to 'keep an eye on' what was emerging from the École Biblique. See Jerome Murphy-O'Connor, *The École Biblique and the New Testament: A Century of Scholarship* (Novum Testamentum et Orbis Antiquus 13; Freiburg/Göttingen: Universitätsverlag/Vandenhoeck und Ruprecht, 1990).

8. The situation of 1943 is appropriately described in *DAS* 56: 'If these things which We have said, Venerable Brethren and beloved sons, are necessary in every age, much more urgently are they needed in our sorrowful times, when almost all peoples and nations are plunged in a sea of calamities, when a cruel war heaps ruins upon ruins and slaughter upon slaughter, when, owing to the most bitter hatred stirred up among the nations, We perceive with greatest sorrow that in not a few has been extinguished the sense not only of Christian moderation and charity, but also of humanity itself'.
9. *DAS* 15 is memorable: 'In like manner ought we to explain the original text which, having been written by the inspired author himself, has more authority and greater weight than any even the very best translation, whether ancient or modern'.

light upon the things of God' (*DAS* 41).[10] He asks that, beyond the Latin Vulgate, Greek and Hebrew texts should 'be published for the benefit of the Holy Church of God' (*DAS* 20). With great astuteness, Pius XII defends the Vulgate, and its role in the Catholic Tradition. However, he rightly points out that 'its authenticity is not specified primarily as critical, but rather as juridical' (*DAS* 21). Would that this pontifical assessment had been recalled in our own time, as *Liturgiam Authenticam* (2001) stipulated that the Latin *Editio Tipica* of all liturgical texts, and the Latin New Vulgate, must serve for the translation of all liturgical texts (*Editio Tipica*) and 'is to be consulted as an auxiliary tool' (New Vulgate) in all biblical translations used in the Liturgy (*Liturgiam Authenticam* 23, 25).

Although couched in a different way, the role of the Word of God in Theology is also found in *DAS*. Speaking directly to Catholic exegetes, Pius XII insists:

> With special zeal should they apply themselves, not only to expounding exclusively these matters which belong to the historical, archeological, philological and other auxiliary sciences . . . but, having duly referred to these, in so far as they may aid the exegesis, they should set forth in particular the theological doctrine in faith and morals of the individual books or texts so that their exposition may not only aid the professors of theology in their explanations and proofs of the dogmas of faith, but may also be of assistance to priests in their presentation of Christian doctrine to the people, and in fine may help all the faithful to lead a life that is holy and worthy of a Christian (*DAS* 24).

An Unresolved Tension

Turning to the task of 'the study of the Sacred Page' as part of the theological reflection of the Church, articulated in principle by *PD* and *DAS* and stated as one of the main objectives of the post-Conciliar period to bring the Word of God to the centre of the life of

---

10. This statement anticipates the fine statement on the rightful autonomy of earthly affairs found in *Gaudium et Spes* 36.

the Church (*DV* 24), the nature of the relationship between the two 'sources' for Revelation (Scripture and Tradition) needs to be raised. *DV* broke genuine new theological ground. In former times, the biblical scholar entertained him- or herself in the playpen of foreign languages, cultures, literary forms, archeology, hermeneutics, and those matters that were proper to a somewhat arcane discipline.[11] The great Tradition was separated from the Word of God, another source of Revelation. Generally speaking, maybe with one eye on useful biblical passages in a 'proof-text' tradition, theologians turned to the great Tradition to articulate—in every different age—Christian and Catholic truths. That this should no longer be the case has been made clear by the Magisterium, from Leo XIII to Vatican II, and beyond.[12]

Following this mounting insistence, Vatican II enhanced the mutuality between the biblical scholar and the theologian by its breakthrough teaching on the relationship between Scripture and sacred Tradition. The Council Fathers, after a bitter debate with those faithful to the 'two-source' theory of Revelation that had been taught at Vatican I (Dogmatic Constitution *Dei Filius*: the two sources of Scripture *and* Tradition [*DS* 3000, 3006, 3011]), Vatican II broke from that tradition to teach that Scripture and Tradition form 'a single sacred deposit of the Word of God' (*DV* 10). The precise nature of the relationship between them, however, can be difficult to determine. The Council simply stated that they flow together from the same well-spring and 'come together in some fashion (*in unum quodammodo coalescunt*)' (*DV* 9). The deliberate vagueness of this description leaves a delicate balance, necessarily calling for the ongoing interpretation of biblical text and sacred Tradition 'under the watchful eye of the Magisterium' (*DV* 23. See *PD* 6). Yet, the Council

---

11. Raymond E Brown, *The Virginal Conception and Bodily Resurrection of Jesus* (New York: Paulist, 1973), 6, described that period as follows: 'Tradition could always correct Scriptural interpretation, but never vice-versa. If the biblical scholar was going to insist on the freedom to play with his new-fangled toys of language and literary form, he was to be kept in a playpen and not let out to disturb the good order of the theological household.'
12. For an earlier reflection on some of the following, see Francis J Moloney, 'L'Écriture Sainte et le Magistère: une relation mouvementée', in *La Responsabilité des Théologiens*. Mélanges offerts à Joseph Doré, edited by François Bousquet, Henri-Jérôme Gagey, Geneviève Médevielle and Jean-Louis Souletie (Paris: Desclée, 2002), 493–505.

insists, 'this Magisterium is not superior to the word of God, but is its servant' (*DV* 10).[13]

Subsequent to the Council, and especially in the time of Pope John Paul II, the Church's leadership has shown increasing interest in what has been called 'the new evangelisation,' which often is expressed in an enthusiastic return to the values and practices of the pre-conciliar period, rather than a critical use of the Sacred Page. The more Euro-centered focus of Pope Benedict XVI, and his very negative understanding of the impact made upon western culture by the Enlightenment, has moved the meaning of 'the new evangelisation' further along the same lines.[14] The relationship between the study of the Sacred Page and the articulation of a relevant theology in an increasingly complex period of rapid cultural change on the one hand, and resistance to it on the other, guiding 'the Church, during its pilgrim journey here on earth . . . until such time as she is brought to see him face to face as he really is (cf John 3:2)' (*DV* 7), is fraught with difficulty.

Biblical Truths

Subsequent to *DAS* (1943), gifted and hard-working scholars gave much to see that historical-critical scholarship took its rightful place in the Catholic tradition of biblical interpretation (see also *DV* 12). The Council's discussions of the role of the Bible in the Church reflects an acceptance of this achievement (see especially, *DV* 7). But since that time biblical interpretation has developed further, encouraged to pursue the 'objective truth' by means of the historical-critical approach to the Bible (see The Pontifical Biblical Commission, *The Interpretation of the Bible in the Church*, 34–41).[15]

---

13. For a careful exegesis of *DV* 10, see Francis A Sullivan, *Magisterium: Teaching Authority in the Catholic Church* (Mahwah, NJ: Paulist Press, 1983), 31–33.
14. Evident in his discomfort with critical biblical scholarship in Joseph Ratzinger, *Jesus of Nazareth*, 2 volumes (New York/San Francisco, CA: Doubleday/Ignatius Press, 2007–2011), 1:xi–xxiv; 2:xiii–xvii. His *Jesus* claims that critical scholarship has nothing further to offer (see 2:xiv). It is largely a pseudo-patristic appeal to believers on the basis of a selected reading of events from the Gospels.
15. The document, The Pontifical Biblical Commission, *The Interpretation of the Bible in the Church* (Vatican City: Libreria Editrice Vaticana, 1993), has no paragraph numbers. I will refer to it throughout by means of the page numbers of the above edition.

A respectful application of historical-critical methods to both text and tradition should benefit the theologian's concern to affirm the 'truths' of the Catholic belief system in a way that was faithful to the Tradition, yet relevant for the world into which it was proclaimed. Biblical historical-critics were confident that they could uncover 'the meaning which the sacred writers really had in mind' (*DV* 12. See *DAS* 23: 'let the Catholic exegete undertake the task, of all those imposed on him the greatest, that namely of discovering and expounding the genuine meaning of the Sacred Books'). In theory, this looked like a good direction for the mutual enrichment of Scripture and theology. This 'genuine meaning' was something to be shared.

The relentless application of the criterion of *objectivity*, so important to historical-critical methods, is dissipating as contemporary biblical criticism recognises the 'worlds' involved in the process of (a) the original production, (b) the ongoing relevance and (c) the interpretation of the Sacred Text. This can create further difficulty for the theologian's oversight of the ongoing interpretation of 'the things (God) had once revealed for the salvation of all peoples' as it is 'transmitted to all generations' (*DV* 7). There are worlds 'behind,' 'within,' and 'in front of' the text. Thus, the Bible, one of the great classical texts of all time, must be approached as a window through which one can look to discover what lies behind it, a portrait with a world of its own, and a mirror in which one may or may not find one's own reflection.[16] But all is not lost. Interpretation of the Bible must attempt to create a 'horizon' which respects all three elements generated by the world behind, within, and in front of the text. This could lead to a greater sense of humility in interpretation. As a contemporary literary critic has written: 'The meaning of a text is inexhaustible because no context can provide all the keys to all its possibilities.'[17] It can with reason be claimed that there has never been an objective reading of any text. The patristic and reformation traditions focussed upon *the world in the text*, but unashamedly read

---

16. For this image, see Murray Krieger, *A Window to Criticism* (Princeton, NJ: Princeton University Press, 1974), 3–70. To my knowledge, it was first applied to the New Testament literature by Norman R Petersen, *Literary Criticism for New Testament Critics*, (Guides to Biblical Scholarship NT Series; Philadelphia, PA: Fortress, 1978), 24–48.
17. Edgar V McKnight, *Post-Modern Use of the Bible: The Emergence of Reader Oriented Criticism* (Nashville, TN: Abingdon, 1988), 241.

their own worlds and their own texts into it. The use of the Johannine literature to develop the language and doctrines articulated at Nicea (325) and Chalcedon (451), and the Reformers' use of Paul, especially Romans, to bolster their fundamental doctrine 'faith alone', are eloquent proofs of that inevitable process in any use of text.

The nineteenth-century quest for the historical Jesus produced a figure who resembled the researcher, the form critics focused upon *the world behind the text*, but their reconstruction of that world is now seen to have been often influenced by their own worlds. The Redaction Critics claimed to have returned, in a more scientific fashion, to *the world in the text*. But their dependence upon form critical conclusions concerning *the world behind the text*,[18] and the risk that they rendered the Evangelists in their own image, makes their work open to the criticism leveled against both form criticism and patristic-medieval exegesis. Rather than producing the 'genuine meaning,' so confidently suggested by the objective historical study of the biblical text, the Scripture scholar asks the theologian to exercise her or his ministry by providing interpretations that are more focussed upon the subjective and culturally conditioned nature of all interpretation, including that of the Tradition itself.

Contemporary Approaches to Biblical Interpretation

Following the larger world of literary criticism, contemporary biblical scholars focus more and more upon *the world in front of the text* (see *The Interpretation of the Bible*, 41–69). But this shift of focus presents its own problems. There are many 'worlds,' cultures, individuals, faith communities and interpretative traditions in front of the text. The emergence of narrative critical and reader-response criticism in the late 1980's initiated a process in which more attention was given to the multiplicity of readers and cultures, and to an increasingly sophisticated literary critique of a the biblical text.[19] In an attempt to devote greater attention to *the world in the text*, narrative critics trace

---

18. See, for example, the comment of a founding father of Redaction Criticism, Hans Conzelmann, *The Theology of St Luke* (London: Faber & Faber, 1961), 9: 'The analysis of the sources renders the *necessary service* of helping distinguish what comes from the source from what belongs to the author' (italics mine).
19. See Francis J Moloney, 'Narrative Criticism of the Gospels,' *Pacifica* 4 (1991): 181–201; also 'Mark as Story: Retrospect and Prospect,' *Pacifica* 25 (2012): 1–11.

implied authors and readers within a text that maintains its status as Divine Revelation. However, many of them have exaggeratedly claimed that the only issue that deserves attention is the text itself and the world receiving it. Thus, questions concerning *the world behind the text* become irrelevant. This approach can have detrimental results. A detachment of the biblical text from its historical setting, and an interest in the reader(s) of the text has led into increasingly subversive readings where the reader and her or his contexts are the determining factors in interpretation. Some attempt, however, even in these more subversive readings, where the text can be regarded as ideologically offensive, to show that it still forms part of a revealing tradition.[20] Others, however, produce an endless multiplicity of interpretations, determined by reading from a post-colonial, feminist, agnostic, or postmodern 'place'.[21] These approaches to the biblical text can become a serious obstacle to the essential and ongoing mutuality between the interpretation of the Word and the theological task. Between these two extremes there are many other interpretations, produced by readers reading 'from their place'.[22]

One of the most significant axioms behind these contemporary so-called postmodern methods of reading a biblical text can hardly be challenged: every interpreter inscribes his or herself in interpretation. On the basis of this axiom a wave of newer scholars suggests that we be honest at all times, admitting that the story I read into my interpretation is my story. But must one accept that biblical interpretation can be no more than a multiplicity of never-ending possible interpretations, reflecting the fragmented story of the reader, the highly mobile result of intertextuality, with no place for a time-honoured canon? Some scholars are developing what is known as autobiographical criticism, claiming that the most honest

---

20. See, for example, Sandra M Schneiders, *The Revelatory Text. Interpreting the New Testament as Sacred Scripture* (second edition; Collegeville, MN: The Liturgical Press, 1999).
21. See The Bible and Culture Collective, in *The Postmodern Bible* (London and New Haven, CT: Yale University Press, 1996); Stephen D Moore, *Poststructuralism and the New Testament. Derrida and Foucault at the Foot of the Cross* (Minneapolis, MN: Fortress Press, 1990).
22. See *Reading from This Place,* edited by Fernando F Segovia and Mary Ann Tolbert (2 volumes; Minneapolis, MN: Fortress Press, 1995–6).

way to interpret a biblical text I still regard as revelatory is to read it as neither his- or her-story, but as my-story.[23]

The theologian faces an impossible task if she or he wishes to dialogue with this multiplicity of contemporary approaches to the Bible. Nevertheless, these approaches indicate an important truth: no interpretation of a given text can lay claim to ultimate authority. It must be admitted that no contemporary religious, historical or cultural context can claim to understand *all the possibilities* of an ancient text, especially one which has remained alive in a reading public, across many cultures and historical eras, for 2,000 years. The traditional theological use of the 'proof text' should be a practice of the past. Paul Ricoeur has done much to indicate that once the act of interpretation has come to its conclusion, there is always a significant 'remainder' which lies beyond the limits of the completed interpretation, 'the residue of the literal interpretation'.[24] However, this same philosopher has also insisted that *many* interpretations are possible, but not *any* interpretation.[25] The contemporary interpreter of the biblical text must serve the theological task within the Christian community by creating a horizon where the worlds meet, behind, within and in front of the text. This should contribute to the role of the theologian who locates this horizon within the faith-tradition of the Catholic Church which reveres the Bible as part of Divine Revelation (*DV* 11-12, 23; *Fides et Ratio* 5-6, 55).[26] There is far more *mutuality* required here than the situation described by Bernard Lonergan in 1971: 'His (the exegete's) principle concern is to understand, and the understanding he seeks is, not the understanding of objects, which pertains to the

---

23. See Jeffrey L Staley, *Reading with a Passion. Rhetoric, Autobiography, and the American West in the Gospel of John* (New York: Continuum, 1995), 'Taking it Personally', edited by Janice Capel Anderson and Jeffrey L Staley, *Semeia* 72 (1995); *The Personal Voice in Biblical Interpretation,* edited by Ingrid R Kitzberger (London: Routledge, 1998).
24. Paul Ricoeur, *Interpretation Theory: Discourse and the Surplus of Meaning* (Fort Worth, TX: Texas Christian University Press, 1976), 55.
25. See, for example, Paul Ricoeur, *Hermeneutics and the Human Sciences,* edited by John Brooke Thompson (Cambridge: Cambridge University Press, 1981), 210-13.
26. For *Fides et Ratio*, see John Paul II, *Fides et Ratio (Faith and Reason)* (Strathfield: St Paul Publication, 1998).

second phase, but the understanding of texts, which pertains to the first phase of theology, to theology not as speaking to the present but as listening, as coming to listen to the past.'[27]

Text and Context

So-called postmodern criticism lays claim to 'point the way toward a more rigorously self-reflective and contextualised biblical criticism.'[28] But such claims have a certain arrogance. At the beginning of the third Christian millenium, after several decades of intense ecumenical activity and scholarly communion, biblical scholars are aware of the motivating principles, scholarly, cultural and ecclesial, of their various (and sometimes conflicting) interpretations.[29] Within this dialectic, Jews and Christians demand that the rights of believing biblical scholars to inscribe *their* age-old stories in Jewish and Christian interpretations be respected. *The limited comprehension created by context is not detrimental until one pretends to be free from it.* Aggressive anti-Jewish and anti-Christian readings of the biblical text cannot be part of a healthy dialectic as 'every investigation is conducted within some horizon'.[30]

How is the theologian, locating him- or herself within two thousand years' experience of reading and responding to the biblical text as Divine Revelation, to play his or her rightful role in the process of interpreting the Bible within the Church (see *The Interpretation of the Bible*, 50–7; *FR* 94–5)? Much culturally driven interpretation invites the reader into the text, giving *primacy* to cultures and a multiplicity of possible reading experiences. Such interpretations correctly point to the subjective nature of any interpretation, but they ignore an even more important hermeneutical principle. Read within the Christian Tradition, not only does the reader shape the text. As any observer of the Christian story can point out, *the text has shaped the reader, and*

---

27. Bernard Lonergan, *Method in Theology* (London: Darton, Longman and Todd, 1971), 167–8. Expanatory parenthesis mine.
28. Anderson and Staley, 'Taking It Personally,' 16.
29. On the rich results that can proceed from this 'dialectic,' part of the journey 'to discover the self-transcendence proper to the human process of coming to know,' see Lonergan, *Method*, 235–66, 239.
30. Lonergan, *Method*, 247. On 'dialectically opposed horizons,' see 247–9.

the practice of reading the Bible, for almost two thousand years.[31] In a Catholic 'study of the Sacred Page' *primacy* must be given to the text and its literary, historical and theological context, not to the socio-cultural context of the contemporary reader, however important the latter may be, especially for the theological articulation of the great Tradition in different times and cultures.

Even a believer might see that everything is 'intertext', the product of a highly volatile number of possibilities which happened to come together at one particular, but passing, point in time. This interpretative stance asks: why bother involve oneself in the process of interpreting a text which exists because of a tradition? Why subject to analysis a cultural, historical and religious moment 'frozen' in the past to generate (and subsequently impose) a normative 'canon,' if all that matters is the enculturated reader who is also the product of an infinite number of possibilities that have come together in one particular reading experience? An exegete working in the Catholic tradition must respond: to displace the primacy of the biblical text in the act of interpretation and to replace it with the cultural context of the reader and the reading community would be a tragic loss. Christians would be faced with the giddy possibility of spiralling through a never-ending whirlwind of interpretative possibilities, accepted today and discarded tomorrow. But this interpretative stance has no place in the exegetical task of the believing biblical scholar. No human community, especially the one served by the biblical scholar and the theologian as members of a Christian community that accepts the Bible as Divine Revelation, can survive in such a whirlwind (*FR* 46, 81, 91). Of course, the opposite destructive stance must also be avoided. The primacy of the biblical text in the act of interpretation can be replaced by the context of the culturally conditioned perspective of a particular Catholic authority or community.

A Contemporary Catholic Approach

Contemporary cultural, postmodern, and biographical interpretations focus more intensely upon the cultural situations of the interpreters

---

31. Artistic and musical expression, every-day language and practices across all the cultures where the Bible is read are eloquent proof of the formative power of the biblical text. See *FR* 24.

and their reading and hearing communities. Catholic biblical scholarship accepts that agenda, but submits that the process must run in two directions. *Biblical exegesis is not only shaped by culture and the cultures. Culture and the cultures have been profoundly shaped by the biblical revelation (FR 69–71).* This essential interplay between text *and* reader and reader *and* text affirms the ongoing importance, and indeed the priority, of the text transmitted in the Tradition above the culturally situated reader.

At least two factors lie behind the Catholic insistence upon the priority of the text over the situated reader, individual or communitarian. The first is the Tradition, which has its beginnings in Israel's recognition that *Torah*, *Nebi'im* and *Kᵉtubim* provided an authoritative word of God determining all aspects of the life and practice of the individual Israelite and the nation. This, of course, was particularly the case with *Torah*, but the commentary upon *Torah* provided by the Prophets and the Writings also gave them an authoritative status as *Tanak*. This sense of 'Scripture' (γραφη) passed rapidly into the early writings of the Christian communities. Widely recognised as Sacred Scripture late in the Second Century, there are indications from the very beginnings of a Christian literature that a Christian Sacred Scripture was emerging. This can be sensed in the Lukan and Matthean use of Old Testament texts and the literary forms in their narrative, and in the explicit Johannine claim that: 'Jesus did many other signs in the presence of the disciples that are not written (γεγραμμένα) in this book; but these are written (γέγραπται) that you may believe that Jesus is the Christ, the Son of God, and that believing you may have life in his name' (John 20:30–31). John is consciously passing on a 'writing' (γραφη), a Scripture to 'those who have believed without seeing' (verse 29), that their belief may be life-giving.[32] The same impression is created for the Pauline Corpus in 2 Peter 3:14–16, early in the second century.

The second factor is the evidence that culture, especially—but not only—European culture, has been shaped by the biblical tradition. Language, art, music, architecture, literature, ethical traditions,

---

32. See Dwight Moody Smith, 'When Did the Gospels Become Scripture?' *JBL* 119 (2000): 3–20; Moloney, 'The Gospel of John as Scripture,' *Catholic Biblical Quarterly* 67 (2005): 454–68. See also, Moloney, 'What Came First—Scripture or Canon? The Gospel of John as a Test Case,' *Salesianum* 68 (2006): 7–20.

national constitutions and modes of government bear its imprint. To use the language of contemporary literary criticism, the biblical text is the essential intertext for much contemporary culture. The English poet, William Blake, described the biblical text as our 'great code'.[33] A rejection of the formative nature of what Jews and Christians regard as the Word of God is the rejection of 4,000 years of human endeavor. Such a rejection, present in some contemporary philosophical and hermeneutical schools, is unacceptable in the Catholic community. Catholic life depends upon a history that, despite its ambivalence, reflects the unfolding of God's design.[34]

Most, even if not all, elements in the Christian Creeds reflect a mutuality between biblical texts and the cultural contexts that generated the Creeds.[35] This mutuality, however, does not detract from the truth that the biblical text has shaped the culture that has, in its own turn, interpreted that text for its credal formulations. One example must suffice, taken from a passage in the Gospel of John. Such examples could be multiplied to form a sizeable volume. *The text* of the encounter between Jesus and Nicodemus recorded in the Fourth Gospel (John 3:1–21) provides formative articulations of a

---

33. See Northrop Frye, *The Great Code. The Bible and Literature* (London: Routledge & Kegan Paul, 1982).
34. The consistent intervention of the Magisterium to stimulate the use of the Bible in the Catholic Church recognises this important truth. As well as *PD* (1893), *DAS* (1943), *DV* (1965) and *The Interpretation of the Bible in the Church* (1993), used for this reflection, recent decades have been marked by two further important documents, one from the Pontifical Biblical Commission, *The Jewish People and their Sacred Scriptures in the Bible* (2001), and the significant post-Synodal Apostolic Exhortation of Benedict XVI, *Verbum Domini. The Word of God in the Life and Mission of the Church* (2010). The continued need for these interventions may be a sign that the Bible still remains little known and used in the life of the Catholic Church. For a reflection on the Australian situation, see Moloney, 'Scripture Since Vatican II,' in *Vatican II. Reception and implementation in the Australian Church,* edited by Neil Ormorod, Ormond Rush, Clare Johnson and Joel Hodge, (Melbourne: Garratt Publishing, 2012), 47–61.
35. The problem of the non-biblically based doctrine that forms part of the Roman Catholic tradition cannot be explored here. It has long been a contentious issue between the Protestant and the Catholic traditions. In the end, it depends upon the careful use of the Paraclete saying in John 16:12–15. It is unacceptable for a Catholic theologian to reject those elements in the Tradition that are not biblical, or cannot be located in a reading of the historical Jesus. See, for example, Roger Haight, *Jesus Symbol of God* (New York: Maryknoll, 1999), especially, 187–212.

number of fundamental elements of the *Christian belief system*. We learn the Christian Tradition was born within Judaism (3:1–2). To see and to enter into the Kingdom (for John, the Christian community), one had to pass through the waters of Baptism and receive the gift of the Spirit from above (3:3–5). Those who wish to belong to that 'Kingdom' must allow the impulse of the Spirit to draw them beyond rituals, accepting the divine origins of their beginning and their end (3:6–10). We are instructed that in both past and present times, many claim to speak authoritatively of God, but there is only one who has come from God, and has made God known (3:11–12). Jesus of Nazareth, the Son of Man, has been lifted up on a cross to show in his flesh the love of God, so that all who gaze upon this unique revelation of a unique God will have life (3:13–15). In this God's love has been made known; God sent Jesus, his Son, not to judge us but to give us life (3:16–17). Christianity is life, not judgment, but we are shapers of our own destiny. Johannine 'realised eschatology' is not just a technical term dear to Charles Harold Dodd, Joachim Jeremias and Rudolf Bultmann. It speaks to those of us who need to be taught that we are responsible for our words and deeds (3:18–21).[36] From this brief example, one can see that the list of Christian 'truth-claims' that flow naturally from a critical acceptance of the biblical text is potentially very long. These claims have an impressive history in the confessed and lived faith of the Church, entrusted to the theologian in the service of the Church and its people (*FR* 7–12, 82).

The theologian and, one would hope, the Magisterium must allow a multiplicity of possible readings of the biblical text and a multiplicity of interpretations resulting from such readings. But the biblical text has shaped and continues to shape a Catholic community and a Catholic Tradition which recognise Jesus as Son of God, Son of Man, the unique revelation of God in the human story (*DV* 2).[37] But there is

---

36. For more detail, see Moloney, *The Gospel of John*, Sacra Pagina 4 (Collegeville, MN: Liturgical Press, 1998), 88–103.
37. There can be no laziness in this pursuit. The biblical meaning of the Christological expressions 'Son of God' and 'Son of Man' must be incorporated into theological discussion. Too often the Patristic association of 'Son of God' with Jesus' divinity (and the Trinitarian debate) and 'Son of Man' with his humanity (and Chalcedon) are taken for granted. This is a serious impoverishment of Christological possibilities that emerge from a serious interaction between biblical scholars and theologians. The biblical uses of 'Son of God' and 'Son of Man' are far richer than

more. The person of Jesus Christ gives the text authority, not the text itself. Christian Tradition pre-existed the text, and gave us the books (βιβλία) of the New Testament to grant access for their own and later generations to the person of Jesus Christ. We continue to read the story of Jesus within that Tradition.[38] Not only is there a narrative world behind, within and in front of the text, but there is also a Christian Tradition which pre-dated the text, generated the text, and which continues to give it life within the many contemporary cultures. The relationship between Tradition and Scripture, however, is never stable; much less 'frozen'. The Tradition gave birth and continues to enliven the Scriptures in a Christian community, but the Scriptures perform the prophetic role of keeping the Tradition honest when it falls to the temptation of absolutising, through accommodation, any age, culture or particular religious practice (*DV* 9–10; *FR* 64–5).[39] Not all will accept this view, but within a postmodern world, where 'différance' is important, we Catholics affirm our 'difference'.[40] It is within this highly volatile interaction of Scripture, Tradition, and the many, increasingly fragmented, cultures addressed by the one Word of God that the Catholic Scripture scholar and theologian exercise their difficult, but exciting ministry.

Conclusion

The narrator in Arundhati Roy's Booker Prize winning novel, *The God of Small Things* (1997), has a reflection appropriate for this setting:

---

the theological debate over the human/divine in Jesus.
38. Parallel affirmations could (and should) be made concerning the place of *Torah*, *Nebi'im* and *Kᵉtubim* within the Jewish Tradition. It is beyond the scope of this paper to do so.
39. For further development of this important point, see Moloney, 'Jesus Christ: The Question to Cultures', in *Pacifica* 1 (1988): 15–43. See also Lonergan's remarks on the interpreter in *Method*, 161: 'He can succeed in acquiring that habitual understanding of an author that spontaneously finds his wavelength and locks onto it, only after he has effected a radical change in himself.'
40. This play on words refers to the practice, developed by Jacques Derrida, of continually deferring meaning, and thus never locating a 'metaphysic' behind text that can constitute a definitive 'meaning'. To describe this practice he invented the neologism 'différer/différance'. As Kevin Hart, *The Trespass of the Sign: Deconstruction, Theology and Philosophy* (Cambridge: Cambridge University Press, 1989), describes it: '*différance* can be neither self-present nor self-identical; it is never constituted, only ever constituting: thus Derrida's talk of the play of *différance*' (37).

> The Great Stories are the ones you have heard and want to hear again. The ones you can enter anywhere and inhabit comfortably. They don't deceive you with thrills and trick endings. They don't surprise you with the unforeseen. They are as familiar as the house you live in. Or the smell of your lover's skin. You know how they end, yet you listen as though you don't. In the way that although you know that one day you will die, you live as though you won't. In the Great Stories you know who lives, who dies, who finds love, who doesn't. And yet you want to know again.[41]

It is important for Catholic Christians that there be a Catholic community where 'the study of the Sacred Page' is treasured. For the Catholic Tradition, the Bible is one of the ways God is made known, it is our Great Story. It is the house we live in . . . the smell of our lover's skin. It has given us the fixed points that support the silken threads upon which the many possible tapestries of Jewish and Catholic responses to that belief can be woven. We know, and yet we want to know again.[42] Our interpretation of the text is not determined by a dogmatic tradition, itself interpretation of text, but inspired by its beauty and the Tradition that continues to give it life (*FR* 79). As Joseph Ratzinger comments, using the image of the 'house':

> The 'house' of theology is not a building erected once and for all, it stands only because theologizing continues to go on as a living activity, and so the foundation (i.e. Sacred Scripture) is always something that is actively founding and hence the constant starting-point for the possibility of theology's existence. Hence the image is changed into one of the organic sphere, and Scripture is described as the rejuvenating force that keeps theology alive.[43]

---

41. Arundhati Roy, *The God of Small Things* (London: Flamingo, 1997), 229.
42. To this point, Lonergan, *Method*, 161, cites Friedrich Schlegel: 'A classic is a writing that is never fully understood. But those that are educated and educate themselves must always want to learn more from it.'
43. Ratzinger, 'Sacred Scripture in the Life of the Church,' in Vorgrimler ,

The theologian continues to construct and watches over 'the house we live in,' 'not superior to the Word of God, but its servant' (*DV* 10). Herein lies the tension, an inevitable 'restless relationship.' The scholar, whether biblical or theological, belongs to a community of human beings grappling with the timeless mysteries of God's action in and through Jesus Christ. There is always the risk of distorting the Word of God by demanding that the interpretation of Scripture correspond to the demands of a particular time, place or culture. Such distortions are understandable, as Joseph Ratzinger pointed out in his 1967 commentary upon *DV*. Addressing the problem of the relationship between Scripture and Tradition described as '*in unum quodammodo coalescunt*' (*DV* 9), the then Professor of Systematic Theology at the University of Tübingen rightly remarked:

> We shall have to acknowledge the truth of the criticism that there is, in fact, no explicit mention of the possibility of a distorting tradition and the place of Scripture as an element in the church that is *also* critical of tradition, which means that a most important side of the problem of tradition, as shown by the history of the church—and perhaps the real crux of the *ecclesia semper reformanda*—has been overlooked. In particular a council that saw itself consciously as a council of reform and thus implicitly acknowledged the possibility and reality of distortion in tradition could have achieved here in its thinking a real achievement in theological examination, both of itself and of its own purpose. That this opportunity has been missed can only be regarded as an unfortunate omission.[44]

In a later article, in the same volume, commenting on *DV* 23 and the use of the Scriptures in the Church, Ratzinger again correctly focuses upon the necessity of the 'restless relationship' which must exist between 'the study of the Sacred Page' and the role of the theologian in the Church:

Commentary, 3:268. Explanatory parenthesis added by author.
44. Ratzinger, 'The Transmission of Divine Revelation', in Vorgrimler, *Commentary*, 3:192–3. Stress in original.

A reference to the ecclesial nature of exegesis on the one hand, and to its methodological correctness on the other, again expresses the inner tension of church exegesis, which can no longer be removed, *but must simply be accepted as tension.*[45]

The interpretation of Sacred Scripture within the Catholic Tradition, and the ever caring, but critical and scholarly role of the theologian, necessarily generate this tension. Neither exegete nor theologian has the right to ease its pain by either a rigid and unbending dogmatism or a playful interaction with the vagaries of some contemporary postmodern biblical scholarship.[46] In the end, neither the exegete nor the theologian can resolve this restless relationship. It is a tension that the Catholic Church embraces willingly, under the guidance of the Holy Spirit, and directed by its teaching authority. It is yet another indication of the mystery and messiness of the Incarnation.[47]

The mystery of the Catholic Church, local and universal, itself a 'world' within and yet beyond the cultures, cannot freeze the Christian

---

45. Ratzinger, 'Sacred Scripture', in Vorgrimler, *Commentary*, 3:268. Stress mine. It is unfortunate that Ratzinger's two volumes on Jesus of Nazareth no longer display this breadth of vision. He rejects the ongoing usefulness of critical scholarship. He writes to 'be helpful to all believers who seek to encounter Jesus and to believe in him' (2:xvii). The stated aim of the work is 'to make possible a personal relationship with Jesus' (2:xvi). See above, note 14. As Krister Stendal ('The Apostle Paul and the Introspective Consciousness of the West', in *Harvard Theological Review*, 56 [1963]: 199–215) pointed out many years ago, European scholarship, under the influence of Augustine and Luther, often reads the introspective situation of the contemporary Christian into first century documents. While never doubting good intentions, a study of the figure of Jesus (*die Gestalt Jesu*) that disregards critical scholarship (1:xi–xvi) cannot hope to produce 'a personal relationship with Jesus.' As nineteenth century Jesus research indicated, such work can only produce the Jesus of Joseph Ratzinger.
46. See the remarks of Raymond E Brown, 'Critical Biblical Exegesis and the Development of Doctrine', in *Biblical Exegesis and Church Doctrine* (New York: Paulist, 1985), 52: 'Neither a fundamentalist interpretation of the NT, which finds later dogmas with great clarity in the NT era, nor a liberal view, which rejects anything that goes beyond Jesus, is faithful to Catholic history'.
47. See the interesting study of a number of contrasting and potentially mutually enriching 'theologies' of the Bible as revelation (*Dei Verbum*, Karl Barth, Sandra Schneiders, Brevard Childs, Stanley Hauerwas, Tony Kelly) in John Thornhill, 'Do We Need a More Adequate Theology of the Scriptures?', in *Pacifica*, 9 (1996): 15–34.

response to the biblical revelation, ever attentive to 'the living voice of the Gospel' (*DV* 8), into an irrelevant past. Nor does it create for the Catholic believer of any particular time a comfortable house to live in. The proclamation of the Kingdom is a never-ending summons to conversion: 'The Kingdom is at hand. Repent and believe in the Gospel' (Mark 1:15. See *Lumen Gentium* 8). Those who 'study the Sacred Page' and the theologians must accept and live their restless relationship that this summons be heard and re-heard until the Lord comes again. It will call for love, humility, and not a little patient pain, from both parties.[48] It is fitting that we close by returning to *DAS*:

> Nevertheless no one will be surprised, if all the difficulties are not yet solved and overcome; but even that serious problems greatly exercise the minds of Catholic exegetes (and theologians). We should not lose courage on this account; nor should we forget that in the human sciences the same happens as in the natural world; that is to say, new beginnings grow little by little and fruits are gathered only after many labors (*DAS* 44).

---

48. I add a personal note. In 1972 I was the student representative on the Academic Board of the Pontifical Biblical Institute, Rome. That year Pope Paul VI visited the faculty. He devoted particular attention to me as the representative of the student body. He directed the following words to me, instructing me to report them to the students: 'Nella Chiesa il biblista avrà sempre delle difficoltà. Abbiate corragio! Il Papa è sempre con voi.' (English: 'In the Church the biblical scholar will always have difficulty. Courage! The Pope is always with you'). (Parenthetic addition mine).

3

Scripture and Tradition in the Patristic Age

Denis P Minns OP

In October 1960 the Preparatory Theological Commission that began the process that would ultimately issue in the Dogmatic Constitution on Divine Revelation presented a working paper bearing the significant title: *A Compendious Schema for the Constitution on the Sources of Revelation.*[1] Famously, the Dogmatic Constitution itself would reject the (traditional) notion of Scripture and Tradition as two separate sources (*fontes*) of Revelation and assert that 'Sacred Tradition and Sacred Scripture are tightly connected and linked with one another. For both flow forth from the same divine, bubbling spring, somehow or other coalesce as one thing, and extend toward the same goal.'[2] To say that the two, having arisen from the same spring, then coalesce 'somehow or other' (*quodammodo*) suggests a surprising degree of wooliness of thought on the part of the Council Fathers. But this formulation, like the use of the unfamiliar word *scaturigo* for 'spring' may have another explanation. For this was one of the most bitterly contested texts at the Council, and, although the text finally approved represents a victory for an understanding of Tradition that had its origins in the nineteenth century Tübingen school[3] over the conservative position of contemporary Roman theology, it was a partial victory,[4] and one that had to be couched in

---

1. Joseph Ratzinger, 'Dogmatic Constitution on Divine Revelation. Origin and Background', in *Commentary on the Documents of Vatican II*, volume 3, edited by Herbert Vorgrimler (New York and London: Burns & Oates/ Herder and Herder, 1969), 159.
2. *Dei Verbum* 9.
3. Ratzinger, 'Dogmatic Constitution', 184.
4. 'Even now, after the Council, it is not possible to say that the question of the

cautious, conciliatory language. To speak of Scripture and Tradition arising from a 'bubbling spring' might be thought to have been chosen because it suggests liveliness in the source, but it also avoided the offence that would undoubtedly have been given to the losing side had the two been said to have arisen from a single *fons*.

The discussion at Vatican II about the relationship of Tradition to Scripture was, broadly speaking, a product, on the one hand, of Protestant-Catholic polemics from about the time of the Council of Trent onwards, and, on the other hand, of developments within Catholic theology from about the time of Vatican I onwards. Throughout those debates appeal was made, naturally enough, to the ways this relationship was viewed in the early Church, and, unsurprisingly, the interpretation of the evidence from the early Church was shaped by contemporary polemical pressures. In what follows, I attempt a sketch of some of the discussions in the early Church on their own terms.

Like Judaism and Islam, Christianity is sometimes described as a 'religion of the book', but it may be wondered if the description is as apt in the case of Christianity as it is for the other two faiths, for which 'people of the Book' can be a self-description.[5] Important as the Bible undoubtedly is for Christianity, aside from those parts of it that came to be dominated by the *sola scriptura* principle of the Reformation, that importance has sometimes also been seen as something relative. It might be a useful exercise to try to imagine not being too deeply shocked by the view that one might be a good and authentic Christian, and sit rather lightly to the sacred books of that faith. St John Chrysostom, for example, wrote as follows:

> It should not have been necessary for us to stand in need of the help of the scriptures; instead we ought to have presented a life so pure that the grace of the Spirit would take the place of books for our souls, and our souls be written upon by the Spirit, just as books are written

---

relation between critical and Church exegesis, historical research and dogmatic tradition has been settled', Ratzinger, 'Dogmatic Constitution', 158.

5. Yves Congar suggests that it was only in the course of the seventeenth century that 'Protestantism became a religion of the Book', *Tradition and Traditions: An Historical and a Theological Essay* (London: Burns and Oates: 1966), 154.

on with ink. But since we have driven that grace away, come, let us at least cleave to the next best thing.[6]

As John made those remarks at the beginning of the first homily of his massive series on the Gospel of St Matthew it is quite likely that he did mean to shock his listeners into paying attention to what he was about to say: having abandoned the best course, so as really to stand in need of the Scriptures, we will be all the more blameworthy if we neglect them as well. It remains the case, however, that necessary though the Scriptures are in fact, they are second best. This 'second best' must be in some way qualitatively inferior, but there is no suggestion here that the Scriptures do not give us access to the same truths, revelation, grace etc. that the Spirit would have bestowed had we allowed it.

Cyril of Jerusalem, a younger contemporary of Chrysostom, believed that, when it came to the divine and holy mysteries of the Creed, nothing at all should be handed on apart from the divine Scriptures.[7] Nevertheless, since not all people were able to read the scriptures, either because they were illiterate or because they were preoccupied by other business, the Creed, confirmed by the whole of Scripture, embraced within the space of a few verses the whole teaching of the faith. It was taught to advanced catechumens orally, not given to them in writing, and they were to take care when they were memorising it that no other catechumen should overhear what had been handed on to them. In the course of their instruction each verse of the creed would be confirmed from Scripture, for it was made up out of the most appropriate selections from the whole of Scripture. The catechumens were to lay hold of the traditions that they were now receiving and inscribe them upon the breadth of their hearts, because, just as a mustard seed contains many branches in a small grain, so the Creed, in a few words, embraces all the religious knowledge of both the Old and the New Testament.[8]

Two hundred years before John Chrysostom, though echoing exactly the same combination of images from 2 John 12 and 2

---

6. *In Matthaeum* 1.1, S. Ioannis Chrysostomi *Homiliae in Matthaeum* . . . textum emendavit . . . F Field, Tomus I, Cambridge, 1839.
7. *Catechesis* IV.17 (S Cyrilli Hierosolymorum Archiepiscopi *Opera quae supersunt Omnia*, Vol I, *Catecheses*, Munich, 1848).
8. *Catechesis* V.12

Corinthians 3:3, Irenaeus of Lyons had thought that not only was it possible that Christians might have their souls inscribed directly by the Spirit, but that, in some places, this was, in fact, the case:

> Amongst those who have faith in Christ there are many barbarian peoples who, without paper and ink, have salvation written on their hearts by the Spirit, and they carefully preserve the old tradition, believing in one God, the creator of heaven and earth . . . [9]

Though Irenaeus is unfazed by the fact that Christians can and in fact do get by quite happily without any access to the Scriptures, he does not suppose, any more than John Chrysostom did, that the salvation written on their hearts by the Spirit gave them access to anything more or anything less than other Christians' access through the Scriptures. Irenaeus does not expressly present 'tradition' as an alternative to 'Scripture' here. His barbarian Christians have salvation written on the hearts *and* they carefully preserve the old tradition, but presumably he means that tradition does the same service for them that Scripture does for literate Christians: both make it possible for salvation to be written on the heart by the Spirit.

It is with Irenaeus that the concept of 'tradition' first becomes a major theological theme in orthodox theology, but it is crucial to our correct understanding of what he means by the term to recall that it was not he who introduced it to theological argument. Epiphanius preserves a letter of instruction written in Rome in the second century by a Christian teacher to a female disciple, whom he calls his dear sister. Towards the end of his letter Ptolemy counsels Flora not to allow herself to be disturbed by the puzzling implications of what he has been teaching, for, he says:

> if God grants it, you will learn [this] later, when you have been made worthy of the apostolic tradition which we too have received by way of succession, along with the

---

9. *Adversus Haereses* III.4.2 (Irénée de Lyon, *Contre les Hérésies*, livre III, édition critique par A. Rousseau et L. Doutreleau [Paris: Les Éditions du Cerf, 1974]).

controlling by rule of all the statements by the teaching of the Saviour.¹⁰

Here Ptolemy deploys a number of concepts that were used in contemporary philosophical schools in order to establish that what was being taught in those schools was consistent with the teaching of the founder of the school. The heads of the schools were called 'successors' (διάδοχοι):¹¹ they stood in a line of succession stretching back to the founder of the school, and the process of 'handing over' (παράδοσις/παραδίδωμι) the teaching and 'receiving' it (παράληψις/παραλαμβάνω), were thought to guarantee that one could control the consistency of current teaching with the teaching of the school's founder.¹² In the context of the philosophical schools there need not have been any implication that current teaching had to be undeviatingly identical with the teaching of the founder, and Ptolemy's suggestion that Flora's participation in the process of handing on and receiving would eventually lead her to a deeper knowledge of that teaching is also consistent with contemporary philosophical usage. While Ptolemy is thus clearly staking a claim to be a teacher within such a context, it is not altogether clear whether by 'we too' he means to be comparing himself with philosophical schools properly so called, or with other Christian teachers who also make a claim to stand in a tradition stretching back to the Apostles. The reference to the Apostles itself also has its counterpart in the philosophical context: like Socrates, Jesus did not leave his teaching in written form, so a connection had to be established with those who heard him speak.

Ptolemy was not the first, however, to make use of this vocabulary to legitimate his teaching. Paul had solemnly introduced his account of the institution of the Eucharist by saying 'I received (παρέλαβον) from the Lord what I also handed on (παρέδωκα) to you' (1 Cor

---

10. Epiphanius, *Panarion* 33.7 (S. Epiphanii Episcopi Constantiensis *Panaria* . . . edidit F Oehler, Berlin, 1859).
11. Martin Lowther Clarke, *Higher Education in the Ancient World* (London: Routledge and Kegan Paul, 1971), 79.
12. Cf George R Boys-Stones, *Post-Hellenistic Philosophy: A Study of its Development from the Stoics to Origen* (Oxford: Oxford University Press, 2001), 58, 103.

11.23); speaking of the good news concerning the saving death and resurrection of Jesus he says 'I 'handed on (παρέδωκα) to you as of first importance what I in turn had received (παρέλαβον)' (1 Cor 15.3); and he warns against 'believers who are living in idleness and not according to the tradition that they received from us (κατὰ τὴν παράδοσιν ἣν παρελάβοσαν)' (2 Thess 3:6).[13]

When Irenaeus of Lyons took upon himself the refutation of contemporaries whom he thought to be teachers of pretended knowledge he conceived his task precisely as a contest about the legitimacy of a doctrinal tradition. He uses all the terms employed by Ptolemy but tightens their meaning. The handing on and reception of teaching by way of a succession does guarantee that the teaching of the Saviour will serve as a means of controlling what is now taught, but, just as in the philosophical schools, the successors must be not a vague cloud of witnesses but real individuals, identifiable by name. So Irenaeus produced, or borrowed,[14] a list of named successors to the Apostles Peter and Paul in the church in Rome.[15] It is possible that such lists were being produced at just this time for just this purpose, and most likely that they were made up from known names in a likely chronological order, rather than representing a genuine succession of monarchical bishops.[16] Irenaeus contents himself with just one succession list, on the ground that if the principle is sound that succession from the Apostles guarantees authentic tradition then one list will do: successors to the Apostles in one place will not be

---

13. For other uses of these verbs with this technical meaning cf 1 Cor 11:2: 'you maintain the traditions (τὰς παραδόσεις) just as I handed them on (παρέδωκα) to you'; Gal 1:9: 'a gospel contrary to what you received (παρελάβετε)'; Phil 4:9 'keep on doing the things that you have learned and received (παρελάβετε) and heard and seen in me'; Col 2:6 'as you therefore have received (παρελάβετε) Christ Jesus'; 1 Thess 2:13 'when you received (παραλαβόντες) the word of God that you heard from us'; 1 Thess 4:1 'as you received (παρελάβετε) from us how you ought to live'; 2 Thess 2:15: 'hold fast to the traditions (τὰς παραδόσεις) that you were taught by us'.
14. Hegesippus tell us (in Eusebius, *Ecclesiastical History* IV.22.3) that when he was in Rome (probably about 160) he made 'a succession list up to Anicetus, whose deacon was Eleutherus, and Soter succeeded to Anicetus, after whom came Eleutherus'.
15. *Adversus Haereses* III.2.1-3.
16. Cf Peter Lampe, *From Paul to Valentinus. Christians at Rome in the first two Centuries* (London: T&T Clark, 2003), 406.

teaching anything different to successors to the Apostles in another place,[17] and, in any case, by the time Irenaeus was writing, the church in Rome was claiming to have been the place of martyrdom of not one, but two, Apostles, and most glorious ones, at that. If his opponents want to claim an apostolic tradition that teaches something other than what is taught in the Church in Rome then they will need to be able to show his succession list to be false and to put forward another one with at least as much claim to verisimilitude. But as what his opponents teach is demonstrably not what is taught in the church in Rome neither can they legitimately claim that it is based on an apostolic tradition. Even if it were the case that Jesus had imparted an esoteric teaching to the Apostles, a teaching that went beyond what was handed on to the generality of his followers,[18] as Ptolemy seems to have supposed, it remains the case that such a teaching must be expected to be found in churches of apostolic foundation, able to point to a succession from those founders.[19]

The word 'tradition', however, was already manifesting something of the slipperiness that would characterise it for most of the subsequent history of the Church.[20] For Ptolemy, as for the philosophical schools, tradition served as a guarantee of authentic continuity between what was now being taught and what had been taught by the founder of the school. If immersion in the tradition made possible a deeper insight into its teaching then it was only to be expected that some difference would be found between what was commonly taught and what the more expert could divine. Irenaeus therefore took a more rigid view of what the notions of tradition and reception implied. The Tradition, he decreed, does not and cannot change:[21] if it could change, it would

---

17. *Adversus Haereses* III.3.2: for the interpretation of this much debated passage see Luise Abramowski, 'Irenaeus Adv. Haer. III.3.2: Ecclesia Romana and Omnis Ecclesia and *ibid*. Anacletus of Rome', *Journal of Theological Studies* 28 (1977): 101–4.
18. *Adversus Haereses* III.2.1.
19. *Adversus Haereses* III.3.1.
20. For a recent survey of the meanings of the word in the early church see Everett Ferguson, '*Paradosis* and *Traditio*: A Word Study', in *Tradition and the Rule of Faith in the Early Church. Essays in Honor of Joseph T Lienhard*, edited by Ronnie J Rombs and Alexander Y Hwang (Washington, DC: Catholic University of America Press, 2010), 3–29.
21. *Adversus Haereses* I.10.2, cf Ellen Flesseman-van Leer, 'Tradition, Schrift und Kirche bei Irenaeus', in *Schrift und Tradition,* edited by KE Skydsgaard and L

cease to be tradition. It is at this point that a distinction began to emerge between tradition as process and tradition as product. What was originally thought of as the act of receiving and handing on came to be seen rather as an object, the teaching itself as received and handed on. Tradition guarantees that the content of the faith is identical wherever it is handed on and received; an eloquent exponent will not enhance it in handing it on, an incompetent one will not diminish it.

Irenaeus' strategy against his opponents was, in its time and place, an effective one, but its usefulness was to prove limited and short-lived. Those he opposed made no secret of the fact that they were putting forward an esoteric, an advanced teaching, albeit one that they claimed had its foundations in what Jesus taught his disciples. It was not all that difficult to expose and explode such pretensions. But even in Irenaeus' own time orthodox Christianity was nowhere near as monolithic in its doctrinal structure as he had supposed, and his simplistic understanding of tradition as the safeguard of an obvious and unproblematic apostolic teaching would not stand up to the probing and testing that would become inevitable as subsequent generations of Christians sought to think that teaching through.

Though they were exacerbated by personal animosities and ecclesiastical rivalries, the crises that engulfed the church in the fourth and fifth centuries were not the product of idle or misguided speculation. When thoughtful Christians asked themselves what they really meant when they asserted that Jesus was divine and what implications this would have for the traditional Christian beliefs that there is only one God and that Jesus is a human being it was inevitable that the common confession of a naive belief-system would fracture into irreconcilable oppositions. Was Jesus God in the strict and proper sense of the term, or only in a (thoroughly appropriate) manner of speaking? If he was God in the strict and proper sense of the term did it make any sense at all to go on asserting that he was also a human being, and if it did make any sense, what was that sense? A theologian of as lofty an eminence as Gregory of Nyssa might scoff at ordinary Christians for becoming excited about such questions,[22] but no serious Christian, whatever the extent of her or his

---

Vischer (Zürich: EVZ-Verlag, 1963), 45–61, 49f.
22. *De Deitate Filii et Spiritus Sancti* in *Patrologia Graeca* (Jacques-Paul Migne, Paris

theological training, should be censured for thinking that the answer to such questions is of vital importance. Are Christians genuinely monotheists, or do they just pretend to be? Does it mean anything for them to say that Jesus was a human being, or is this, though true, of no real theological significance? Such questions ought to matter. But where does one find the answer to them? Clearly not in the Scriptures alone, for all the various and conflicting views arose precisely from the reading of the same Scriptures.

Opponents of the Creed adopted at Nicaea in 325 complained that it had employed terms not found in Scripture, such as 'of the essence' and 'of the same essence' in accounting for the relationship between the Father and the Son.[23] Athanasius counters this by claiming that it is the mark of true teachers that they agree with one another and with their ancestors. In contrast to the squabbling schools of Greek philosophy, Christian teachers, though they lived in different times, yet hold the same teaching, as prophets of the one God, preaching the same Word in harmony.[24] And if the expressions they used are not to be found in Scripture in so many words, yet they contain and express the meaning of the Scriptures,[25] and these words were not invented by the Fathers at Nicaea, but were taken by them from their predecessors.[26] Athanasius proceeds to quote from the writings of theologians of the preceding century to show that the words used in the Nicene Creed were transmitted from fathers to fathers, handed down to us from the beginning by those who were eye-witnesses and ministers to the Word.[27] Athanasius is not here appealing to Tradition as a source of doctrine separate from Scripture, but arguing that the way Nicaea speaks of the relationship of Father and Son is consistent with the understanding of the Scriptures that has been handed down in the church. This is not an easy case to make, and Athanasius had to devote a separate treatise to the defence of the orthodoxy of one of the 'fathers' he had quoted, seeking to show that, properly understood, the words of Dionysius, one of his predecessors as bishop of Alexandria,

---

    1863), 46, col 557 BC.
23. Athanasius, *De Decretis Nicaenae Synodi* 1, in *Patrologia Graeca* (Jacques-Paul Migne, Paris, 1884), vol 25, col 416 A.
24. *De Decretis* 4, col 421 CD.
25. *De Decretis* 21, col 453 B.
26. *De Decretis* 25, col 460 B.
27. *De Decretis* 27, col 465 C–468 A.

were consistent with the doctrine of Nicaea, and with the teaching of the Apostles.[28]

Later in the fourth century, when the debate had moved on to impugn the full divinity of the Holy Spirit, Basil the Great had to contend with the argument of his opponents that theological statements should not go beyond the strict datum of Scripture.[29] In *On the Holy Spirit*, written about 375, he says:

> Of the doctrines and proclamations that have been preserved in the church we have some from written teaching but others we have received as given to us mystically from the tradition of the apostles: both of these have the same force for sound religion.[30]

This could be construed as making a claim for Tradition as a second source of teaching, separate from Scripture, and a mistranslation of the Greek behind 'some . . . but others' as 'partim . . . partim' influenced the phrasing of the Draft Decree presented at Trent on 22 March 1546: 'the Council clearly perceives that this truth is contained partly in written books and partly in unwritten traditions.'[31]

Basil proceeds to list a number of ecclesiastical customs that do not have scriptural authority, such as marking with the sign of the cross, praying towards the East, the words of the preface and the Eucharistic Prayer, the threefold immersion and the blessing of the water, oil and candidate at baptism, and the renunciation of Satan and his angels (it should be noted that all these refer to liturgical practices). There is no scriptural support for any of these things but we owe them to the 'silent and mystical tradition', to

> that unpublicised and unspoken teaching which our fathers, having been well taught that this holiness of

---

28. *De Sententia Dionysii* in *Patrologia Graeca*, Jacques-Paul Migne, Paris, 1884 vol 25, coll 480–521.
29. *On the Holy Spirit* (Basile de Césarée, *Sur le Saint-Esprit*, introduction, texte, traduction et notes par Benoît Pruche, second edition [Paris: Les Éditions du Cerf], 58).
30. *On the Holy Spirit*, 66.
31. *Concilium Tridentinum*, Volume 5, edited by Sebastian Merkle (Freiburg, 1901), # 21; cf. Congar, *Tradition and Traditions*, 48.

the mysteries is preserved from danger in silence, kept safe in a silence that was not to be subject to the prying investigations of the curious. How could it have been fitting for them to make a public display in writing of the teaching about things that it is not lawful for the uninitiated to encounter? . . . Moses . . . well knew by means of wisdom that disdain lies ready to hand for what is common and to be apprehended of its own accord while an eager longing is, as it were, naturally associated with what is rare and has been withdrawn from view. In just the same way, from the beginning, the apostles and fathers, when they made ordinances with respect to the churches, preserved reverence for the mysteries in what was kept hidden and unspoken. For there is no mystery at all in what is divulged to the casual hearing of the populace. This is the reason for the unwritten tradition, so that the knowledge of the doctrines might not become ignored and readily despised by the multitude on account of familiarity.

Perhaps the best argument that Basil is not here claiming that a 'secret, unwritten' tradition stands beside Scripture as a distinct source of revelation is that, despite all his ponderous insistence on such a tradition, he does not, in fact, call upon it to support any doctrine that he believes cannot be found in Scripture. We need to remember that Basil's opponents insist that only formulations used in Scripture are to be allowed. They do so because they want to argue that different words, and in particular different prepositions, used in Scripture in connection with Father, Son, and Spirit point to different natures for each, with the consequence that Son and Spirit cannot be of the same nature as the Father, and thus cannot be God in the strict sense of the term.[32] In 1 Corinthians 8:6 Paul says 'there is one God, the Father, *from* (ἐξ) whom are all things and *for* (εἰς) whom we exist, and one Lord Jesus Christ *through* (διὰ) whom are all things and *through* (διὰ) whom we exist'. Basil's opponents concluded from this that *through* is the preposition appropriate to the Son, betokening that he is the instrument through which the Father acts, and, as instrument,

---

32. *On the Holy Spirit*, 4.

different in nature from the agent that uses him.[33] And if *through* is the preposition appropriate to the Son it cannot be used of the Father or the Spirit and so, in the doxology, we pray *to* the Father, *through* the Son, *in* the Holy Spirit. All Basil really needs to do to overturn this logic-chopping he does very early in *On the Holy Spirit*. He shows that Paul, for example, can say of God (the Word, as Basil thinks): '*from* him and *through* him and *to* him are all things' (Rom 11:36). It does not matter if in Paul's mind the Father was the object of these prepositions because, in either case, we have *from* and *through* used of the same person and they cannot therefore indicate a difference of nature.[34] Similarly, the preposition *through* is used in Scripture of the Father and the Spirit as well as of the Son, and the preposition *in*, which his opponents wish to reserve to the Spirit, is used of the Father and of the Son.[35]

That might have been thought a sufficient rebuttal, but Basil's opponents seem to have struck a raw nerve when they accused him of using unusual and contradictory language in the liturgy when he had employed two forms of the doxology: on one occasion giving glory to the Father *with* (μετὰ) the Son *together with* (σὺν) the Holy Spirit and on another occasion to the Father *through* (διὰ) the Son, *in* (ἐν) the Holy Spirit.[36] Basil's opponents thought that *in* (ἐν), the preposition proper to the Spirit, was altogether adequate for every conception concerning him, while *with* (σὺν) was in no way necessary or customary in the churches.[37] For Basil, on the other hand, to be able to describe the Spirit as co-existing *with* the Father and the Son was a necessary corollary of the co-equal divinity of the Spirit. *In* is an appropriate preposition to use when thinking of the relationship of the Holy Spirit to created things, at work in us, dwelling in us, and so on, but when we think of the relationship of the Spirit to the Father and the Son it is more in keeping with sound religion to say that he is *with* them than that he is *in* them: 'for existing *with* is properly and truly predicated of those that are *with* one another eternally.'[38] Basil

---

33. *On the Holy Spirit*, 6.
34. *On the Holy Spirit*, 8.
35. *On the Holy Spirit*, 10, 11.
36. *On the Holy Spirit*, 3.
37. *On the Holy Spirit*, 65.
38. *On the Holy Spirit*, 63.

does not base his belief in the co-eternal divinity of the Spirit on a proof-text in which the preposition *with* is used in conjunction with the Spirit, though it would be polemically convenient if he could make reference to one. As he cannot find such a usage in the Scriptures, the liturgy will have to do, and it is in order to bolster the status of the liturgy as a suitable source of corroborative usage that he speaks of it in the way he does. The liturgy is not an alternative, secret and mystical source of doctrine. It is not Scripture but it is a reality that is vital to the Church and one that, by its very nature, is secret and mystical: it re-enacts and celebrates the mysteries of salvation, mysteries reserved for those who had been initiated. Though there are liturgical texts the liturgy is not contained in them in the way the Scriptures are contained in books. The liturgy is a living action: though the words used in it contain scriptural passages and reminiscences, it is not itself scriptural, and that is what Basil means by describing it as an *unwritten* tradition. Were it not that 'unwritten tradition' has become such a loaded term it would be much more accurate to translate him as speaking of 'non-scriptural tradition'.[39]

Almost incidentally, then, Basil has drawn attention to the liturgical life of the Church as a living Tradition, as indispensable to the life of the Church as the Scriptures themselves and therefore to be regarded as having the same force with respect to sound religion.[40] Basil does not suppose that, by itself, the liturgy will give one access to revealed truth that would not otherwise be available. What he does claim is that the liturgical life of the Church may legitimately be expected to corroborate a revealed truth to which one already has access by other means. His whole argument might be reduced to this: we know that the Holy Spirit is coeternal with the Father and the Son, therefore it is appropriate to say that he is worshipped and glorified with the Father and the Son. If we cannot find this monosyllable *with* used of the Holy Spirit in the Scriptures that is nothing to the point: because it is used in the august mysteries of the liturgical life of the Church, handed down to us from the Apostles, a tradition that has the same force with respect to sound religion as the Scriptures themselves: it is used

---

39. Cf Emmanuel Amand de Mendieta, *The 'Unwritten' and 'Secret' Apostolic Traditions in the Theological Thought of St Basil of Caesarea*, Scottish Journal of Theology Occasional Papers No. 13 (Edinburgh: Oliver and Boyd, 1965), 25–39.
40. *On the Holy Spirit*, 66.

in the doxology that gives glory to the Father *with* the Son *together with* the Holy Spirit, a doxology that Basil had himself used, though not exclusively, and which his opponents, because of their insistence that doctrine must be derived solely from a minute inspection of the use of syllables and words found in Scripture and nowhere else,[41] had claimed to be novel and contradictory.

Though he recognises that Basil 'is not really claiming that he possesses in unwritten tradition a second source of doctrine parallel to the Bible and independent of it', RPC Hanson says that Basil has invented a legend of apostolic origin for rite and custom, so that tradition, 'instead of being left as the word to describe doctrinal development and exploration in continuity with the original Gospel, becomes an historical fiction'.[42] But I do not think we should credit Basil with the invention of such a fiction. He has drawn attention to the liturgy as a place where something of vital significance for the Church, something other than Scripture, is handed on, and he has taken offence at the accusation that a doxology that he received in the liturgical celebration traditional in his own church and that was supported by the language used about the Spirit by eminent earlier Christian writers[43] is not customary and cannot be used to support what he knows, on other grounds, to be the truth about the divinity of the Holy Spirit. What Basil has to say about the secret and mystical tradition may contain more than a little bluster, but he makes no extravagant claim for a secret, unwritten source of revelation to be set beside Scripture.

---

41. *On the Holy Spirit*, 4.
42. *Tradition in the Early Church* (London: SCM Press, 1962), 184.
43. *On the Holy Spirit*, 71.

4

'I handed on to you . . . what I also received' (1 Cor 15:3) The Scripture-Tradition Connection/Controversy

Dianne Bergant CSA

'The living Tradition is essential for enabling the Church to grow through time in the understanding of the truth revealed in the Scriptures.'[1] These words from the Post-Synodal Apostolic Exhortation of Benedict XVI throw light on the relationship between Scripture and Tradition as understood by the Roman Catholic Church. It speaks of the revelatory character of the Scriptures, and of the Tradition as being living and dynamic as it opens the Church to the revelation of God. However, within the broader Christian Church, the relationship between Scripture and Tradition has been a source of contention and, despite the strides that have been made in this area down through the centuries, this question continues to challenge believers today. It is important to place this controversy within the historical circumstances out of which it sprang. This essay will trace the ongoing causes of the controversy and identify some of the ways in which it has been addressed. It will begin with an overview of the development of the biblical tradition. This step is deemed necessary in order to appreciate the fact that Scripture itself is the specific written articulation of ancient Israel's and early Christianity's fundamental tradition, and its interpretation is a continuation of the tradition process that produced it. This overview will be followed by a consideration of Tradition's inherent connection with the Scriptures. Here, discussion will focus on the tradition that began to emerge during the apostolic period of the early Christian era, tradition that itself came to be considered revelatory. The essay

---

1. Benedict XVI, *The Word of the Lord: Post-Synodal Apostolic Exhortation* (Boston: Pauline Publishing House, 2010), 30.

will end with a consideration of the contemporary debate within the Christian Church over the role played by Tradition in the process of biblical interpretation.

Traditioning Process

Tradition is part of the historical reality of any people. 'Human life is simply unthinkable without the element of tradition.'[2] It enables a people to identify who they are and to direct how they are to live. Because it represents the truths and experiences of previous generations, it provides solidarity with the past and influences directions into the future. The core tradition of ancient Israel was grounded in belief in YHWH. The principal features of this core tradition included belief in YHWH's constant presence to them in their movements, in YHWH's concern for and readiness to ease the plight of the oppressed, and in YHWH's promise of new and decisive benefits to come. It is difficult to determine how this core tradition originated. It probably emerged out of Israel's own experience of marginality and relative insignificance in the ancient world. This core tradition has been preserved in Israel's story of deliverance from bondage in Egypt and in its subsequent self-perceptions and theological understandings that developed out of it. This course of development has come to be known as the traditioning process.

The relationship between the actual events and the tradition that grew out of them is complex and often difficult to trace. The major shift in understanding brought on by the Enlightenment only served to accentuate this lack of clarity. Traditional people, as was ancient Israel, often possess a ready tendency to perceive God's presence and activity in many phenomena, which is due to their particular view of reality and their capacity to apprehend it.[3] In Israel, stories took shape as the people reported these experiences, and the character of the stories reflected the people's metaphorical, non-linear view of reality. These stories were handed down orally from one generation to the next, thus establishing a testimony to the early perception of the divine. The stories varied because of the wide-ranging experience

---

2. Gerald O'Collins, *Fundamental Theology* (New York/Ramsey, NJ: Paulist Press, 1981), 193.
3. We see this even today in the Aboriginal people of Australia.

of the individual groups of people, leading to various streams of tradition (for example, the Pentateuchal traditions known as Yahwist, Elohist, Deuteronomic, Priestly). Thus the overall tradition became both rich and complex. Despite this complexity, the core tradition remained basically the same.

While the originating experiences of the divine might be seen as revelation, what can be said about the testimonies to those experiences? What of the traditions that they engendered? Rather than argue that tradition itself is a mode of revelation, some biblical theologians maintain that:

> The term 'locus' is more appropriate, because the tradition, both in *traditum* (tenets of faith) and *traditio* (traditioning process), constitutes the context of revelation. It does this in two respects: it provides the categories for apprehending and understanding revelation, and it is the springboard for new revelatory occasions.[4]

In other words: '... tradition carries structures of meaning and ... the tradition process creates new meaning.'[5]

While they recognise the importance of new meanings, scholars insist that: 'An interpretation should not tend to petrify earlier revelation or its interpretation, absolutising it into a convention that stifles rather than promotes life. This would pervert revelation by thwarting its original purpose.'[6] This gradual emergence of new meanings, which might be seen as a dialogue between a testimony and a new context, brought elements of the core tradition into a new time period, allowing the force of the theological insight to impact a new historical context. This enabled diverse understandings to exist side by side as each new insight bore contemporary, theological testimony.

Canonisation of a testimony is the step of stabilising in this traditioning process. Decided upon at a particular time in history,

---

4. Douglas A Knight, 'Revelation Through Tradition', in *Tradition and Theology in the Old Testament*, edited by Douglas A Knight (Philadelphia: Fortress Press, 1977), 165.
5. Knight, 169.
6. Knight, 175.

canonisation determines which versions of testimony are to be seen as authoritative and which, though meaningful, are not. Such stabilisation does not put an end to the traditioning process. Rather, those traditions that continue to develop out of contemporising interpretation (for example, preaching; up-to-date theological development) are not considered part of the canon of biblical tradition. Most of the selection of authoritative testimonies occurred gradually, over time, and through usage by the believing community. However, statements canonising a particular version and not others were ultimately affirmed by various authoritative bodies.

Three references in the *Forward* to the Book of Sirach indicate that, by the second century BCE, Israel had a tripartite collection of sacred tradition consisting of the Law, the Prophets, and the Writings. However, it was not until after the destruction of the Second Temple (ca 70 CE) that a group of rabbis gathered at the northern Israelite town of Jamnia (Jabneh or Jabneel) to finalise the Jewish canon. The Christian community continued the traditioning process, developing new testimonies to the life, death, and resurrection of Jesus as its core tradition. The same processes of contemporising earlier testimonies and the development of streams of tradition (for example, various gospels) followed. Twice in the First Letter to the Corinthians (11:23; 15:3), Paul uses the Greek terms παραδίδωμι (I hand on) and παραλαμβάνω (I receive). These verbs soon became technical terms within the traditioning process. In many ways, the believing community itself determined by its regular usage what were the acceptable components of various testimonies. However, final decisions regarding the canonisation of these testimonies were made at the time of the Council of Trent (ca 1547).

The community's reflection upon and interpretation of testimonies to God's self-revelation eventually resulted in the Scriptures we have today. Further reflection upon and interpretation of the canonical texts continues to produce new traditions.[7] Thus it is clear that from the very beginning, an inherent connection exists between tradition and Scripture. However, the way this relationship has been understood is at the core of significant theological controversy.

---

7. For a discussion of the development of traditions during the time of ancient Israel down through Christian eras, see Yves M-J Congar, *Tradition and Traditions: An Historical Essay and a Theological Essay* (London: Burns & Oates, 1966).

Scripture and Tradition

The sixteenth century is remembered as a time of great unrest. The Church's unchecked accumulation of various traditions in its teaching and practice came under fire. The Christian world was entrapped by many of the controversies, both theological and political, spawned by the Great Schism of Western Christianity (1378-1416). The relationships between the Church and many of the prominent secular powers were convoluted and difficult to unravel. The insertion of the *filioque* clause into the Nicene Creed by the Roman Church was strenuously opposed by the Eastern Church. Disputes in the Balkans challenged the claims of both the Western Church and the Eastern Church, and these led to uprisings and wars. The role played by the Bishop of Rome in relation to the other four Patriarchs, as well as to the bishops of the Western Church, was in dispute. The exchange of decrees of excommunication between the Bishop of Rome and the Patriarch of Constantinople exacerbated the rift between the Church in the West and the Church in the East. The final breach came as the result of the sack of Constantinople by the Fourth Crusade in 1204.

The Church itself was enmeshed in widespread corruption, which also became the concern of many monarchs. Ecclesiastical as well as secular leaders were reluctant to initiate a reform, for that might mean a diminishment of their power and a curbing of the opulent lives they were living. Reformers such as John Wycliffe and Jan Hus spoke out against these abuses. The Council of Constance (1414-18) condemned these men and the corruption within the Church continued, preparing the way for Martin Luther's opposition and his issuance of *The Ninety-Five Theses* which he nailed to the door of a church at Wittenberg.[8]

Luther's protest began with a denunciation of certain Church practices, but then evolved into a criticism of some of the Church doctrine. Since many within the Church were appealing to Scripture for justification of various religious practices, Luther sought a 'pure' understanding of Scripture, one that was not encumbered by mediaeval piety and ecclesiastical bias. Basing many of his theological positions on the New Testament teachings of Paul, he

---

8. John W O'Malley, *Trent: What Happened at the Council?* (Cambridge, MA/London: The Belknap Press of Harvard University Press, 2013), 24-38.

insisted on salvation by faith alone, not by observance of current religious practices. This led to his rejection of any Church teaching that could not find its grounding in Scripture. Luther's censure of what he considered spurious doctrine gave rise to the expression *sola scriptura* (scripture alone), which implies rejection of the prevalent Church Tradition. This expression soon became the battle cry of the Reformation.

The Council of Trent (1545-63), convened to address the challenges posed by the Reformers, took up questions regarding Scripture almost immediately. On 8 April 8 1546, only four months into the Council, the assembly issued a decree stating that Scripture alone is not sufficient for understanding revelation; Tradition, defined as that which developed out of the apostolic tradition, also contains authoritative gospel teaching.[9] One of the goals of the Council of Trent may have been the reunification of the several factions within the Christian Church. However, this decree brought about the opposite result—it solidified the rift and laid the ground for continued controversy over issues of Church teaching and authority.

While this council decree stated that both Scripture and Tradition are sources of revelation, it did not clearly indicate how the two sources are related to each other. In fact, the Council Fathers' statements were ambiguous about this relationship. It seems that the original text affirming their mutual authority stated that Revelation is found partly in the written books and partly in the unwritten Tradition. However, in the final version, the word 'partly' was changed to 'both'.[10] Thus the first version suggests that there is one source of revelation made up partly of Scripture and partly of Tradition; the second version suggests two distinct sources. The ambiguity of this relationship has been the source of discussion and disagreement down through the centuries. It would take the Second Vatican Council to take steps toward resolving this ambiguity.[11]

---

9. O'Malley, *Trent*, 97–8.
10. John E Thiel, *Senses of Tradition: Continuity and Development in Catholic Faith* (Oxford/New York: Oxford University Press, 2000), 20–3.
11. The relationship between Scripture and Tradition was a pressing question just before and during the Second Vatican Council. For treatment of the various views on this topic that surfaced at this time, see James P Mackey, *The Modern Theology of Tradition* (New York: Herder and Herder, 1963), 150–69; Gabriel Moran, *Scripture and Tradition: A Survey of the Controversy* (New York: Herder

At Vatican II, the original schema on the Bible, *On the Sources of Revelation* dealt with Scripture, Tradition, and the Magisterium and their relationship to one another. Discussion of the contents of this schema was long and contentious. The revelatory character of Scripture was not questioned; the crux of the matter was the character of Tradition and the role of the Magisterium in interpreting Scripture. Some participants feared that any lessening of Tradition's revelatory authority would throw into question certain earlier pronouncements of the Magisterium, such as dogmas concerning Mary, which could claim no solid Biblical grounding. These men supported the original version of the schema which implicitly gave Tradition a privileged role in Church teaching. However, many other participants felt that the original schema lacked the open, fresh, pastoral spirit intended by Pope John XXIII. According to them, that inadequate schema presented revelation as a collection of truths or doctrines, rather than as God's self-revelation which expressed itself both in action in history and in authoritative pronouncements. They argued that God, not Tradition nor even Scripture, was the source of revelation.[12]

After much debate, the addition of a great number of amendments, several furtive interventions by Pope Paul VI, and despite a degree of opposition, the council fathers agreed upon a final document on revelation. Entitled *Dogmatic Constitution on Divine Revelation (Dei Verbum—DV)*, it devoted an entire chapter to the relationship between Scripture and Tradition. There we read:

> Hence there exists a close connection and communication between sacred tradition and Sacred Scripture. For both of them, flowing from the same divine wellspring, in a certain way merge into a unity and tend toward the same end (*DV* 9).
>
> Therefore both sacred tradition and Sacred Scripture are to be accepted and venerated with the same sense of loyalty and reverence (*DV* 9).
>
> Sacred tradition and Sacred Scripture form one sacred

---

and Herder, 1963).
12. O'Malley, *What Happened at Vatican II* (Cambridge, MA/London: The Belknap Press of Harvard University Press, 2008), 226–28.

deposit of the word of God, committed to the Church (*DV* 10).

The language used is noteworthy. It sets forth the major components of the relationship between Scripture and Tradition: 'both of them, flowing from the same divine wellspring', 'merge into a unity', which is 'one sacred deposit of the word of God'.[13] Distinct in their origin, these two authoritative sources merge into one sacred deposit.

We read earlier in the document:

> This tradition which comes from the Apostles develops in the Church with the help of the Holy Spirit. For there is a growth in the understanding of the realities and the words which have been handed down. This happens through the contemplation and study made by believers, who treasure these things in their hearts . . . through a penetrating understanding of the spiritual realities which they experience, and through . . . preaching (*DV* 8).

This statement underscores the dynamic character of Tradition, stating that it is not a static collection of doctrines, but 'the way the teaching authority of the church related to Scripture',[14] and continues to relate in its witness, life, and worship. Tradition functions in:

> a symbiotic relationship to Scripture and as the vital principle in the church of the transmission and interpretation of what God has revealed. In other words, in this approach the key question is not so much what Tradition contained as how it operated.[15]

The role of the Magisterium is also clarified:

> This teaching office is not above the word of God, but serves it, teaching only what has been handed on, listening to it devoutly, guarding it scrupulously and explaining it faithfully in accord with a divine

---

13. Ronald D Witherup, *Scripture: Dei Verbum* (New York/Mahwah, NJ, 2006), 35–6.
14. O'Malley, *Vatican II*, 6.
15. O'Malley, *Vatican II*, 228.

commission and with the help of the Holy Spirit, it draws from this one deposit of faith everything which it presents for belief as divinely revealed (*DV* 10).

Contrary to the title of the original schema presented for acceptance, the final document does not consider the Magisterium a source of revelation. Nor, despite what some maintained, is the function of Tradition hardly distinct from the teaching Magisterium.[16] Finally, again in contrast to the original schema, the Magisterium is not comparable to Scripture as a source of revelation. Rather, it serves the word of God.

Though *DV* offered a clearer explanation of the relationship between Scripture and Tradition, it did not resolve all the issues. It did not provide directions on how scholars might engage Tradition in the interpretation of Scripture. Hence, various attempts at understanding this relationship continue to surface.[17] Furthermore, once the impetus to employ critical methods of interpretation took hold, a new gulf within the Church seems to have developed. Critical interpretation of Scripture was assumed by the academy of scholars, while teaching of the Tradition was done by the Church.

Interpretation of the Bible

The dynamic relationship between Scripture and Tradition can be traced throughout the history of biblical interpretation, beginning in the Bible itself. For example, the passage from Isaiah—'The virgin shall be with child, and bear a son, and shall name him Immanuel' (Isa 7:14)—is given Christological meaning when employed by the author of the Gospel According to Matthew to explain the conception and birth of Jesus (Mt 1:23). This form of reinterpretation was not original with the Gospel writers. At least three centuries earlier, the author of the Book of Wisdom refashioned the stories of the plagues and Israel's deliverance from bondage in Egypt (Exod 7–12) in order to encourage Jews living in Alexandria to remain steadfast in their faith (Wisdom 11–19). Many exegetes saw this form of reinterpretation as an attempt to uncover the fuller meaning of the biblical message.

The importance of the Apostolic Tradition in biblical interpretation

---

16. O'Malley, *Vatican II*, 278.
17. See Thiel, *Senses of Tradition*.

became clear in the very earliest centuries of the Christian era. Patristic teachers such as Justin Martyr (100–ca 165) and Tertullian (ca 160–225) interpreted many passages of the Old Testament through the christological lens of their own day. They were followed by teachers like Clement of Alexandria (ca 150–215) and Origen (184–253), who honed an allegorical method of exegesis that became very popular, thus establishing Alexandria as an important center of biblical interpretation. Exegetes in Antioch were not slow to follow. Men like Theodore of Mopsuestia (ca 350–428), John Chrysostom (ca 347–407), Gregory of Nyssa (ca 335–95), and Basil (339–79) continued to employ the developing Tradition as their focus for reading the Bible. Though Jerome seems to have been more interested in the literal sense of the Bible, in his earlier days he too employed Origen's allegorical approach. These early Christian teachers were interested in what came to be known as the spiritual sense, a fuller sense that becomes clear when the Bible is read through the lens of the Christian mystery and under the influence of the Holy Spirit.

Medieval exegesis followed the four senses of interpreting Scripture through the lens of Tradition proposed by John Cassian: the literal or historical, the allegorical or christological, the tropological or moral, and the anagogical or eschatological. Though Cassian developed these approaches, aspects of each can be found in Scripture itself. In his insistence that we are saved through faith and not works, Paul employs a literal reading of Abraham story where that ancestor's righteousness through faith (Gen 15:6) precedes his carrying out the prescription of circumcision (Gen 17:23). In his reproach of the Judaisers who insisted that Christians were bound to observe the Law, he allegorised Sarah and Hagar as the covenants of freedom and slavery, respectively (Gal 4:21–31). The tropological sense is seen in his claim that events surrounding Israel's exodus from Egypt and sojourn in the wilderness 'happened to them as an example, and they have been written down as a warning to us, upon whom the end of the ages has come' (1 Cor 10:11). Finally, the anagogical sense appears in the Letter to the Hebrews and Revelation where the authors consider the city of Jerusalem as an image of heaven (Heb 12:22; Rev 21:2, 10).

These four senses of Scripture held sway until the sixteenth century when the Reformers reacted against the Church's excessive allegorising to justify some of its traditional practices and teachings.

This reaction gave birth to a new interest in history and the beginning of historical-critical interpretation. In its resistance to Protestant teaching, the Catholic Church time and again denounced this historical approach, promoting various forms of spiritual exegesis. Those within the Church, such as the priest of the Oratory, Richard Simon (1638–1712), who advocated the historical approach, were condemned by the Church. It was not until the twentieth century that critical exegesis was espoused by the Church.

Another approach to interpretation developed during the first part of the twentieth century. Referred to as 'fuller sense' (*sensus plenior*), it resembled aspects of both the Patristic approaches and the medieval four senses, though it recognised a role for the human author. It claimed that there was a deeper meaning intended by God, though not clearly anticipated by the human author. This meaning could be perceived when the passage was studied in the light of later Christian passages. This theory developed out of the scholastic concept of instrumental inspiration, the notion that God inspires through human agency.

Pius XII's encyclical *Divino Afflante Spiritu* (1943) opened the door to critical biblical interpretation for Roman Catholics. Nonetheless, most biblical understanding that followed still flowed from some form of spiritual interpretation or was a method of proof-texting in which the use of a biblical passage was employed to provide biblical legitimacy to a doctrinal formulation. However, once Roman Catholic scholars were authorised to employ historical methods of analysis, they advanced by leaps and bounds in this critical approach. Still, they generally failed to include aspects of Tradition in their investigations. This omission may have resulted from their deep-seated dissatisfaction with ecclesiastical proof-texting and their criticism of overly pious spiritual interpretation.

The late twentieth and early twenty-first centuries have witnessed a plethora of critical interpretive approaches. Among them were various forms of narrative-criticism, reader-response, semiotic analysis, as well as types of literary deconstruction. Various liberationist methods such as cultural exegesis, feminism, and post-colonial studies also developed. However, like historical-criticism, these approaches are generally disengaged from the long Christian tradition of biblical interpretation. Still, while Tradition may not enjoy a role in the employment of these critical analyses, its importance is recognised when pastoral ceremonies and/or practices call for the contemporary realisation of the biblical message. Even then, Tradition is less an active factor in the actual analytical process itself than it is the standard against which the meaning of the passage that is derived from the analysis is judged acceptable.

This is generally the state of the relationship between Scripture and Tradition today. However, over the last two decades, the lacuna resulting from the disengagement of Scripture and Tradition has long concerned many scholars from various Christian denominations. This has given rise to seminars that investigate Scripture and hermeneutics, professional groups dedicated to the study of sound critical theological interpretation, monographs, a scholarly journal, and biblical commentary series, all of which are informed by principles of theological interpretation. These endeavors reflect the premise that 'Christian interpretation of scripture needs to involve a complex interaction in which Christian convictions, practices, and concerns are brought to bear on scriptural interpretation in ways that both shape that interpretation and are shaped by it'.[18]

Those who champion contemporary theological interpretation hold very different views on its nature. Some deny the value of findings derived from modern critical approaches and endorse approaches similar to Patristic or medieval methods that appeal to the Bible as the norm for judging Christian faith and works. Others accept the findings of critical approaches but insist that the standard of theological understanding is found outside of the biblical text, within the Tradition of the Church. Still others accept the findings of the critical approaches, but place the authority of the Scripture, not in its origin as coming from God or in the Tradition of the church, but in the theological subject matter of the Scriptures.

The benefits derived from historical-critical methods and the hegemony they have enjoyed within scholarly circles have made the large majority of interpreters wary of a return to theological interpretation:

---

18. Stephen E Fowl, *Engaging Scripture* (Malden, MA/Oxford: Blackwell Publishing, 1998), 8.

On the other hand scholars who have found in historical-critical approaches to the Bible a liberation from scholasticism, authoritarian dogmatism, or fundamentalism are often suspicious of renewed proposals for theological interpretation. For the ready appeal to theological concepts seems to be unwitting surrender of the freedom so painfully gained. Those suspicious remain confident that (this) is merely old wine in new wine skins.[19]

In 1994, the Pontifical Biblical Commission issued a document entitled 'The Interpretation of the Bible in the Church'. After it reviews many of the current interpretive approaches employed by scholars, as well as some pressing hermeneutical issues, it discusses some of the major characteristics of Catholic biblical interpretation. Chief among them is the deliberate placing of interpretation within the living tradition of the Church.

An example of theological interpretation that includes both historical-critical analysis and interpretation within the Tradition of the Church is the trilogy of books on Jesus recently published by Pope Benedict XVI.[20] In the Forward to the first volume, Benedict states that historical-criticism is a 'fundamental dimension of exegesis, but it does not exhaust the interpretive task for someone who sees the biblical writings as a single corpus of Holy Scripture inspired by God'. Believing in the unity of the Scriptures (a tenet of Tradition), he employs principles of canonical criticism (a critical approach). He then clearly places the interpretation of Scripture within the Tradition of the Church: 'The people of God—the Church—is the living subject of Scripture; it is in the Church that the words of the Bible are always in the present.'[21]

---

19. RWL Moberly, 'What is Theological Interpretation of Scripture?' in *Journal of Theological Interpretation*, 2/3 (2009): 161-78, 175.
20. Pope Benedict XVI and Adrian Walker, *Jesus of Nazareth: From the Baptism in the Jordan to the Transfiguration* (New York: Doubleday, 2007); *Jesus of Nazareth: Holy Week: From the Entrance Into Jerusalem To The Resurrection* (San Francisco, CA: Ignatius Press, 2011); *Jesus of Nazareth: The Infancy Narratives* (New York: Crown Publishing, 2012).
21. Benedict XVI, *Jesus of Nazareth: From the Baptism in the Jordan to the*

In many ways, this new kind of theological interpretation is only in its infancy. Some maintain that it has moved away from critical approaches. Others accuse it of inconsistency, because it employs both critical and spiritual methods. Those who strive to be faithful both to faith and critical analysis have a formidable task ahead of them, for biases on both sides must be addressed and resolved. Still, the Scriptures belong to the Church, not to the academy, and the living Tradition is meant to open these riches for believers.

Transfiguration, xxi.

5

'The Unity of the Whole of Scripture'

Justin Taylor SM

The editors of this volume have asked me to discuss the following question: 'Given modern critical awareness of difference and disagreement within the biblical tradition (viewpoints, manuscript and translation variants, etc.) can one continue to speak of the "unity of the whole of Scripture" as in *Dei Verbum* chapter 3, paragraph 12?'

The question admits of several possible approaches to an answer. I have chosen to examine closely the text of the Conciliar Constitution, then that of relevant portions of Emeritus Pope Benedict XVI's Apostolic Exhortation *Verbum Domini*.

In the words of a contemporary commentator, 'the discussion of the Council [of what became its Dogmatic Constitution on Divine Revelation] took place in an atmosphere of restless theological ferment and sometimes almost risked being overwhelmed by it'. As a consequence, 'The text ... naturally reveals traces of its difficult history; it is the result of many compromises'. The writer is a certain Joseph Ratzinger, who served, along with Yves Congar, Alois Grillmeier, Karl Rahner and others, as a *peritus* to the special Sub-Commission of the Council's Theological Commission set up on 7 March 1964 to work on a final text of the Constitution. He was therefore in an excellent position to make these comments, which were published in 1967.[1]

---

1. Joseph Ratzinger, 'Dogmatic Constitution on Divine Revelation: Origin and Background', in *Commentary on the Documents of Vatican II*, volume III, general editor Herbert Vorgrimler (English translation of German original published in Freiburg, 1967; London and New York: Burns and Oates, Herder and Herder, 1968), 155–66, 155 and 164.

It is fascinating to see in this light the Constitution *Dei Verbum* (*DV*) as a kind of analogue of the Scripture that the conciliar document takes as its subject. In the one case as in the other the text as we have it 'reveals traces of its difficult history'; the careful listener can discern echoes of past debates—whether lasting over many centuries or only a few years—and is invited to a reading that is not only synchronic but also diachronic. It can well be the case that, with a given biblical text (or even, perhaps, with the biblical canon itself), as with the conciliar document, we have in our hands 'the result of many compromises'. Yet in both cases—so we are assured—there is a deeper unity. Ratzinger continues:

> But the fundamental compromise which pervaded [*Dei Verbum*] is more than a compromise, it is a synthesis of great importance. The text combines fidelity to Church tradition with an affirmation of critical scholarship, thus opening up anew the path that faith may follow into the world of today.[2]

Now this compromise, synthesis or combination is at the heart of the Constitution's paragraph 12, which both affirms diversity in the biblical texts, often underlined by 'critical scholarship', and also asserts the 'unity of the whole of Scripture' assumed by 'Church tradition'; and so we arrive at our problem.

This paragraph is situated in the Constitution's chapter 3, on the divine inspiration and interpretation of Sacred Scripture.[3] Paragraph 11 has just dealt with biblical inspiration and our paragraph 12 goes on to deal with biblical interpretation. This discussion is not situated—as often in the past—exclusively in the context of scriptural inerrancy and in particular the problems of the 'historical truth' of the Scriptures. Rather, in accordance with the formula that is to be

---

2. Ratzinger, 'Dogmatic Constitution on Divine Revelation', 164.
3. In what follows, for all conciliar and papal documents, I am quoting the Latin original texts and English translations published on the official website of the Holy See (<www.vatican.va>. Accessed 12 October 2012). For chapter 3 of *Dei Verbum* I am following, unless otherwise noted, the historical and theological commentary of Alois Grillmeier, 'The Divine Inspiration and the Interpretation of Sacred Scripture', in *Commentary on the Documents of Vatican II*, volume III, 199–246.

found near the end of the preceding paragraph 11, scriptural exegesis seeks 'that truth which God wanted put into sacred writings for the sake of salvation'.[4]

In this search the exegete is guided by the fundamental principle that 'God speaks in Sacred Scripture through men in human fashion (*per homines more hominum*)'. This aphorism, with which the Council opens paragraph 12, is adapted from St Augustine, in *De Civitate Dei*. After quoting 1 Samuel 13:14, which he read in his Latin Bible as 'the Lord is seeking (*quaeret*) for himself a man according to his own heart', Augustine comments: 'God seeks a man for himself—not as if God does not know where he (David) is; but God speaks through a man (Samuel) in the fashion of men (*per hominem more hominum*); and also by speaking in this way God seeks us'.[5] The Council finds in this formula an apt description of the way in which the Word of God addresses human beings in Scripture.

Since this is so, the Council continues, 'the interpreter of Sacred Scripture, in order to see clearly what God wanted to communicate to us, should carefully investigate what meaning the sacred writers really intended, and what God wanted to manifest by means of their words'. We note in passing—for the question is not ours—that the Council Fathers appear to assume that the meaning of a text is simply that which the writer 'really intended': they do not consider the question whether a text may have a meaning of its own, independently of the intention of the writer. Further, the formulation 'what meaning the sacred writers really intended and what God wanted to manifest by means of their words' is, it seems, deliberately imprecise and leaves open the question whether the two are exactly coextensive or whether God may have wanted to manifest more by means of their words than the writers themselves intended.[6]

The rest of the paragraph is concerned with the rules of scriptural interpretation, which are arranged in two groups. The first group consists of the means to be employed in order to 'search out the intention of the sacred writers'. Among the rules of interpretation

---

4. Thus Grillmeier, 'Inspiration and Inerrancy', 237.
5. St Augustine, *De Civitate Dei*, 17.6.2 (Migne, *Patrologia Latina*, volume 41, column 537).
6. Thus leaving open the question of the *sensus plenior*; see Grillmeier, 'Inspiration and Interpretation', 217–19.

in the second group we find 'the unity of the whole of Scripture'. It is interesting to note that, until a fairly advanced stage of the discussion, the Council's draft document dealt only with the methods of establishing the meaning of Scripture that are to be found in the first set; it was only in 1964 that a second group of hermeneutical rules was formulated.[7]

So that exegetes may see clearly what God intends to communicate by means of human language, the Council instructs that 'attention should be given, among other things to "literary forms" (*genera litteraria*)' and goes on to develop this statement.[8] The expression *litteraria genera*, translated here as 'literary forms', had made a famous first appearance in Pope Pius XII's encyclical of 30 September 1943, *Divino Afflante Spiritu* (*DAS*).[9] The encyclical apparently means it to be taken in a fairly wide sense, to refer generally to modes of expression, and not only to those that are strictly literary: the synthesis offered in *DAS* 38 speaks of 'the manner of expression or (*seu*) the literary mode adopted by the sacred writer'. In the last analysis, the task of the exegete is nothing less than to make known the 'mentality (*mens*)' of the ancient writers (*DAS* 40).[10]

The Council briefly resumes the teachings of Pius XII, to which it refers at the end of the paragraph, while transposing them to its own perspective. Truth—that is, the truth that 'God wanted put into sacred writings for the sake of salvation'—is expressed differently in different sorts of texts (historical, prophetic, poetical, etc). In fact the Constitution means to go beyond a consideration

---

7. Grillmeier, 'Inspiration and Interpretation', 225.
8. The phrase 'among other things' implies that the means of interpretation that follow, in particular giving attention to 'literary forms', are not the only ones that might be employed to determine the intention of the sacred writers. Vatican II did not discuss them. The Pontifical Biblical Commission's document of 15 April 1993, on 'The Interpretation of the Bible in the Church', might be regarded as an attempt to complete the teachings of the Council at this point.
9. 'For what they [the ancient authors of the East] wished to express is not to be determined by the rules of grammar and philology alone, nor solely by the context; the interpreter must, as it were, go back wholly in spirit to those remote centuries of the East and with the aid of history, archaeology, ethnology, and other sciences, accurately determine what modes of writing, so to speak, (*litteraria, ut aiunt, genera*) the authors of that ancient period would be likely to use, and in fact did use' (*DAS* 36).
10. Compare Grillmeier, 'Inspiration and Interpretation', 217–18.

of the literary forms of written texts to recommend study of their cultural background.[11] So, the interpreter's task is to investigate 'what meaning the sacred writer intended to express and actually expressed in particular circumstances by using contemporary literary forms (*generum litterariorum illo tempore adhibitorum*) in accordance with the situation of his own time and culture (*pro sui temporis et suae culturae condicione*)'. Hence, a correct understanding of the author's meaning involves paying attention also to 'the customary and characteristic styles of feeling, speaking and narrating (*ad suetos illos nativos sentiendi, dicendi, narrandive modos*)' employed at the time, and to those normally used at that period in people's 'everyday dealings with each other'.[12]

The expression *pro . . . temporis . . . condicione* is borrowed once again, with due reference, from St Augustine, this time his *De Doctrina Christiana*. St Augustine is occupied, at this point of his work on the understanding and interpretation of Scripture, with the problems that can arise from trying to apply the literal sense of some biblical passages in the Old Testament directly to Christian life in his own day, especially in the domain of ethics. So, he writes:

> We must also be on our guard against supposing that what in the Old Testament, making allowance for the condition of those times (*pro illorum temporum conditione*), is not a crime or a vice even if we take it literally and not figuratively, can be transferred to the present time as a habit of life.[13]

---

11. As indicated in the Latin original by the conjunction *porro* ('further') at the beginning of the sentence, which is not represented in the English translation. Grillmeier ('Inspiration and Interpretation', 221) quotes a decision of the Theological Commission, on 21 September 1965: '*porro* is to be retained because a new idea (*nova idea*) is introduced concerning the various circumstances of the composition of the books'.
12. Here Grillmeier finds an advance on *Divino Afflante Spiritu*. By comparison, *Dei Verbum* gives greater prominence to forms of feeling and thinking, as well as to 'pre-literary ways of speech and narration', which are 'expressions of a total understanding of the world and life' and 'may penetrate all literary forms' ('Inspiration and Interpretation', 222).
13. St Augustine, *De Doctrina Christiana*, 3.8.26 (Migne, *Patrologia Latina*, volume 34, columns 75–6). English translation from *Select Library of Nicene and Post-Nicene Fathers*, online at: <http://www9.georgetown.edu/faculty/jod/augustine/

In other words, 'other times, other *mores*'—even in the Bible. This is a nice reminder that the Church Fathers—sometimes treated as a kind of deposit of timeless biblical interpretation—could also be aware of the historical dimension of the Bible and find in it a way of resolving difficulties presented by the text. The drafters of *DV* have expanded these three words and thus adapted them to refer generally to the influence of contemporary conditions upon the way biblical writers expressed themselves.[14]

After thus highlighting the fact of diversity, of various kinds, in the Bible, the Council now declares that 'no less serious attention must be given to the content and unity of the whole of Scripture (*contentum et unitatem totius Scripturae*) if the meaning of the sacred texts is to be worked out'. The exegete must also take into account the 'living tradition of the whole Church' and the 'harmony which exists between elements of the faith (*analogiae fidei*)'.

In order to locate this second group of interpretative rules in the whole paragraph 12, we need to return to the statement with which the paragraph begins: 'God speaks in Sacred Scripture through men in human fashion'. Up till now *DV* has been dealing with the second part of this sentence, how the fact that God speaks through human authors in human fashion must be taken seriously in all its aspects by exegetes. Now the document considers how the fact that Scripture is the Word of God ('God speaks') must also govern its interpretation. It would, however, be a mistake to separate these two groups. In the first group, the historical-critical rules are applied in order to search for 'that truth which God wanted put into sacred writings for the sake of salvation'; and in the second group, the exegete does not abandon the use of reason and historical investigation.[15] In the practice of Scriptural exegesis in the Church, both sets of rules are to be applied.

The paragraph begins by enunciating a principle from which flows the second set of rules. In the official English translation it reads: '. . . since Holy Scripture must be read and interpreted in the sacred spirit in which it was written . . .' This, on the face of it, appears to be a reminder of the religious character of the scriptural texts: they cannot be treated just like any other writings emanating from the ancient world.

---

ddc.html>. Accessed 12 October 2012.
14. Compare Grillmeier, 'Inspiration and Interpretation', 221–22.
15. Compare Grillmeier, 'Inspiration and Interpretation', 243.

Another translation, published shortly after the end of the Council, has: '... since holy Scripture must be read and interpreted according to the same Spirit by whom it was written'.[16] The use of the capital letter and of the pronoun 'whom' seem to mean that, for these translators, the 'Spirit' in question is the Third Person of the Trinity. But does the Council really mean to teach that the Scriptures were not only 'written *under the inspiration of* the Holy Spirit', as stated already in paragraph 11, but also that Holy Scripture was 'written *by* the Holy Spirit'. And in that case, what would they have meant by that?

So, what does the Latin original say? '... *cum Sacra Scriptura eodem Spiritu quo scripta est etiam legenda et interpretanda sit...*' The use of the capital letter would indicate that it is indeed the Holy Spirit who is meant, so that the pronoun *quo* is to be translated 'whom' and not 'which'. On the other hand, if the Council had meant to say 'the same Spirit *by whom* [Holy Scripture] was written', one might have expected that the Latin original would read *a quo* and not simply *quo*.

Immediately after the words '*interpretanda sit*', the Council inserts references to Pope Benedict XV's encyclical *Spiritus Paraclitus*, of 15 September 1920, written to commemorate the 1500th anniversary of the death of St Jerome, and to Jerome's own commentary on Galatians, 5:19–21. Benedict XV writes that, since St Jerome was

> aware that 'in expounding the holy Scriptures we are always in need of the coming (*adventu*) of the Spirit of God' and that Scripture is not to be read and understood 'otherwise ... than the meaning intended by the Holy Spirit in whom it was written demands (*aliter ... quam sensus Spiritus Sancti flagitat quo conscripta est*)', the most holy man of God ... suppliantly implores the aid and lights of the Paraclete.[17]

---

16. *The Documents of Vatican II, in a New and Definitive Translation with Commentaries and Notes by Catholic, Protestant and Orthodox Authorities*, general editor Walter M Abbot sj (New York: Herder and Herder, Associated Press, 1966), 120. Despite the use of the adjective 'definitive' in the title, the translation expressly disclaims the status of 'official' (Preface by Joseph Gallagher).
17. Benedict XV, *Spiritus Paraclitus* 35. The Vatican website gives only the Latin text of the encyclical, and the above translation is mine.

This latter quotation is precisely the passage in Jerome's commentary on Galatians to which reference is made in *DV* 12.[18] It is not without some ambiguity: does *quo* refer to *sensus*—if so, it should be translated 'in which'—or to *Spiritus Sancti*? (In the latter case, it is probably better rendered 'in whom', rather than 'by whom'). So, unfortunately, neither in itself nor in its use by Benedict XV does the quotation from St Jerome really resolve our problem beyond doubt.[19]

Before leaving Benedict XV, let us take a look at the first of his two quotations from St Jerome, which is not explicitly cited by *DV*. At this point in his commentary on the prophet Micah (1:10), Jerome is facing the numerous and significant differences between the Hebrew text he is translating (not always identically with the Vulgate) and that of the Septuagint.[20] After giving both forms of the text, he exclaims:

> The Hebrew disagrees greatly with the interpretation of the Seventy, and both my translation and theirs is wrapped with so many difficulties that if ever we needed the Spirit of God (but in expounding the holy Scriptures we are always in need of his coming), now most of all we desire him to be present and to explain what he spoke in the prophets . . .

Jerome assumes the single divine authorship of the Bible, but is acutely aware of the diversity of the Bible's human authors and texts. In the case that he highlights here, for all his preference for the '*Hebraica veritas*', he is not free to dismiss or ignore the Septuagint. Clearly, the reconciliation of unity and diversity in the Scriptures is not a new problem.

DV does not explain what it means by the 'content and unity of the whole of Scripture', or how precisely it is to be used as a rule of interpretation. Where can we turn for further light?

---

18. St Jerome, *In Gal.* 5, 19-21 (Migne, *Patrologia Latina* volume 26, column 417 A).
19. The translation in *Vatican Council II: The Conciliar and Post-conciliar Documents*, general editor Austin Flannery op (Wilmington, Delaware: Scholarly Resources, 1975), 758, seems to despair of clarity: '. . . since sacred Scripture must be read and interpreted with its divine authorship in mind'.
20. St Jerome, *In Mich.* 1:10 (Migne, *Patrologia Latina* volume 25, column 1159).

Given Joseph Ratzinger's involvement in the formation of *DV*, we might expect to find in Pope Benedict XVI's post-synodal Exhortation *Verbum Domini* (*VD*), of 30 September 2010, on 'The Word of God in the Life and Mission of the Church', elements of a *relecture* of the Council's Constitution, in which the pope might attempt to clarify or develop the teachings of the earlier document. This in fact turns out to be the case; although the new document does not solve all difficulties and even has some inconsistencies of its own.

In *VD* 29 of the Exhortation, Benedict XVI writes that the 'interpretation of sacred Scripture in the Church' was a major topic of discussion at The Twelfth Ordinary General Assembly of the Synod of Bishops, meeting in the Vatican from 5–26 October 2008. Following on from the discussions held there, he formulates the following 'fundamental criterion of biblical hermeneutics: *the primary setting for scriptural interpretation is the life of the Church*'. This is not to be taken as an extrinsic rule, obliging the exegete to submit to the 'ecclesial context'. Rather, it is 'something demanded by the very nature of the Scriptures and the way they gradually came into being'. For 'faith traditions formed the living context for the literary activity of the authors of sacred Scripture'. Here the pope quotes a phrase from *DV* 12, that we have already studied: 'since sacred Scripture must be read and interpreted in the light of the same Spirit through whom it was written . . .'.[21] He draws from it the consequence that 'exegetes, theologians and the whole people of God must approach (Scripture) for what it really is, the word of God conveyed to us through human words (cf 1 Thess 2:13)'. In the last analysis, 'The Bible is the Church's book, and its essential place in the Church's life gives rise to its genuine interpretation'.

Coming to a consideration of 'the development of biblical studies and the Church's Magisterium', the former pope writes (*VD* 32): 'Before all else, we need to acknowledge the benefits that historical-critical exegesis and other recently-developed methods of textual analysis have brought to the life of the Church'. This clear statement should suffice to silence those in the Church today who are opposed

---

21. Note the wording of the official (Vatican) English translation of this passage as quoted in *Verbum Domini* ('*through* whom'), which differs from that given for the passage in its original context in *Dei Verbum* (and from other translations seen above).

to historical-critical exegesis and similar methods and regard them as somehow un-Catholic—at any rate, they cannot claim the support of Benedict XVI for their views. Against any such tendencies, he is forthright: 'For the Catholic understanding of sacred Scripture, attention to such methods is indispensable, linked as it is to the realism of the Incarnation'. On the other hand, if they are indispensable, they are not by themselves sufficient for a fully Catholic understanding of the Scripture. Pope Benedict follows his predecessors in rejecting (*VD* 33) 'a split between the human and the divine, between scientific research and respect for the faith, between the literal sense and the spiritual sense',[22] and quotes with approval the 1993 document of the Pontifical Biblical Commission:

> in their work of interpretation, Catholic exegetes must never forget that what they are interpreting is the word of God. Their common task is not finished when they have simply determined sources, defined forms or explained literary procedures. They arrive at the true goal of their work only when they have explained the meaning of the biblical text as God's word for today.[23]

'Against this background', Benedict XVI suggests, 'one can better appreciate the great principles of interpretation proper to Catholic exegesis set forth by the Second Vatican Council, especially in the Dogmatic Constitution *Dei Verbum*'. He reaffirms that the Council's biblical hermeneutic is 'a directive to be appropriated'. *VD* 34 presents in summary form the teachings of *DV* 12, including the quotation of the key sentence:

> Seeing that, in sacred Scripture, God speaks through human beings in human fashion, it follows that the interpreters of sacred Scripture, if they are to ascertain what God has wished to communicate to us, should carefully search out the meaning which the sacred

---

22. Quoting John Paul II, 'Address for the Celebration of the Centenary of the Encyclical *Providentissimus Deus* and the Fiftieth Anniversary of the Encyclical *Divino Afflante Spiritu*' (23 April 1993), 5: *Acta Apostolicae Sedis* 86 (1994), 236.
23. Pontifical Biblical Commission, 'The Interpretation of the Bible in the Church' (15 April 1993), III, C, 1: *Enchiridion Vaticanum* 13, No. 3065.

writers really had in mind, that meaning which God had thought well to manifest through the medium of their words.

So, on the one hand,

> the Council emphasizes the study of literary genres and historical context as basic elements for understanding the meaning intended by the sacred author. On the other hand, *since Scripture must be interpreted in the same Spirit in which it was written*, the Dogmatic Constitution indicates three fundamental criteria for an appreciation of the divine dimension of the Bible.

It will not have escaped the reader's notice that, in the words that we have italicised, the pope once again quotes (in a slightly adapted form and without an express citation) the difficult expression of *DV* that he cited a few paragraphs above. The fact that the official English version gives yet another translation of *Spiritu quo scripta est*, shows how obscure is the Council's formula.

In repeating the 'three fundamental criteria for an appreciation of the divine dimension of the Bible', Benedict XVI abbreviates the first, which interests us: 'the text must be interpreted with attention to the unity of the whole of Scripture'—he has tacitly dropped the words 'content and', which occur in the original formulation. He also glosses the 'unity of the whole of Scripture' by adding: 'nowadays this is called canonical exegesis'. He does not develop this. He probably means us to take the expression 'canonical exegesis' in a quite loose sense, which is perfectly compatible with other methods and indeed complements them.[24] So an exegete would look beyond the immediate context of a Scriptural passage—even beyond the individual book in which it occurs—and situate it ultimately in the context of the entire Bible. In this way, one passage can be read in the light of another.[25]

---

24. For Brevard Childs, who is regarded as its founder, the 'canonical approach' (as he preferred to call it) is not simply another method of criticism to be practised alongside the historical-critical method. Rather, it seeks to establish 'a stance from which the Bible can be read as sacred scripture'. See Brevard Childs, *Introduction to the Old Testament as Scripture* (London: SCM Press, 1979), 82.
25. Compare Grillmeier, 'Inspiration and Interpretation', 243.

The pope expresses concern that Catholic exegetes should employ both 'historical-critical' and 'theological' methods of interpretation: he seems to feel that there has been a certain imbalance to the disadvantage of the latter. He finds it necessary to warn against the 'danger of dualism'—of separating the two approaches as if they were alternative instead of being complementary—and also against a 'secularized hermeneutic', which is 'ultimately based on the conviction that the Divine does not intervene in human history' (*VD* 35). Both faith and reason are to be employed in 'the approach to Scripture' (*VD* 36).

The pope writes (*VD* 37) that a 'significant contribution to the recovery of an adequate scriptural hermeneutic, as the synodal assembly stated (*Propositio* 6), can also come from renewed attention to the Fathers of the Church and their exegetical approach'. Notably, their theology still has 'great value' today because at its heart is the 'study of sacred Scripture as a whole'. Furthermore, quoting the Congregation for Catholic Education, their example can 'teach modern exegetes' two things of which they apparently stand in need. One of these is 'a truly religious approach to sacred Scripture'; another is 'an interpretation that is constantly attuned to the criterion of communion with the experience of the Church, which journeys through history under the guidance of the Holy Spirit'.[26] At the same time, it should be noted that this strong recommendation to pay attention to the Church Fathers for what they still have to offer, is not an imposition of their precise methods or particular interpretations on today's exegetes.[27] The same is to be said of what amounts to a brief excursus, which follows, on the patristic and medieval distinction of the senses of Scripture.

Finally, writes Pope Benedict,

> we learn from the Fathers that exegesis 'is truly faithful
> to the proper intention of biblical texts when it goes not
> only to the heart of their formulation to find the reality

---

26. Congregation for Catholic Education, 'Instruction *Inspectis Dierum*' (10 November 1989), 26: *Acta Apostolicae Sedis* 82 (1990), 618.
27. We might note that Fr Marie-Joseph, Lagrange, op, who advocated the use of modern critical methods in biblical exegesis, also gives a large place to the Church Fathers in his commentaries.

> of faith there expressed, but also seeks to link this reality
> to the experience of faith in our present world.[28]

Here, again, it seems to this writer, if the Fathers offer an example of how to 'link this reality [of faith expressed in the biblical texts] to the experience of faith in our present world', we are not restricted to their characteristic ways of doing so. It is a not uncommon experience that, after one has paid close attention to the wording and the life-situation of, say, an Old Testament passage, and discovered the 'reality of faith there expressed', far from ending up being a 'text belonging only to the past',[29] it speaks to our 'experience of faith in our present world'. This writer would respectfully submit that such a reading is 'truly religious' and even 'attuned to the criterion of communion with the experience of the Church'.

The 'passage from letter to spirit' (*VD* 38) is not 'automatic' or 'spontaneous'. Rather, writes Pope Benedict, to arrive at the spiritual meaning of Scripture 'involves a progression and a process of understanding guided by the inner movement of the whole corpus, and hence it also has to become a vital process'.[30] In the last analysis, one might say, his understanding of the 'spiritual sense' is profoundly existential: 'an authentic process of interpretation is never purely an intellectual process but also a lived one, demanding full engagement in the life of the Church, which is life "according to the Spirit" (Gal 5:16)'. So, 'an individual literary fragment' must be 'seen in relation to the whole of Scripture'. This is ultimately because 'the goal to which we are necessarily progressing is the one Word'.[31] At the same time,

> there is an inner drama in this process, since the passage
> that takes place in the power of the Spirit inevitably

---

28. *Verbum Domini* 37, quoting the Pontifical Biblical Commission, 'The Interpretation of the Bible in the Church' (15 April 1993), II, A, 2: *Enchiridion Vaticanum* 13, No. 2987.
29. Cf. *VD* 35, where Pope Benedict lists the 'most troubling consequences' of a 'sterile separation' between exegesis and theology.
30. The Pope is here quoting his own 'Address to Representatives of the World of Culture' at the Collège des Bernardins in Paris (12 September 2008): *Acta Apostolicae Sedis* 100 (2008), 726.
31. '*Unum enim est Verbum, quod nos transcendere vocamur*': is there a hint here of the Platonic ascent from the many to the One?

> engages each person's freedom. Saint Paul lived this passage to the full in his own life. In his words: 'the letter kills, but the Spirit gives life' (2 Cor 3:6), he expressed in radical terms the significance of this process of transcending the letter and coming to understand it only in terms of the whole.

Finally, the Exhortation comes to the subject that has been in the background for some time: 'the Bible's intrinsic unity' (*VD* 39). Pope Benedict quotes Hugh of Saint Victor: 'All divine Scripture is one book, and this one book is Christ, speaks of Christ and finds its fulfilment in Christ'.[32] He admits that,

> viewed in purely historical or literary terms, of course, the Bible is not a single book, but a collection of literary texts composed over the course of a thousand years or more, and its individual books are not easily seen to possess an interior unity; instead, we see clear inconsistencies between them.

We may not, however, be satisfied with a simple assertion of the Bible's unity, specifically of its unity in Christ, and may seek literary symptoms of unity within the Bible itself. Exegetes frequently underline the unity between the two Testaments—or within either corpus—by pointing out the frequent allusions that one book will make to another.[33] Other examples of literary unity can be cited: cases of influence, either directly or by provoking a response; recourse to a system of symbols embedded in a common culture.[34]

Pope Benedict is, of course, perfectly well aware of these and similar literary elements that tend to unify the Scriptures; but he does not mention them here. His interest is theological. To put it simply, in their diversity the Scriptures are God's Word, and that is one. So,

---

32. *De Arca Noe*, 2, 8 (Migne, *Patrologia Latina*, volume 176, column 642C-D).
33. It has become fashionable to call this phenomenon 'intertextuality'; however, if it is not intended thereby to define this expression in terms of its original meaning within 'post-structuralism', one might doubt its usefulness.
34. On this last point, see, for instance, Northrop Frye, *The Great Code: The Bible and Literature* (San Diego and New York: Harcourt, 1982).

the 'unity of all Scripture' is 'grounded in the unity of God's word'.[35] Now that word is not simply to be heard or studied; it 'challenges our life and constantly calls us to conversion'. For the Word of God is a Person, incarnate in Jesus Christ. 'In this way', he concludes, 'we can understand the words of Number 12 of the Dogmatic Constitution *Dei Verbum*, which point to the internal unity of the entire Bible as a decisive criterion for a correct hermeneutic of faith.'

If there is already an interplay of diversity and unity within 'the Bible of Israel', it is brought to a new level of intensity when the 'Bible of Israel' becomes the 'Old Testament' within the 'Christian Bible'. In other words, we cannot leave the question of the 'unity of the whole of Scripture' without discussing the unity of that Scripture as comprising also the 'New Testament'.

This is the subject of *VD* 40. The former Pope outlines several aspects of 'the relationship between the Old and the New Testaments', beginning with elements of continuity between them. First is the obvious fact that 'the New Testament itself acknowledges the Old Testament as the word of God and thus accepts the authority of the sacred Scriptures of the Jewish people'.[36] This it does in two ways: 'implicitly... by using the same language and by frequently referring to passages from these Scriptures'; 'explicitly... by citing many parts of them as a basis for argument'. Even more fundamentally, 'Jesus of Nazareth was a Jew and the Holy Land is the motherland of the Church'[37]; therefore, the 'roots of Christianity are found in the Old Testament, and Christianity continually draws nourishment from these roots'. Benedict XVI rejects 'all new forms of Marcionism, which tend, in different ways, to set the Old Testament in opposition to the New'.[38]

---

35. '... quandoquidem unicum est Verbum Dei'—perhaps a better translation would be: 'the unicity of God's Word'.
36. Citing *Propositio* 10 of the Synod; Pontifical Biblical Commission, 'The Jewish People and their Sacred Scriptures in the Christian Bible' (24 May 2001): *Enchiridion Vaticanum* 20, Nos. 748–55.
37. Synod's *Propositio* 52.
38. See also Pontifical Biblical Commission, 'The Jewish People and their Sacred Scriptures in the Christian Bible' (24 May 2001), 19: *Enchiridion Vaticanum* 20, Nos. 799–801; Origen, *Homily on Numbers* 9, 4: *Sources Chrétiennes*, volume 415, 238–42.

The relationship between the Old and the New Testaments is not, however, one of simple continuity—all the more so as the New Testament itself claims (for example Luke 24:44-48) 'that in the mystery of the life, death and resurrection of Christ the sacred Scriptures of the Jewish people have found their perfect fulfilment'. In fact, 'the concept of the fulfilment of the Scriptures is a complex one, since it has three dimensions: a basic aspect of continuity with the Old Testament revelation, an aspect of discontinuity and an aspect of fulfilment and transcendence'.

The resolution of this complex relationship between the Old and the New Testaments proposed by Benedict XVI in *VD* 41 is the traditional one of Typology, which, to quote the *Catechism of the Catholic Church*, 128, 'discerns in God's works of the Old Covenant prefigurations of what he accomplished in the fullness of time in the person of his incarnate Son'. We are all familiar with this way of thinking: the New Testament presents 'antitypes', beginning with Jesus himself, of 'types' that are presented in the First Testament. So King David is a type (Greek *typos*)—or, to use the corresponding word of Latin origin, 'figure' (Latin *figura*)—of Jesus.

In recent times, however, some unease has been felt about Christian use of typology to understand the 'Bible of Israel'. Does it not necessarily involve or lead to 'supersessionism', to the idea that the Jewish dispensation has simply been superseded or replaced by the Christian? After all, if the point of a type is to be fulfilled by an antitype, does not that mean that, once fulfilled, it is no longer needed? Has it not been replaced?

This worry occurred to Erich Auerbach, the great German Jewish literary critic who made a lifetime's study of *figura* and its role in the development of European literature. At the end of the second chapter of his book *Mimesis*, Auerbach reflects on the moment when the young Church, disappointed with the response from Jesus' own people, turned to the Gentiles:

> With that, an adaptation of the message to the preconceptions of a far wider audience, its detachment from the special preconceptions of the Jewish world, became a necessity and was effected by a method rooted in Jewish tradition but now applied with incomparably

greater boldness, the method of revisional interpretation. The Old Testament was played down as popular history and as the code of the Jewish people and assumed the appearance of a series of 'figures,' that is of prophetic announcements and anticipations of the coming of Jesus and the concomitant events . . . The total content of the sacred writings was placed in an exegetic context which often removed the thing told very far from its sensory base, in that the reader or listener was forced to turn his attention away from the sensory occurrence and toward its meaning. This implied the danger that the visual element of the occurrences might succumb under the dense texture of meanings . . . What is perceived by the hearer or reader or even, in the plastic and graphic arts, by the spectator, is weak as a sensory impression, and all one's interest is directed toward the context of meanings.[39]

VD does not directly take up this objection. On the other hand, Benedict is clearly aware of it, as he quickly makes the point that 'we must not forget that the Old Testament retains its own inherent value as revelation, as our Lord himself reaffirmed (cf Mk 12:29 31)'.[40] He also quotes 'the Synod Fathers' who state that 'the Jewish understanding of the Bible can prove helpful to Christians for their own understanding and study of the Scriptures'.[41]

The question merits a much more extensive discussion than we can give here.[42] Briefly, in the second century the Christian Church recognised, against Marcion, that she could not do without the Scriptures of Israel. This was because precisely those Scriptures, interpreted figurally or typologically, gave meaning to Jesus and to

---

39. Erich Auerbach, *Mimesis: The Representation of Reality in Western Literature* (Fiftieth Anniversary Edition, English translation by Willard Trask; Princeton: Princeton University Press, 2003), 48–9.
40. VD 41.
41. *Propositio* 52; the whole question is, of course, discussed at length by the Pontifical Biblical Commission in 'The Jewish People and their Sacred Scriptures in the Christian Bible'.
42. See, for example, John David Dawson, *Christian Figural Reading and the Fashioning of Identity* (Berkeley, CA: University of California Press, 2002).

the significant events of the Gospels. If we know that Jesus is Messiah, it is because we understand his life, death and resurrection as the fulfilment of 'all that is written about him in the Law of Moses, in the Prophets and in the Psalms' (cf Luke 24:44). Type and antitype point to one another: the type confers meaning on the anti-type, which in turn 'fulfils' the type. However, the reality of the type abides even after it has been fulfilled by the antitype to which it has given meaning: David does not—despite Christian figural reading of the Books of Samuel or of the Psalms—disappear once Jesus is proclaimed as Messiah.[43]

A further consideration might be added. The types of the Old Testament do not find their final fulfilment in the antitypes of the New Testament. They continue to look forward to an ultimate accomplishment in the *eschaton*. In the last analysis, eschatology is the best preventative of all forms of Christian supersessionism. This is the real function of the Book of Revelation or Apocalypse considered as the completion not only of the New Testament, but of the entire Christian Bible. This book is a 'mosaic of allusions to the Old Testament: that is, it is a progression of antitypes'.[44] As such it draws together into a final unity the great themes and symbols that are first stated in Genesis and recur throughout the Bible: spirit, light, garden, tree, river, bride and bridegroom and others. For the unity of the whole of Scripture is also poetic. But that would be another subject.

---

43. Erich Auerbach insists on the abiding reality of the type, even after its fulfillment by the antitype, citing Tertullian and other Church writers; see his article 'Figura', originally published in *Dantestudien*, Istanbul, 1944, and reproduced in English translation in *Scenes from the Drama of European Literature* (Minneapolis, MN: University of Minneapolis Press, 1984), 11–71.
44. Frye, *The Great Code*, 135.xs

6

Dei Verbum
Literary Forms and Vatican II—An Old Testament Perspective

Antony F Campbell SJ

The invitation offered by the fiftieth anniversary of a Council document is a marvellous opportunity to look at the nature of an ecumenical council (such as Vatican II) and the nature of its documents. The nature of neither can be taken for granted. In days gone by, Council documents culminated in a series of propositions, each ending with 'anathema sit'—let any person holding this view be considered anathema, an outsider. Vatican II did not do this. At the earlier Councils, it was probably felt that the anathema would hold its force for all time. The passage of time would make clear that with the changing circumstances of Church and culture that was not the case. 'Anathema sit' might be best understood as 'we're really serious about this'. It is the responsibility of historians to determine how long that seriousness lasted. It is also the responsibility of historians to determine whether Council documents were a base from which the future might be developed or a culminating crown summing up the preceding developments or a stopgap while a process of theological reflection continued. Which was *Dei Verbum* (*DV*) and how does it look fifty years later?

John O'Malley is emphatic that the literary form of the documents from Vatican II is radically different from what preceded it, going back to the beginning with the Council of Nicaea.[1] Most of the documents of Vatican II sought to address the world; those of its predecessors addressed the Church. The code for the former would be 'pastoral';

---

1. John O'Malley, *What Happened at Vatican II* (Cambridge, MA: Harvard University Press, 2008), 11 and *passim*.

for the latter, 'legislative and judicial'. The two must therefore be used quite differently. As a rule, in the 'legislative and judicial', the Council laid down the law for what was to be believed and condemned the errors opposed to that belief. The 'pastoral' quality of the Vatican II documents means that quite opposed positions can be found within the same document because quite opposed positions could be found within the same Church.

DV provides as good an example of this as any. Early in the piece (1962), dissatisfaction with the initial schema for discussion was registered at sixty per cent. In 1965, after four years of stubborn resistance from a group favouring tradition over scripture as the primary vehicle of revelation, the final vote was almost unanimous, 2,344 in favour and 6 against. One side was not massively outvoted; the stubborn minority had not seen the light and caved in under pressure; instead, the text was such that both sides could vote for it. As one participant put it: 'We must not simply substitute the declaration of a different school of thought, but rather produce something acceptable to all'.[2] Yves Congar clearly understood 'that Paul VI wanted to secure a large consensus of the Fathers and that that presupposed compromise'.[3] These Vatican II documents must be read very differently from their predecessors.

It is standard practice for Latin documents emerging from the Vatican to be known by their opening words. In this case, *Dei Verbum* (Word of God) can be misleading. The document is a Dogmatic Constitution on Divine Revelation, as it is correctly entitled. It is not exclusively concerned with the inspired word of Scripture, as the title *Dei Verbum* might suggest. Its concern goes beyond the biblical word to touch on the many ways in which God is revealed to God's creatures, some dealt with in detail and some in a passing reference.

Close inspection makes clear that *DV* intends to affirm an overall image of the past and encourage a sure march into the future. In its own words: 'Following in the footsteps of the councils of Trent and of First Vatican, this present Council wishes to set forth the authentic teaching about divine revelation and about how it is handed on' (*DV*

---

2. Dom Basil Butler, President of the English Benedictine Congregation, in Yves Congar, *My Journal of the Council* (Adelaide: ATF Press, 2012), 198.
3. Congar, *My Journal*, xxii.

1).[4] The document *Dei Filius* from Vatican I leaves open the possibility of access to God by reason. Vatican II affirms it bluntly: 'God ... can be known with certainty from created reality, by the light of human reason' (*DV* 6). On the complex question of Scripture and Tradition, Trent's 'scripture and tradition' [*et*] is dealt with far more extensively by Vatican II (*DV* 7–10).

It is desirable that space should be given to the issue of Scripture and Tradition. It was a major sticking point at the time of the Reformation; Luther's *sola scriptura* (scripture alone) was a rallying cry of significance. A proposal at Vatican I affirmed that revealed truth was to be found *partly* in Scripture and *partly* in Tradition (*partim ... partim*). The Council rejected this formulation, because the evidence for it was not there; instead it adopted the alternative, more flexible, formulation 'scripture and tradition' (*et*).[5] I have seen a 'penny catechism' from the Archdiocese of Sydney in the 1930s that asked the question whether all revelation was to be found in Scripture. In flat contradiction to Trent, it replied: certainly not; divine revelation was to be found partly in Scripture and partly in Tradition. Within the Roman Catholic Church of those days, Sydney was probably not alone in knowing what to do when it was a question of denying Protestantism or adhering to Trent. Let the Protestants lose.

That Trent's idea was right is clear; that its formulation was unsatisfactory is evident. Given the importance of the matter, it is small wonder that Vatican II devoted considerable effort on the issue. Anyone with ecclesial experience of ecumenism will be well aware that the Roman Catholic Church's approach to issues of divine revelation will often be different from that of other Churches. That difference can be summed up globally by the term 'tradition'. Exegetes (aka biblical interpreters) may struggle with words, sentences, or passages; Churches more often grapple with matters of greater weight. Of course, Tradition plays a role, along with Scripture, in keeping faith alive and well—and moving in the right direction.

At this point it is time for a moment to take a look at the reality of an ecumenical council. It is not a wondrous gathering of mystical

---

4. Translation throughout from *The Documents of Vatican II: All Sixteen Official Texts Promulgated by the Ecumenical Council, 1963–1965*, translated from the Latin, edited by Walter Abbott (London: Chapman, 1966).
5. Council of Trent, Decree concerning sacred books and traditions to be received; Denzinger-Schönmetze1501).

truth-sayers who have the insight and intelligence to guide the Roman Catholic Church securely for the next century or two. It is a cross-section of the present-day Roman Catholic Church, with its conservative factions and its liberal factions, with its wise folk and its weirdos. The leadership will be tugged forward and backward. The future of the Church will be reflected in that tugging.

When a couple of thousand bishops, archbishops, and cardinals meet in a single place (St Peter's) for a relatively short period of time (four sessions) for a major ecumenical Council, it is a moment of massive significance for the whole of Western Christendom. The participants in such a gathering will reflect a wide range of people—as for believers, so for bishops—from astute front ends of thoroughbreds at one extreme of the range to the rear ends of hard-working draught horses at the other. An ecumenical council is not a gathering of learned theologians; it is not a gathering of naïve believers; it is not a gathering of specialist guides to lead the faithful toward the future. Far from it. A council is a mirror of the Church it represents. Its role is to reflect on where that Church is now and where it might best be going in living to the full the good news of Jesus Christ, of God's love for us in the ordinariness of our lives. It is a gathering of a couple of thousand leaders, reflecting a billion or so believers, including the learned and the naïve, the high-power administrators and the pastorally committed, the elite and the common-or-garden, the wise and the stupid. It is precisely the wide-ranging complexity of this variety that makes this gathering of such massive significance.

Vatican II was summoned by the much loved Pope John XXIII. The word primarily associated with both Pope John XXIII and the Second Vatican Council was *aggiornamento*. Modernisation, updating, bringing up to date are all accurate enough as translations go but a bit facile. It is not easy to catch the force of the image. It is not a matter of throwing open the doors and windows and letting daylight into the structure. The force of the image is day rather than light. Left untouched by the word is whether doors and windows are thrown open to invite 'day' into the structure or to invite the contents and people within the structure to move out into the 'day'. When revelation is under scrutiny, the issue then is whether the forces of day are to enter the structure and further burnish the understanding of revelation or whether the occupants of the structure are freed to move out into the day and inspect the revelation that is being understood out there. This may be very abstract imagistic language. What it points to is highly significant. Where is revelation to be sought? Inside the bureaucracy of the Church or outside the bureaucracy among the believing faithful? The answer 'both' is easy; articulating what this answer means is not easy at all. It is this *'aggiornamento'*, this openness of the Church to its surrounds, that is probably the high point and lasting contribution of Vatican II.

The dogmatic constitution on divine revelation, *DV*, as its readers will gratefully acknowledge, casts its net wide, embracing whatever is of value to those who believe. So, for example, the document speaks early on of God buoying us up with the hope of salvation, with 'His promise of redemption' and it quotes Genesis 3:15 (*DV* 3). A little later on, it insists that attention must be paid, among other things, to *literary genres* (*DV* 12). In the reference to Genesis 3:15 as a promise of redemption and in the reference to the importance of literary genres for understanding the meaning of a text, *DV* invokes two widely different approaches to the understanding of biblical text, approaches as different as the front and rear ends of a thoroughbred. For the historical-critical exegete, Genesis 3:15 has as its purpose 'to describe the phenomenon that enmity exists not merely in a determined situation but has grown to a continual state, something like an institution'.[6] Tradition, on the other hand, reaches back to Irenaeus (second century) for an understanding of the passage as a prophecy about Christ (seed of Mary) and the devil (seed of the serpent). Says Westermann, a relatively conservative modern exegete, 'there are two main reasons that do not allow such an interpretation'[7]—which we will pass over here.

Irenaeus was the second Bishop of Lyons, in France, and was a major figure in the writings of the early Church; he lived a couple of hundred yards down the road from where, for four years, I lived and studied theology. It is said that Irenaeus first moved the interpretation of Genesis 3:15 from Eve's descendants and snakes to Jesus and Satan. This is a perfect example of what, since the term was coined in 1925, has been called *sensus plenior*. In the *New Jerome Biblical Commentary* the *sensus plenior* is described as

---

6. Claus Westermann, *Genesis 1–11* (Minneapolis, MN: Augsburg, 1984; German original, 1974), 259.
7. Westermann, *Genesis 1-11*, 260.

the deeper meaning intended by God but not clearly intended by the human author, that is seen to exist in the words of Scripture when they are studied in the light of further Revelation or of development in the understanding of Revelation.[8]

Its discussion peaked in the work of Fr Raymond Brown SS;[9] interestingly, there has been almost no discussion of *sensus plenior* since 1970. Further comment in the *NJBC* 71.50, almost certainly from Raymond Brown, goes on to say:

> the fact that advocacy of the SPlen [*sensus plenior*] had its roots in distrust of excesses in patristic typology and allegory gave SPlen exegesis a more cerebral and cautionary aura. Reasonable homogeneity with the literal sense was insisted on, and the SPlen was seldom invoked even by strong supporters.

Two points can be underlined: (i) the *sensus plenior* was distinguished from the literal sense; (ii) reasonable homogeneity with the literal sense was insisted on.

There is a notion that recurs almost as a mantra in various formulations in a hugely important book on the Eucharist, *In Breaking of Bread:* 'The heritage of our belief is unsatisfactory, but that does not stop it from being revered.'[10] That applies precisely to what *DV* has done in this case: it combines an unsatisfactory interpretation of Genesis 3:15 that is part of a past to be revered with an insistence a little later on the importance of attention to *literary genres*.[11]

This is not an isolated example. The document *DV* quietly insists on the reverence owed to tradition and equally quietly insists on the openness to the future owed to biblical studies.

---

8. *The New Jerome Biblical Commentary (NJBC)*, edited by Raymond E Brown, Joseph A Fitzmyer, Roland E Murphy (Englewood Cliffs, NJ: Prentice Hall, 1990), 71.50.
9. Raymond E Brown, *The Sensus Plenior of Sacred Scripture* (STD Dissertation. Baltimore, MD: St Mary's University, 1955).
10. PJ FitzPatrick (a Catholic priest, in the department of philosophy at the University of Durham), *In Breaking Of Bread: The Eucharist and Ritual* (Cambridge: Cambridge University Press, 1993), 322.
11. Or 'literary forms'; original Latin, 'genera litteraria'.

The Council has done what it had to do and what has such massive significance. It has dressed the vine in such a way as to yield maximum fruit to the members of its Church, both learned exegetes and generalist believers. There are some, for example, who find the bridal language of late Isaiah ('with everlasting love I will have compassion on you', Isa 54:8) a superb base for prayer; there are others for whom other passages echo spousal abuse ('double for all her sins', Isa 40:2) and cause revulsion more than anything else. Both sorts of passages are in canonical Scripture; both sorts of passages have meaning in the right moments. Ecumenical councils must be careful not to exclude what may have meaning in the various right moments of our lives, whether in Scripture, in theology, or in faith.

The full text of *DV* on literary genres reads: 'In determining the intention of the sacred writers, attention must be paid, among other things, to *literary genres*'. With ancient texts, authors can only be reached through the text. So the phrase 'the intention of the sacred writers' is a convenient shorthand for the exact meaning of the text around the time of its composition. Scholars need to know this; often believers need not. There is often no one single reading of the text that alone is right and proper. There is the text to be read by scholars, the text to be read by preachers, the text to be read for prayer and reflection and so many more. The danger of cross-pollination is real but avoidable. The beauty of a conciliar document is its ability to leave room for many such readings.

Form criticism, the primary discipline relating to the literary genres, was and is a scholarly means of getting at the appropriate academic meaning of a text. It asks the question that must be asked: what sort of a text is this? All too often that question has been answered glibly and wrongly: this text is history or this text is divine communication. In all cases, this text is to be proclaimed as the word of God. But as Msgr Raymond Collins has put it in the *NJBC*, 'This traditional formula, apparently simple, is extremely complex and polyvalent'.[12]

The polyvalence is evident. There are many words attested in Scripture that provoke reflection on the 'traditional formula' word of God. For example: there is the psalmist at prayer, marvelling at God's concern for us (Ps 8); there is David mourning for his Jonathan (2 Sam

---

12. Raymond Collins, 'Inspiration', in *NJBC*, 1023–33 (# 67).

1:25-26); there is a psalmist venting his rage most horribly (Ps 137:8-9); there is God's word, from a prophet wrapped in mystery, 'just as the LORD loves the people of Israel, though they turn to other gods' (Hos 3:1); there is God's contradictory word, powered by identical motivation (the evil inclination of the human heart) brought together by the mythmaker, 'I will blot out from the earth the human beings I have created . . . nor will I ever again destroy every living creature as I have done' (Gen 6:7; 8:21); there is God's word that must witness to a theologian at work, 'Let us make humankind in our image, according to our likeness' (Gen 1:26). 'Complex and polyvalent' is putting it mildly.

However there is more complexity and more polyvalence to deal with. Sayings such as 'thus says the LORD', 'the word of the LORD', 'saying of the LORD' are common in the prophetic books, as might be expected. But there are also three prophetic stories (1 Kgs 13; 22; and Jer 28) that suggest the presence of thought in this area then and the need for it now. One prophet lies to another in the name of the LORD; acceptance of the lie brings the other prophet to his death (1 Kgs 13). In the divine council, one of the host of heaven proposes to be a lying spirit in the mouths of the royal prophets and God approves; it leads to the divinely willed death of Israel's king (1 Kgs 22). The conclusion of the scene is the statement: 'So you see, the LORD has put a lying spirit in the mouth of all these your prophets; the LORD has decreed disaster for you' (1 Kgs 22:23). Finally, at the start of a carefully structured story, the prophet Hananiah, in all the solemnity of the temple in the presence of priests and people, proclaims: 'Thus says the LORD of hosts, the God of Israel: I have broken the yoke of the king of Babylon' (Jer 28:2). At the end of the story, Jeremiah is given the last word:

> And the prophet Jeremiah said to the prophet Hananiah, 'Listen, Hananiah, the LORD has not sent you, and you made the people trust in a lie. Therefore, thus says the LORD: . . . Within this year you will be dead . . .' In that same year, in the seventh month, Hananiah died (Jer 28:15-17).

The chilling conclusion is formulated by Robert Carroll: 'when the divine word may be a lie, prophecy itself becomes an activity in which true and false are indistinguishable'.[13] Carroll's concluding quote from ER Dodds (in the context of the Pythian oracle) may stifle criticism of Hananiah, but it does little to reassure: 'Anyone familiar with the history of modern spiritualism will realise what an amazing amount of virtual cheating can be done in perfectly good faith by convinced believers'.[14] Clearly, in the world of ancient Israel the complexity and polyvalence of the word of God was troublesome.

For *DV*, the phrase 'word of God' cannot be applied exclusively to the sacred Scriptures; on occasion, it is given a wider meaning. 'Sacred tradition and sacred Scripture form one sacred deposit of the word of God, which is committed to the Church' (*DV* 10). While such a statement may betray the origins of the document, it needs to be taken into account for understanding the final form. Reflection on the books of the Old Testament emphasises the *imperfect* and the *provisional*. 'These books, though they also contain some things which are incomplete and temporary, nevertheless show us true divine pedagogy' (*DV* 15).

In all this, it is probably not unfair to smell some confusion. A wise course is to allow the future to sort out that confusion. That is precisely what *DV* does when it turns to literary forms. But first, as noted earlier, an element bearing on that wisdom is worth noting. The commission responsible for *DV* had been given a preliminary draft prepared by the Theological Commission, with a first chapter, 'Two Sources of Revelation' (Scripture and Tradition). In due course, a vote was taken whether the draft should be returned for rewriting. Sixty percent voted to return it, falling short of the two-thirds majority required for this step. John XXIII pulled papal rank, sided with the sixty percent majority, and constituted a new joint commission to recast the text.[15] This accounts for the place of Scripture and Tradition early in the document, more in line with Trent's final text than the more polemical and inaccurate 'partly... partly' of an earlier version at Trent. Rather more important, this early vote in 1962 pointed to the need for delicacy on the part of the commission's authors who could only count on about sixty percent of the votes of their commission.

---

13. Robert Carroll, *Jeremiah* (OTL. London: SCM, 1986), 548
14. *Jeremiah*, 550.
15. Roderick MacKenzie, 'Introduction' to *Dei Verbum*. Pages 107–10 in *The Documents of Vatican II*, edited by Walter Abbott (London: Chapman, 1966).

Bold innovation was not to be the order of the day. The success of the approach adopted is indicated by the final vote of the full council: 2,334 for and 6 against.

The language of the document is:

> Those who search out the intention of the sacred writers must, among other things, have regard for '*literary forms*'. . . The interpreter must investigate what meaning the sacred writer intended to express and actually expressed in particular circumstances as he used contemporary literary forms in accordance with the situation of his own time and culture (*DV* 12).

There is a phrase here that is a quiet reminder that any Council document is a creature of its time and that also serves to banish any whiff of infallibility that might be about. The phrase, 'the intention of the sacred writers', was a helpful shorthand for invoking the historical-critical method and turning one's back on some of the fallacies of centuries past—which of course is precisely what *DV* is doing. By now, any interpreter of text should know that the intention of a writer is mediated by the meaning of the writer's text. There is no other way of reaching an ancient writer's intention. What should be said is not 'the intention of the writer' but 'the meaning of the text'. A quibble of this kind is critical for interpreters of text; it is of no concern to ordinary people and of no concern to bishops, archbishops, and cardinals. The presence of the phrase is a valuable reminder that the document is a creature of its time.

DV is emphatic on the role of the exegete: 'It is the task of exegetes to work according to these rules towards a better understanding and explanation of the meaning of sacred Scripture so that through preparatory study the judgment of the Church may mature' (*DV* 12). Naturally enough for a council document, this task is performed within the Church: 'All of what has been said about the way of interpreting Scripture is subject finally to the judgment of the church' (*DV* 12). The portrayal of this may be more easily said—'it is clear, therefore, that sacred tradition, sacred Scripture and the teaching authority of the Church, in accord with God's most wise design, are so linked and joined together that one cannot stand without the others' (*DV* 10)—than made tangible in the flow of church life.

There is an adage that applies in many professions: it is not so much what is said but what is not said that can be so very revealing. That is certainly the case with *DV*. The insistence on the necessary place of literary forms in interpretation is not hedged around with prohibitions or cautions. The reality of literary forms is to be embraced by those searching out the meaning of God's communication. Naturally, since the communication is with the Church, in order that 'the judgment of the Church may mature' (*DV* 12), the Church's oversight is present.

The choice of 'literary forms' as the shorthand for modern biblical studies is peculiarly apt. At the core of these literary forms is the discipline of form criticism. It came on the scene at the beginning of the twentieth century, with a view to supplementing source criticism (German: *Literarkritik*), which was considered by scholars such as Hermann Gunkel and Hugo Greßmann to have completed a necessary job.[16] About the time of *DV*, form criticism was at its peak; that peak has passed and form criticism today is waning. It was hoped that scientifically describable literary forms could be identified and associated with specific settings (*Sitz-im-Leben*). That hope has been disappointed and replaced by an enhanced trust in intuition, validated by careful study. The question, however, has been raised and will not go away: what sort of a text is this? No longer can it be automatically assumed that texts are either history or divine communication. *DV*'s picture of the 'principal purpose to which the plan of the Old Covenant was directed' (*DV* 15) may be challenging; the identification of smaller units may be more troubling yet. The question 'what sort of a text is this?' must be asked, even if answering it is troublesome. The necessary follow-up to this question cannot be avoided; it must be answered. This follow-up question is: why has this text, in this form, been preserved in sacred Scripture? One answer is the invitation to go think, the invitation to reflection on the matters involved, an invitation that can be offered by both creator and creature and that can be relevant down the ages. Other answers may be revealed as the future unfolds.

DV has the comment that these books (Old Testament]) 'contain some things which are incomplete and temporary' (*DV* 15). The

---

16. For details, see Antony Campbell, 'The Emergence of the Form-critical and Traditio-historical Approaches', chapter 31 in volume III/2 of Magne Saebø (editor) *Hebrew Bible/Old Testament: The History of Its Interpretation* (Göttingen: Vandenhoeck & Ruprecht, forthcoming).

New Testament reflects the reality of a God who has embraced the weakness and fallibility of human life, 'true God and true man', in no way 'exempt and cut off from the divinely given but flawed world in which we live and die'.[17] Because we do not escape the vulnerability and incompleteness of the world in which we find ourselves and which we have been given, not escaped in the person of Jesus Christ, not escaped either in the words of sacred Scripture, how then are troubling passages in Scripture to be dealt with? The Talmud, the authoritative body of Jewish tradition, comments on two passages in Deuteronomy that are rightly troublesome. Regarding the first (Deut 13), 'The destruction of a whole community because of idolatry (verses 13 ff) never occurred nor will it ever occur. The sole purpose of the warning is that it might be studied and that one might receive reward for such study';[18] regarding the second, according to which the wayward or defiant son will be stoned to death (Deut 21:18–21), commenting on a tradition that says this law was never operative, the Talmud records the following: 'If so, why was it written in the Torah? To study (more) and to obtain reward therefrom'.[19] Study, presumably, reached the conclusion that such a law was inappropriate, that such a view could not be held. We might reach similar conclusions. In relation to following another god (Deut 13:3), the use of common sense is commended:

> Is it really possible to 'follow' God, who is described (Deut 9:3) as a 'devouring fire'? Rather, you should follow His attributes: as He clothes the naked, so must you; as He visits the sick, comforts the mourners, and buries the dead, so must you.[20]

Early on, I borrowed the terms 'complexity and polyvalence' from Msgr Collins; with them we are not at a great distance from the term 'mystery'. The final chapter of *DV* takes us in this direction. The chapter opens with the affirmation that

---

17. FitzPatrick, *Breaking of Bread*, 341.
18. Tosefta San 14:1.
19. San 71a.
20. Sotah 14a. The material above has been taken from Gunther Plaut, *The Torah: A Modern Commentary* (New York: Union of American Hebrew Congregations, 1981).

> The Church has always venerated the divine Scriptures just as she venerates the body of the Lord, since from the table of both the word of God and of the body of Christ she unceasingly receives and offers to the faithful the bread of life, especially in the sacred liturgy (*DV* 21).

We might do well to see an invitation here to place our understanding of the role of God in the ownership of the Scriptures in much the same category as our understanding of the eucharist. Over two or three thousand years, believers have associated the Bible with God in an intimate and sacred way. Various believing bodies and various believers have articulated this association between God and Bible in various ways. What may best embrace this variety is the concept of mystery.

I have borrowed earlier from PJ FitzPatrick the notion that 'the heritage of our belief is unsatisfactory, but that does not stop it from being revered'.[21] This is said after careful study of medieval language around transubstantiation and equally careful study of recent attempts to replace it (courtesy of phenomenology). A summary of FitzPatrick's work may be drawn from his own words:

> What matters in eucharistic belief is what has always mattered, namely that the reality of what we receive is the Risen Lord; and what matters in the belief is not constricted by the categories of obsolete modes of thought, and not compromised by the incapacity of language to seize it.[22]

To paraphrase for sacred Scripture:

> What matters in belief regarding God's role in sacred Scripture is what has always mattered, namely that the reality of what we have in Scripture has God in some way ultimately responsible for it; and what matters in the belief is not constricted by the categories of obsolete modes of thought as to how that is to be understood,

---

21. *Breaking of Bread*, 322.
22. *Breaking of Bread*, 309.

and God's role is not compromised by the incapacity of language to seize it.

DV, the document that began with Trent and the traditions that preceded it, that looked to the future with unfettered endorsement of literary forms, and that ended with the word of God and the body of Christ in the eucharist, is a document that has surely done well. Familiarity with the Council leaves no doubt that the battle raged on many fronts between the Curia and the *Ecclesia*, with the latter victorious while on the scene. The words of Paul VI at the United Nations, *Jamais plus la guerre* ('no more war') can be taken to heart. The Curia should never again be at war with the *Ecclesia*. It may take a century or two to work out the balance, but the balance between centre and periphery is essential to the leadership of the Church.

7

Dei Verbum and the Witness of Creation: Reading Ecclesiastes 3:9–22 Ecologically

Marie Turner

In recent times, biblical interpreters have drawn on a range of interpretive approaches in order to ensure that the biblical text 'may not simply be a word from the past, but a living and timely word'.[1] Among the more recent approaches have been ecological readings, which have arisen as a response to the ecological crisis and as a result of a growing sense of responsibility among biblical scholars and theologians towards God's creation. The Old Testament book of Ecclesiastes (or Qoheleth) has evoked many conflicting responses over the centuries, mainly because of its recurring refrain of 'vanity of vanities' or 'absolute absurdity'. This refrain would, on a superficial reading, pose a challenge to the requirements of *Dei Verbum* that 'Holy Scripture must be read and interpreted in the sacred spirit in which it was written' (*DV* 12) and that those who exegete the word should do so in such a way that it helps ministers of the word to provide the nourishment of the Scriptures for the people of God (*DV* 23).

Nevertheless, the status of the book as canonical was settled long ago, and new interpretive approaches such as ecological readings may uncover fresh insights for readers who might otherwise consign it to the 'too enigmatic' category. The book of Ecclesiastes is rich in reference to the natural world and perceives the fruits thereof as witness to God as gift-giver. As such, it invites a reading as a scriptural text which attests to creation as an enduring witness to God's goodness (*DV* 3).

In Roman Catholic understanding, all the biblical books, both Old and New Testaments, canonical and deuterocanonical, are

---

1. Benedict XVI, Post-Synodal Apostolic Exhortation *Verbum Domini* 5.

unequivocally Sacred Scripture. At the same time, Catholics afford a special honour to the four Gospels since, as paragraph 18 attests, they have a 'special pre-eminence'. This proper and understandable emphasis on the Gospels often goes hand-in-hand with a corresponding reserve towards the Old Testament among Catholic Christians. This reserve is not the attitude of *DV*, which makes abundantly clear that in the Old Testament is found the salvific word of God. Paragraph 14 of the document states:

> The plan of salvation foretold by the sacred authors, recounted and explained by them, is found as the true word of God in the books of the Old Testament: these books, therefore, written under divine inspiration, remain permanently valuable. 'For whatever was written in former days was for our instruction, that by steadfastness and the encouragement of the Scriptures we might have hope' (Rom 15:4) (*DV* 14).

This paragraph reiterates Church teaching on the significance of the Old Testament as Scripture and it relates its saving word to the New Testament hope, articulated by Paul in the Letter to the Romans. Paragraph 3 of the same Document outlines the events which are incorporated in God's plan of salvation:

> God, who through the Word creates all things (see John 1:3) and keeps them in existence, gives humans an enduring witness to himself in created realities (see Rom 1:19–20). Planning to make known the way of heavenly salvation, he went further and from the start manifested himself to our first parents. Then after their fall his promise of redemption aroused in them the hope of being saved (see Gen 3:15) and from that time on he ceaselessly kept the human race in his care, to give eternal life to those who perseveringly do good in search of salvation (see Rom 2:6–7). Then, at the time he had appointed he called Abraham in order to make of him a great nation (see Gen 12:2). Through the patriarchs, and after them through Moses and the prophets, he taught

this people to acknowledge himself the one living and true God, provident father and just judge, and to wait for the Saviour promised by him, and in this manner prepared the way for the Gospel down through the centuries (*DV* 3).

The salvific events outlined in the above paragraph can be summarised as the enduring revelation of God in creation from the beginning, continuing from the first humans right through the patriarchs and the prophets, and culminating in the coming of Jesus. *DV* thus sees the whole of salvation history from the very beginning of creation, recounted as the word of God in the Old Testament Scriptures, as preparation for the Gospel. Consequent upon this teaching, *DV* expects Catholic biblical interpreters to read the Sacred Scriptures in the light of Christ. This requirement necessarily creates a tension between honouring Christian belief while at the same time avoiding supersessionism. Some of the Old Testament writings facilitate an honouring of both commitments. Jesus as son of David, Jesus continuing his mission to the death as the prophets of old did, Jesus' message of God's option for the poor as based in the Psalms, all point to Jesus' own Jewish tradition. The Christian interpreter, by attending closely to the messages of the Old Testament in its own right, can have an ever deeper understanding of Jesus and the tradition and promise which gave birth to him. But *DV* means something deeper than this. It sees the whole of the Old Testament as precursor to the fulfilment of God's plan of salvation in the Incarnation. When the Christian interpreter reads the Old Testament through a christological lens, he or she can do so with integrity, always with the proviso that the interpreter acknowledges that this was not the original intention of the ancient authors, and in fact is an approach which diverges from historical-critical approaches. It also requires an acknowledgement that the Old Testament is not superseded, but is indeed an integral part of God's plan of salvation.

One example of a reading of the book of Ecclesiastes in the light of Christ will suffice to show how this might operate at a supersessionist level. Our contemporary ears are quite scandalised by past readings, such as the careful, scholarly yet time-conditioned reading of JA Loader who, in reference to the fate of humans and beast being the same, states, 'By drawing that conclusion, the Preacher has also lopped the future off the Jewish religion . . . his reproduction of reality is a reliable sketch of what life is really like apart from Christ'.[2] In reference to the uncertainty of justice being seen to be done in 3:18, Loader claims,

> By taking this position the Preacher has knocked the foundation out from under the Jewish religion. If no distinction can be made between the righteous and the wicked, then it makes no sense to keep the law, and with that the whole religion collapses.[3]

A more contemporary, and less insensitive reading, is offered by Sidney Greidanus in his 2010 monologue, *Preaching Christ from Ecclesiastes*.[4] Greidanus' aim is to provide Christian preachers with homiletic material for their congregations. He draws analogies with the time of Qoheleth and the Christian era. While the validity of hermeneutical applications in general is accepted, how this analogical practice might be done authentically must always be qualified with the acknowledgement that analogies are simply a means to make a biblical text relevant to a world far removed from the biblical context. My reading of Greidanus' book affirms that he performs his chosen task with care to respect the sense that Qoheleth portrays in his text.

It is not my intention here to read Ecclesiastes explicitly in the light of Christ but to read it in the light of *DV's* concern that the Christian interpreter should acknowledge that the Old Testament, as well as the New, attests to God's salvific plan. Paragraph 3 of the document states that 'God, who through the Word creates all things (see John 1:3) and keeps them in existence, gives humans an enduring witness to himself in created realities (see Rom 1:19–20)'. Paragraph 12 advocates in particular the historical method of exegesis. At the same time the document encourages interpreters of the Scriptures to 'investigate what meaning the sacred writers really intended, and what God wanted to manifest by means of their words' (*DV* 11).

---

2. JA Loader, *Ecclesiastes* (Grand Rapids, Michigan: Eerdmans, 1986), 42, 44.
3. Loader, *Ecclesiastes*, 44.
4. Sidney Greidanus, *Preaching Christ from Ecclesiastes* (Grand Rapids, MI: Eerdmans, 2010).

It is in respect to this 'real meaning' that there is an opening for an ecological reading. One of the chief ethical concerns of contemporary scripture interpretation is environmental responsibility. In recent decades ecological readings of biblical texts have been seen as a way to honour the world of the original author, while at the same time encouraging this responsibility. This is not to suggest that when Qoheleth wrote his book he would have thought of his search after wisdom in terms of ecology. But it is evident that Qoheleth looked to God's creation in his quest to understand God's ways. Qoheleth looked upon Earth and its fruits as gifts of God, to be enjoyed but not exploited. An ecological reading of the book of Ecclesiastes unearths some insights which, I believe, show how this difficult book can indeed be true to the spirit of *DV* and, at the same time, authentic to Qoheleth's meaning.

As ecological readers of biblical texts we are encouraged to declare that we are members of a human community that has exploited, oppressed, devalued and endangered the existence of the Earth community. Ecological readings have several aims, among them the following:

1. to recognise Earth as a subject in the text with which we seek to relate to empathetically rather than as a topic to be analysed rationally;
2. to take up the cause of justice for Earth and to ascertain whether Earth and the Earth community are oppressed, silenced or liberated in the text;
3. to develop techniques of reading the text to discern and retrieve alternative traditions where the voice of Earth and Earth community has been suppressed.[5]

These aims provide a good starting-point for an ecological reading of Ecclesiastes 3:9–22, since these verses encourage the reader to relate to Earth as an active subject in the text. The verses show that Qoheleth sees creation, and the fruits thereof, as given by God, to be enjoyed responsibly by the human members of Earth community. As

---

5. Norman Habel, *The Birth, the Curse and the Greening of Earth: An Ecological Reading of Genesis 1-11*, The Earth Bible Commentary (Sheffield: Sheffield Phoenix Press, 2011), 1.

such, Earth can be seen as an active participant in God's creation, and as a liberating force for humankind. God works through Earth to reveal the divine identity as one of gracious gift-giver.

One of the most debated issues in Ecclesiastes is the meaning intended by Qoheleth in reference to the Hebrew word *habel*. If *habel* carries the negative connotations that biblical interpreters almost unanimously believe, then how can the created realities with which Qoheleth deals act as a witness to God? The thematic claim of the book that all is '*habel*' is instrumental in leading many readers to neglect it as a book where 'nihilism' reigns supreme, and therefore of limited value as far as providing the nourishment that the Scriptures should provide (*DV* 23). Two senses in particular of the word *habel*, when held in tension, challenge the interpretation of the word as indisputably negative. If we translate the word as 'absurdity', correctly understood, and 'breath', which is the root meaning of the word, then a new, more positive meaning emerges. Michael Fox has influenced scholarly interpretation of the word with his reading of it through the lens of Albert Camus' work on *Sisyphus*. In his Preface to *Sisyphus*, Camus explains the stance he takes in the book towards the concept of 'absurdity'. Camus was writing during the chaos and tragedy of World War II. He discusses the question of suicide and comes to the conclusion that nihilism should not have the last word. He uses the discussion to assert his conviction that in the midst of the absurd, there is 'a lucid invitation to live and to create, in the very midst of the desert'.[6]

The other meaning of *habel* which is helpful in understanding Qoheleth's stance is 'breath'. This is a translation which seems to be attuned to an ecological reading, since it is of the very substance of Earth. It also carries overtones of 'elusive', which is an apt rendering of Qoheleth's meaning that there is little in life that human beings can count upon. Holding both senses of *habel* in tension evokes a picture which seems true to the book's overall vision: in the midst of the uncertainties of life, there is enjoyment to be had from Earth's gifts, but like breath, they are elusive to one's grasp.

For the most part, Earth is designated as a place apart from the realm of God. But when Earth is first mentioned (Eccles 1:4),

---

6. Albert Camus, *The Myth of Sisyphus and Other Essays*, English translation by Justin O'Brien (New York: Vintage International, 1955), v.

Qoheleth describes Earth as *'olam*, that is, it is as an eternal presence against which the cycles of life are played out. It is only of God that this word is otherwise used. Everything takes place on the world's stage, but everything is ephemeral. Qoheleth's frustration and sense of *habel* in its negative connotation comes from his life experiences. In Qoheleth's economic system, property grants were given to favoured individuals, who could in turn grant portions of the property to others in return for taxes and military service as needed. The right to the property was not absolute, however, nor was there an automatic right of inheritance and the property could be taken away or, upon the death of the grantee, could be given to another rather than an heir.[7] It is this unpredictable world, where financial stability can never be taken for granted, that so frustrates Qoheleth. Against this world of fluctuating economic fortune, Earth speaks of life-cycles which ebb and flow, but continuously and consistently, and which will outlast the most vociferous and self-interested economic system. Much of the anxiety and exhortations of Qoheleth to enjoy what pleasure one may, while one can, begins to make sense. Qoheleth pits the fluctuation and arbitrariness of economic fortune alongside the stability of an Earth which is *'olam*, eternal. In Qoheleth's world nothing can be taken for granted, including life itself. Thus everything is *habel* in the sense that all is ephemeral, all is breath.

For Qoheleth, God's *'olam*, God's eternal 'otherness' is specifically encapsulated in the notion of God as gift-giver. This is expressed in Ecclesiastes 3:9–13:

> [9] What gain have the workers from their toil?
> [10] I have seen the business that God has given to everyone to be busy with.
> [11] He has made everything suitable for its time; moreover he has put a sense of past and future into their minds, yet they cannot find out what God has done from the beginning to the end.
> [12] I know that there is nothing better for them than to be happy and enjoy themselves as long as they live;

---

7. See the overview of Qoheleth's social setting in Choon Leong Seow, *Ecclesiastes: A New Translation with Introduction and Commentary* (The Anchor Yale Bible; New Haven and London: Yale University Press, 1997), 23.

> ¹³ moreover, it is God's gift that all should eat and drink
> and take pleasure in all their toil.

In these verses toil is not a curse as in Genesis, but an enjoyable, productive activity. The one possibility for humans to deduce something of the nature of God can be gleaned only from God's actions in the world. The language generally used for this understanding of God's action in the world is 'sacramentality'. In this passage, God is known to humankind through God's actions as gift-giver. It is precisely because God's gifts are given through Earth that there is a sense that God and Earth are working together for the good of Earth community. It is God's will that we enjoy the fruits of the Earth and take pleasure in productive work. To be in right relationship with God, we must respond to God's nature as gift-giver; to resile from this invitation would be to reject the nature of God as gift-giver and thus would constitute a break in the relationship between humankind and God.

Qoheleth's admonition that 'all should eat and drink and take pleasure in all their toil' presumes a productive and an enjoyable toil, otherwise there would be no produce of the Earth to eat and drink. Qoheleth does not have any qualms about enjoying economic prosperity. He is constantly aware, however, of its ephemerality and volatility. According to Seow, Qoheleth sees God in similar terms to the earthly rulers who give grants of land. The grantee can enjoy the fruits of such economic activity, but at the cost of uncertainty and possible disaster. This observation of Qoheleth, however, does not presume an ill-will on the part of God, but refers instead to the inscrutability of God who, as Walther Zimmerli observed in his 1964 article on 'The Place and the Limit of the Wisdom in the Framework of the Old Testament Theology', acts always in freedom'.[8] Breath is a particularly pertinent metaphor for the life-giving spirit of God, with its sense of elusiveness and intangibility. While constantly aware that the search for God's wisdom is akin to a 'chasing of the wind', Qoheleth nevertheless has confidence in God's justice:

---

8. Walther Zimmerli, 'The Place and Limit of the Wisdom in the Framework of the Old Testament Theology', in *Scottish Journal of Theology*, 17/2 (June 1964 ET): 146–58, 157.

> ¹⁶ Moreover I saw under the sun that in the place of justice, wickedness was there, and in the place of righteousness, wickedness was there as well.
> ¹⁷ I said in my heart, God will judge the righteous and the wicked, for he has appointed a time for every matter, and for every work.

This sense of the appointed time and the consequent urge to *carpe diem* may seem little comfort in an uncertain world in which the *dies* may be very short, but Zimmerli convincingly rescued Qoheleth from the charge of nihilism. Zimmerli was a forerunner of eco-justice readings of wisdom texts when he pointed out that behind Ecclesiastes 3 is the doctrine of the proper time or *'eth* (cf 3:11): God 'has made everything suitable for its time'. As Zimmerli says, Wisdom must be willing to enjoy the gift that God gives today and remain open to the free and living God.[9] Zimmerli recognises that it is through the enjoyment of Earth's gifts that Qoheleth encounters God. Indeed, as Zimmerli clearly articulates, Qoheleth 'encounters the reality of the creator more clearly than any other Israelite wise man before him'.[10] That encounter takes place in the created realities which give witness to God as gift-giver.

There is negativity in Qoheleth's view of God indicated in his statement in 3:18–22:

> ¹⁸ I said in my heart with regard to human beings that God is testing them to show that they are but animals.
> ¹⁹ For the fate of humans and the fate of animals is the same; as one dies, so dies the other. They all have the same breath, and humans have no advantage over the animals; for all is vanity.
> ²⁰ All go to one place; all are from the dust, and all turn to dust again.
> ²¹ Who knows whether the human spirit goes upward and the spirit of animals goes downward to the earth?
> ²² So I saw that there is nothing better than that all should enjoy their work, for that is their lot; who can bring them to see what will be after them?

---

9. Zimmerli, 'The Place and Limit of the Wisdom', 158.
10. Zimmerli, 'The Place and Limit of the Wisdom', 156.

The meaning seems to be simply that God intends humankind to see that it shares a common fate with all creation, namely death. Humankind is not immortal, for that is a quality reserved for God. This would make sense of the word, 'testing'. It is a lesson which humankind must learn. There is an echo here of Genesis 3:22–3:

> [22] Then the LORD God said, 'See, the man has become like one of us, knowing good and evil; and now, he might reach out his hand and take also from the tree of life, and eat, and live forever'—
> [23] therefore the LORD God sent him forth from the garden of Eden, to till the ground from which he was taken.

Both texts remind us that we are made of the stuff of Earth, or in contemporary understanding, of stardust, subject to mortality. We are not *'olam*, as God and Earth are *'olam*.

Conclusion

As we return to *DV's* reminder of revelation in creation, an ecological reading of Ecclesiastes has shown the significance of Qoheleth's search to understand something of the nature of God from created realities. Through Earth, the identity of God as gift-giver has been brought to light. Through Earth, God has been able to enact God's nature as gift-giver. This is a high view of creation that is shared by the Christian doctrine of the Incarnation. It follows that any undervaluing and cavalier attitude to Earth constitutes a cavalier attitude to God's gifts in creation.

Qoheleth claims in 3:11 that God has given humans a sense of past and future, but that we cannot know how to use it. In today's world, this may not be so impossible. A hermeneutical outcome of the acceptance of the produce of Earth as God's gift will be to ensure that these gifts are left for the *yitron*, the advantage, of future generations. This action of humankind in leaving fruits of the Earth for others may well be a way of partaking in the nature of God, the gift-giver and thus a call to respect God's creation. In our era, thanks to scientific advances and mass communication, we do have a sense of what happens in the future (Eccles 3:11) in the long term. We do know now that something of the Earth's destiny lies in our hands. Perhaps, then, this is the call to right relationship with God and God's Earth that modern humans can hear in the text of Ecclesiastes. We have the legitimation of Qoheleth to enjoy what fruits of the earth we can in whatever time we may be allotted. But we are to be mindful of the future, for God has indeed put a sense of it in our hearts.

Biblical exegetes and theologians alike are becoming more aware that environmental responsibility is not an option, but is an obligation incumbent upon all who regard respect for God's creation as a sacred duty. In the words of Denis Edwards,

> Commitment to ecology has not yet taken its central place in Christian self-understanding. It is far from central in terms of its structure, personnel and money. As the church itself is called to conversion to the side of the poor in the struggle of justice and to the side of women in their struggle for full equality, so the church itself is called to conversion to the side of suffering creation.[11]

It is worth noting here that Edwards views ecological conversion through the same lens as the 'option for the poor' perspective. He places suffering creation on the side of the marginalised. Edwards takes his cue from the General Audience Address in January 2001 of Pope John Paul II who introduced the need for an ecological conversion. Catholic theologians such as Edwards have promoted this concept as integral to the development of ecotheology.[12] The context of this concept is the growing ecological crisis and our emerging awareness of its implications. The Address stated:

> We must [therefore] encourage and support the 'ecological conversion' which in recent decades has made humanity more sensitive to the catastrophe to which it has been heading. Man is no longer the Creator's 'steward', but an autonomous despot, who is

---

11. Denis Edwards, *Ecology at the Heart of Faith* (Maryknoll, New York: Orbis Books, 2006), 3.
12. Edwards, *Ecology at the Heart of Faith*, 2–4.

finally beginning to understand that he must stop at the edge of the abyss. 'Another welcome sign is the growing attention being paid to the quality of life and to ecology, especially in more developed societies, where people's expectations are no longer concentrated so much on problems of survival as on the search for an overall improvement of living conditions (*Evangelium vitae*, n. 27).' At stake, then, is not only a 'physical' ecology that is concerned to safeguard the habitat of the various living beings, but also a 'human' ecology which makes the existence of creatures more dignified, by protecting the fundamental good of life in all its manifestations and by preparing for future generations an environment more in conformity with the Creator's plan.[13]

To reiterate the message of *DV* 3 in a slightly different expression, an ecological reading of Ecclesiastes 3:9–22 respects the original meaning of Ecclesiastes and at the same time honours the teaching of *DV* of the witness of creation to God. Even more than this, it shows that, through Earth, God's own nature is able to be expressed in the gift-giving that identifies the gracious God known to Christianity, and which knowledge was much earlier bequeathed to us through this ancient Jewish writing.

---

13. John Paul II, *The Ecological Conversion,* General Audience Address, 17 January 2001.

8

A Review and Assessment of the Church's Engagement with Historical Critical Analysis of the New Testament as outlined in *Dei Verbum*

Jerome Murphy-O'Connor OP

The more conciliar documents of bygone years are studied, the extent to which they were conditioned by historical circumstances becomes more and more evident. It is important, therefore, to first situate *Dei Verbum* (*DV*) in the history of the twentieth century Church. Then I shall examine what exactly *DV* said about the New Testament, and conclude with an assessment of the impact of this document on the Church. It will appear that while authorities in the Church adhere faithfully to the directives of *DV*, there remains a ground swell of bitter discontent among those who have not been brought up to date on Church teaching, and which manifests itself in ill-informed criticism of biblical scholarship.

The Background to Vatican II

It was an unfortunate accident of history that the end of the Modernist crisis coincided with the advent of form-criticism. This approach to the New Testament, which became popular among Protestants in Germany after World War I, was seen by conservatives in the Church as a threat. The vigilance that it inspired put a break on the tentative steps towards freedom that exegetes had expected after the end of the repressive regime of Pius X and his Secretary of State Cardinal Rafael Merry del Val (1903–1914).

Form-criticism originated in the simple observation that episodes in the Gospel of Mark glow with vivid colour and sparkle with life. The links between them, however, are dull and prosaic. The Gospel, in other words, is like a necklace of precious stones linked with fittings of inferior metal. What the form-critics did was to set the links aside, and to focus on the episodes. Thus they were able to line up all the miracle stories, for example, and to highlight their common features. This permitted them to define the 'literary form' of a miracle story. From such observations, which are totally innocuous, the form-critics jumped to an assumption regarding the sources of the gospels. This leap of faith had far ranging consequences.

The stories, they assumed, had been circulating anonymously in the Christian community. All that Mark did was to select a number and string them together, thereby creating his Gospel. Previously, conservative Christians had taken it for granted that the gospels came with the guarantee of a recognised tradition. It was believed, for example, that Mark wrote down what he recalled of the preaching of Peter, who had been an eyewitness of the ministry of Jesus. For the form-critics, on the other hand, the stories were simply anonymous rumours circulating in a post-paschal community boiling with the creativity of the Holy Spirit.

Moreover, the form-critics had learnt from those researching folk tales that stories were preserved as long as they served a useful function in the community. Thus today virtually everyone knows a story or a song likely to put fractious children to sleep. The form-critics, in consequence, attemped to fix the life-situation (*Sitz-im-Leben*) implied by the 'literary form' of each story. Their research, however, did not seek evidence but focused on the creation of hypotheses. Not surprisingly, the result was a perfect match between story and situation. Usually it was so neat and tidy that the suspicion that the story was created to fit the situation became inevitable. For example, to solve the question of whether Christians could work on Saturday someone in the community would have suggested, 'Did not Jesus say somewhere that the sabbath is made for man not man for the sabbath?'.

Finally, the origin of folk takes was lost in the mist of history; they had been around for unknown ages. This fostered the implicit belief that there was a long time-span between the life of Jesus and the composition of the gospels. Thus there were no eyewitnesses to control the final result, which might have been seriously distorted or corrupted.

In a word, not only did the stories lack the guarantee of a name, but it seemed very likely that they were invented at a significant remove from the life of Jesus. As practiced, therefore, form-criticism led straight to complete scepticism regarding the historicity of the gospels.

In a series of reviews of books by form-critics in the 1920s Marie-Joseph Lagrange OP ruthlessly exposed the unwarranted character of many of the underlying assumptions and highlighted the corrupting influence of the personal beliefs and philosophies of its practitioners on what was speciously presented as a scrupulously objective scientific method.[1] His authority was so great that Catholics were not seduced by the fad of form-criticism that dominated New Testament scolarship in Germany and the English-speaking world for the next generation. Nonetheless, Church authorities lived in fear that scholarship would lead to scepticism and intrusive vigilance was the order of the day.

Self-censorship, in consequence became a way of life. A culture of delation to Rome was not only tolerated but encouraged. Cardinal Merry del Val had moved from the Secretariate of State to the Holy Office, which he headed from 1914 to 1930. It was enough to report that someone was thought to have 'advanced ideas'. No specific accusation or page numbers were required. The blatantly unchristian character of this reign of terror led to its formal repudiation by Pope Benedict XV (1914–22).[2]

Subsequent popes showed themselves equally protective of biblical scholars. Pope Pius XI (1922–39) showed his support for the Pontifical Biblical Institute (PBI) by personally presiding at two of its doctorate defenses.[3] The historical-critical approach of the PBI had been criticised by Italian bishops. The papal gestures did not deter them. They prefered a certain 'spiritual' type of exegesis, which drew a blistering letter of condemnation from the Pontifical Biblical

---

1. As a representative sample of such reviews one might mention *Revue Biblique*, 3 1 (1922): 286–92 (on Rudolf Bultmann); *Revue Biblique*, 32 (1923): 442–5 (on Georg Bertram); *Revue Biblique*, 33 (1924): 280–2 (on Karl L Schmidt); *Revue Biblique*, 39 (1930): 623–5 (on K Kundsin). See also the revised edition of Lagrange's *Évangile selon Marc* (EBib; Paris: Gabalda, 1929), lv–lviii.
2. Jean Levie, *La Bible. Parole humaine et message de Dieu* (Paris: Desclée de Brouwer, 1958) 84, 145.
3. For the details of these events, see Maurice Gilbert, *L'Institut Biblique Pontifical. Un siècle d'histoire (1909–2009)* (Rome: Editrice Pontificio Istituto Biblico, 2009), 117–120.

Commission (PBC) in 1941.[4] It was formally approved by Pope Pius XII (1939–1958), who realised that the tensions within the Church of Italy were probably at least latent in other parts of the world. A more authoritative document addressed to the whole church was a necessity. Thus on 30 December 1943, the fiftieth anniversary of *Providentissimus Deus* (henceforth *PD*) of Pope Leo XIII, he issued the encylical *Divino Afflante Spiritu* (*DAS*), which has rightly been hailed as the charter of modern Catholic biblical study.

The crucial issue in biblical studies within the church has always been the question of historicity. Conservatives took the text of the Bible at face value; what is said is exactly what happened. Those aware of the realities knew that a more subtle approach was necessary. This involved sophisticated judgments, whose complexity clashed with the simplicity of the world-view of the conservatives, leaving critical scholars at a definite disadvantage in trying to justify themselves. The most important contribution of *DAS* was to formally state that what is said in the Bible is not necessarily what happened.

> What is the 'literal' sense of a passage is not always as obvious in the speeches and writings of the ancient authors of the East as it is in the works of our own time. For what they wished to express is not to be determined by the rules of grammar and philology alone nor soley by the context; the interpreter must, as it were, go back wholly in spirit to those remote centuries of the East and with the aid of history, archaeology, ethnology, and other sciences accurately determine what modes of writing, so to speak (*litteraria, ut aiunt, genera*) the authors of that ancient period would be likely to use, and in fact did use. For the ancient peoples of the East, in order to express their ideas, did not always employ those forms or kinds of speech that we use today but rather those used by men of their times and countries. . . . Hence the Catholic commentator, in order to comply with the present needs of biblical studies in explaining the Sacred Scripture and in demonstrating and proving

---
4. Text in Dean P Béchard, *The Scripture Documents. An Anthology of Official Catholic Teachings* (Collegeville, MN: Liturgical Press, 2002), 212–20, here 213.

its immunity from all error, should also make prudent use of this means, determining, that is, to what extent the manner of expression or the literary mode (*dicendi forma seu litterarum genus*) adopted by the sacred writer may lead to a correct and genuine interpretation.[5]

Catholic scholars were offered the freedom they had long desired. One might have thought that such a clear and formal statement might have silenced the conservatives, who claimed to be totally obedient to papal teaching and to act always in the best interests of the Church. Such was not to be the case. The undercurrent of dissent was so marked that the PBC underwent a radical change. Instead of defending the traditional understanding of the truth of the Bible, it became the promotor of a genuinely critical approach.[6] Nonetheless Catholic exegetes were still bound by the *responsa* of the PBC issued during the height of the Modernist controversy (1905-14).[7] As time went on, however, the extent to which these highly restrictive decrees were historically conditioned became ever clearer, to the increasing embarassment of the Holy See. Eventually they were set aside by the PBC itself but in a most unhelpful way. Instead of a formal admission that the PBC had been wrong, the Secretary of the PBC and its Sub-secretary published simultaneous reviews of the third edition of the *Enchiridion Biblicum* in which they said in virtually identical words,

> As long as these decrees [of the PBC] propose views that are neither immediately or mediately connected with the truths of faith and morals, it goes without saying that the interpreter of Sacred Scripture may pursue his research with complete freedom.[8]

---

5. Béchard, *Scripture Documents*, 128-9.
6. Notably in the Letter to Cardinal Suhard on the historicity of Gen 1-11 (text in Béchard, *Scripture Documents*, 221-3) and on the Teaching of Scripture in seminaries; Latin text in *Enchiridion Biblicum. Documenta Ecclesiastica Sacram Scripturam Spectantia* (fourth edition; Romae: Arnodo/Neapoli: d'Auria, 1961) 241-54
7. Texts in Béchard, *Scripture Documents*, 187-211.
8. Anastasius Miller, OSB, 'Das neue biblische Handbuch', in *Benediktinische Monatschrift*, 31 (1955): 49-50. Arduin Kleinhans, OFM, 'De nova Enchiridii Biblici editione', in *Antonianum*, 30 (1955): 63-5. Translation from Béchard, *Scripture Documents*, 327.

Senior Roman curial officials do not publish their personal opinions on crucial matters, and particularly in an obviously concerted way. Manifestly the message was intended as an authoritative indication of 'the mind of the Church'.[9] The way in which it was articulated, however, permitted conservatives to dismiss the words of Miller and Kleinhans as lacking the authority of an official pronouncement; it was no more than a private option worthy of censure.

The fact that the PBC had backed down profoundly shocked the integretrists whose reaction was a fierce attack on the PBI, which they claimed practiced and encouraged a methodology that diminished the historicity of the OT and the gospels. The end result was that in June 1962 Stanislas Lyonnet, SJ, and Max Zerwick, SJ, were suspended from teaching at the PBI.[10] Such an action indicates that displeasure with the PBI had percolated to the highest levels of the Church, where action was taken by cardinal Ernesto Ruffini of the Congregation of Seminaries and Universities and by Cardinal Alfredo Ottaviani of the Holy Office.

The Production of *Dei Verbum*

It was in this tense atmosphere that Vatican II opened on 11 October 1962. The first discussions were focused on liturgy, but on 14 November 1962 attention shifted to the schema on 'The Sources of Revelation'. It had been circulated previously with the result that it was known to be a rehash of the Councils of Trent and Vatican I with little sympathy for the modern approach to critical biblical study. Acceding to well merited opposition, Pope John XXIII ordered it withdrawn and rewritten. That was on 21 November 1962, which gave the conciliar fathers a free day the next day.

The PBI took advantage of that freedom to stage what can only be considered a unique clerical demonstration in Rome. They invited all the conciliar fathers to attend the defense of the brilliant doctorate of

---

9. See Edward F Siegmann, 'The Decisions of the Biblical Commission: A Recent Clarification', *Catholic Biblical Quarterly*, 18 (1956): 23–9.
10. For a bibliography and excellent summary of this controversy, see Gilbert, *Institut Biblique Pontifical*, 160–6. More expansive summaries are given in Joseph A Fitzmyer, 'A Recent Roman Scripture Controversy', *Theological Studies*, 22 (1961): 426–44.

Norbert Lofink, SJ, *Das Hauptgebot. Eine Untersuchung literarischer Einleitungsfragen zu Dtn 5-11*.[11] The defence had orginally been scheduled for 8 November, but recalling that Pius XI had shown his support for the PBI by presiding at doctorate defenses, the Jesuits calculated that they might possibly get greater mileage out of it. They were right; 12 cardinals were present that day as were some 400 bishops. Among the lower classes, who filled the great hall of the Gregorian University, were a young *peritus*, Joseph Ratzinger, and myself. It was a wonderful occasion full of hope and committment.

The gesture greatly fortified those who fought for a schema that would both consolidate the advances made by modern Scripture studies and point the way to a fruitful future of research. Much work, however, was still to be done. The schema was to be rewritten several times before the fourth revision was accepted on 18 November 1965 by a vote of 2344 to 6 out of 2350 voting.[12]

The decisive intervention was the promulgation of the *Instruction on the Historical Truth of the Gospels* by the PBC on 21 April 1964. Its tone and content graphically illustrate how far the PBC had moved to the left since its foundation by Pius X. The *Instruction*, for example, strongly reiterates *DAS* to the effect that it is the duty of a responsible Catholic exegete to use the 'form-critical method' when purified of its corrupting adventitious elements.[13] This is highly significant in view of the fact that the most vocal and influential opponent of the 'form-critical method', Cardinal Ernesto Ruffini, was himself a member of the PBC that issued the *Instruction*![14] He would have ensured that every possible objection was raised. There can be little doubt,

---

11. Gilbert, *Institut Biblique Pontifical,* 169–70.
12. For details see *La révélation divine. Constitution dogmatique 'Dei Verbum'*, edited by Bernard-Dominique Dupuy, Unam Sanctam, 70 (Paris: Cerf, 1968), 573–6.
13. Many, if not all, of these had been exposed in Lagrange's reviews (see note 1 above). The good is systematically separated from the bad in Pierre Benoit, 'Réflections sur la *Formgeschichte Methode*', *Revue Biblique,* 53 (1946): 481–512, and in his collected essays *Jesus and the Gospel* (NY: Herder, 1971/London: Darton, Longman, & Todd, 1973), volume 1.11–46.
14. He considered the view of Pius XII 'an absurdity' and the Congregation of Seminaries and Universities sent his article 'Generi letterari e ipotesi di lavoro nei recenti studi biblici', in *L'Osservatore Romano* (24 August 1961), 1 to the rectors of all Italian seminaries. The notorious American conservative John C Fenton published an English translation in the *American Ecclesiastical Review,* 145 (1961): 362–5.

therefore, that the issue was thoroughly thrashed out in meetings before the words of the Instruction were finalised. This makes its lack of ambiguity all the more remarkable; there is no hint of compromise.

Recognising the influence of Ruffini at the Council, it would seem that the timing of the promulgation of the Instruction was a carefully calculated move designed to influence the content of *DV*. The bishops had plenty of time to read the Instruction before returning to Rome in the autumn. In the end the Instruction had a definite impact on the final version of the schema,[15] whose improvement was greatly aided by a series of submissions by professors of the PBI between September 1964 and September 1965.[16]

The fifth chapter of the final version was devoted to the New Testament.[17] Pride of place is given to the four Gospels because 'they are the principal witness to the life and teaching of the Incarnate Word, our Savior'. This formulation is not entirely satisfactory, because it is evident that the key to the Gospels is the paschal mystery of the death and resurrection of Jesus. It has been well said that the Gospel stories are merely the prelude to the passion narrative with its climax on Easter Sunday. It would appear, therefore, that 'life of Jesus' is to be given the widest extent possible. Whether this was the intention of the Council must remain open. There can be little doubt, however, that the formulation adopted reflected the concern of the Council for the historicity of the Gospels.

According to *DV,* their historical value is rooted in the fact that

> the four gospels are of apostolic origin. For what the apostles preached by the command of Christ they and others of the apostolic age, at a later time and under the inspiration of the Spirit, handed on to us in writing as the foundation of our faith, namely, the fourfold Gospel (*DV* 18).

---

15. Xavier Léon-Dufour, 'Sur le Nouveau Testament', in *La révélation divine. Constitution dogmatique 'Dei Verbum'*, 401–31, 418.
16. Gilbert, *Institut Biblique Pontifical,* 185–9.
17. The text supposed by what follows is that in Béchard, *Scripture Documents,* 27–8, with the paragraph numbers.

There is here an important distinction. The writing of the Gospels is attributed to 'the apostles' and 'others of the apostolic age'. The 'apostles' must be understood to be those sent out by Jesus (Mk 6:7) who, in consequence, were eyewitnesses of his ministry (Acts 1:21-22). One is forced to conclude, therefore, that 'others of the apostolic age' who contributed to the Gospels were not eyewitnesses but had only second-hand knowledge of the words and deeds of Jesus.

When approved in 1965 this distinction accurately reflected the thinking of critical scholars. Subsequent research, however, has shown that they were not quite as critical as they thought. They were still influenced by the unstated assumption of the form-critics that a temporal abyss separated the writing of the Gospels from the life of Jesus. In fact, men and women who followed Jesus personally in their 20s would only have been in their 60s when Mark's Gospel was written in the 70s. In reality the time-span was in fact very short, one generation, two at the most.[18]

This simple observation is transformed into fact by Papias (c 60-130), bishop of Hierapolis. He is the first Christian to tell us how he researched the historical Jesus.

> If by chance anyone who had been in attendance on the elders should come my way, I inquired about the words of the elders—[that is,] what [according to the elders] Andrew or Peter said (*eipen*), or Philip or Thomas or James or John or Matthew or any other of the Lord's disciples and whatever Aristion and the elder John, the Lord's disciples, were saying (*legousin*). For I did not think that information from books would profit me as much as information from a living and surviving voice (Eusebius, *Hist. Eccl.* 3.39.3-4).

Clearly two eyewitness were still alive ('were saying'), probably in nearby Smyrna or Ephesus, whereas others had died ('had said'). In the former case there was only one intermediary who spoke from

---

18. This point is argued most thoroughly by Richard Bauckham, *Jesus and the Eyewitnesses: The Gospels as Eyewitness Testimony* (Grand Rapids, MI/Cambridge, UK: Eerdmans, 2006). Without being in any way fundamentalist, not everything in this book is of equal value; see my critical review in *Revue Biblique*, 114 (2007): 621-30.

personal knowledge of his source. The 'living voice', in consequence, is not that of anonymous oral tradition but an informant whom Papias knew. This activity of Papias can hardly be later than the decade 80–90 AD, precisely when others were collecting material for their Gospels.

What Bauckham has done for the Jesus story on the basis of oral history, Dunn has confirmed from the perspective of oral tradition.[19] The first disciples of Jesus had to justify their new vocation to family and friends. Such stories quickly coalesced into a commonly agreed presentation of Jesus. This was the founding narrative of Christianity. In oral societies the community as a whole is concerned to control the retelling of stories that contribute to its self-understanding or identity. Each retelling reinforces the retention of the story in the corporate memory. The community is not there to be informed, but to be reaffirmed in its identity. Hence, it will insist on absolute fidelity in the essential core of a story, while permitting a high degree of flexibility in ancillary details.

One is forced to conclude that in the light of modern research the Gospels are seen to be much more trustworthy than the form-critics ever supposed.[20] A genuine life of Jesus is no longer the absurdity it was once assumed to be.

The text from *DV*, which we are discussing, is also important for what it does *not* say. The first version of the schema said, 'Holy Mother Church has believed and continues to believe without the slightest hesitation (*firma et constantissima fide credidit et credit*)' that the four Gospels give a sincere account of the deeds and words of Jesus.[21] This gives the impression (no doubt intended) that questions such as the authenticity and date of the Gospels were matters of faith, and thus closed to discussion. *DV* restores to them their status as

---

19. James DG Dunn, *Christianity in the Making*. Volume. 1. *Jesus Remembered* (Grand Rapids, MI/Cambridge, UK, 2003); see my review in *Revue Biblique*, 111 (2004): 578–85.
20. The illegitimacy of the exclusive focus of the form-critics on the creativity of the Spirit-filled post-paschal Christian community was ruthlessly exposed by Heinz Schürmann using their own methodology, 'Die vorösterlichen Anfänge der Logientradition. Versuch eines formgeschlichtlichen Zugangs zum Leben Jesu' in *Der historische Jesus und der kerygmatische Christus. Beiträge zum Christus verständnis in Forschung und Verkündigung,* edited by Helmut Ristow and Karl Matthiae (Berlin: Evangelische Verlagsanstalt, 1962), 342–70.
21. See the useful synoptic presentation by Léon-Dufour in *La révélation divine*, 414–5.

matters of scholarly debate, and does not venture any suggestion as to the identities of the authors of the Gospels.

In the next paragraph *DV* takes up the crucial point of the historicity of the Gospels.

> Holy Mother Church has firmly and constantly held and continues to hold that the four gospels just named, whose historicity the Church affirms without hesitation, faithfully hand on what Jesus, the Son of God, while he lived among men and women, actually did and taught for their eternal salvation, until the day when he was taken up (*Sancta Mater Ecclesia firmiter et constantissime tenuit ac tenet quattuor recensita Evangelia, quorum historicitatem incunctanter affirmat, fideliter tradere quae Iesus Dei Filius, vitam inter homines degens, ad aeternam eorum salutem reapse fecit et docuit*) (*DV* 19).

The underlined words were not in this place in previous versions of the schema. Their insertion reveals the concern of the Council that the historicity of the Gospels was not adequately emphasised. What, then, is meant by 'historicity'?

The simple answer would appear to be that 'history' means 'what really happened'. Today, however, secular historians have a much more pessimistic view of what they can achieve in their reconstructions of the past. It should be assumed, therefore, that 'historicity' in *DV* carries a built-in limitation. In fact, the text itself embodies a qualification; it is a question of what Jesus 'actually did and taught for their eternal salvation'. 'History' it would appear is first and foremost sacred history.

Further light is shone on our question by chapter 3 of *DV* which is entitled 'The Divine Inspiration of Scripture and Its Interpretation'. Commentators have been quick to notice that the co-relative of 'inspiration' is no longer 'inerrancy', as it was in previous versions of the schema, but 'truth'. A move from a negative approach (what Scripture is not) to a positive one (what Scripture really is) is typical of the general approach of Vatican II. The baggage of the past is set aside. The abandonment of the term 'inerrancy', however, does not mean that the *idea* of inerrancy was repudiated. The fact that scripture is 'without error' is formally stated. Thus the consequence of inspiration is that 'we must acknowledge the Books of Scripture as teaching firmly, faithfully, and without error the truth that God wished to be recorded in the sacred writings for the sake of our salvation' (*DV* 11). The text goes on to quote 2 Tim 3:16–17 which stresses the 'utility' (ὠφέλιμος) of scripture.

The qualification of *DV* 19 apropos of 'historicity' also appears here apropos of 'truth'; 'the truth that God wished to be recorded in the sacred writings for the sake of our salvation'. The intention of the Council becomes evident if this is contrasted with the repudiated formulation of the first schema on revelation: 'divine inspiration of itself necessarily excludes and refuses all error in matters both sacred and profane (*divina Inspiratio per se ipsam tam necessario excludat et respuat errorem omnem in qualibet re religiosa vel profana*)'. The 'truth' that one must look for in the Scriptures is not the enlargement of our knowledge of the past but the sacred truth of salvation. This point is emphasised by the fact that even though 'truth' appears thirteen times in *DV* it is always in the singular.[22] To appreciate the 'truth' of the Scriptures one must view it from the perspective of the revelation of God's saving plan. In more scholastic language one might say that in order to appreciate the value of a proposition one must know, not only the material object, but the *objectum formale quo* (the perspective of the author) which is the only way to specify the *objectum formale quod* (what is actually meant).[23]

It is not surprising, therefore, that *DV* continues

> Since in Sacred Scripture God has spoken through human agents and in human fashion, the interpreter . . . should carefully search out what the sacred writers truly intended to express . . . To determine the intention of the sacred writers, one must attend to such things as 'literary forms'. For truth is differently presented and expressed in various types of historical writings (*'genera literaria' respicienda sunt. Aliter enim atque aliter veritas*

---

22. Ignace de la Potterie, 'La verité de la Sainte Écriture et l'Histoire du salut d'après la Constitution dogmatique *Dei Verbum*', *La Nouvelle Revue Theologique*, 88 (1966): 149–69, here 156 note 16.
23. Pierre Grelot, 'L'inspiration de l'Écriture et son interpretaton (commentaire du chapitre III)', in *La révélation divine*, 347–380, 367.

in textibus vario modo historicis), in prophetic or poetic texts, or in other modes of speech (*DV* 12).

The emphasis on the fact that there are different kinds of 'truth' in different kinds of 'historical' texts is not only interesting in itself but underlines the necessary connection between 'truth' and 'historicity'. The 'truth' of scripture presupposes the reality of certain historical events insofar as these are linked to the mystery of salvation. For example, it would be meaningless to speak of the salvific death of Jesus or of his resurrection unless he had in fact died according to the most objective historical standards.

Perhaps at this point an illustration of what the rather abstract language above implies might be useful. What is the 'truth/historicity' of Mark's narrative (1:9-11) of the baptism of Jesus? The answer reveals the complexity of the subject and the careful discriminatory judgments required of the interpreter.

The account begins with a simple statement of fact 'In those days Jesus came from Nazareth of Galilee and was baptised by John in the Jordan' (1:9). These few words constitute a complete account of the event: the two actors are named, the place is specified, and the nature of the encounter is identified. Then follows, 'When he came up from the water, immediately he saw the heavens opened and the Spirit descending upon him like a dove. And a voice came from the heaven, "You are my beloved Son with whom I am well pleased"' (1:10-11). Is this description of the same order of reality as that in verse 9? Did it really happen in the same way as Jesus' immersion in the river?

Some scholars answer in the affirmative because the event is so crucial to the life and mission of Jesus. But, noting that there is a greater stress on corporeity in later versions, they surmise that originally it was an entirely subjective experience of Jesus and possibly John the Baptist.[24] Such harmonising of the text with contemporary expectations is not scientific exegesis. What we have in verses 10-11 is nothing more than a type of interpretative technique common among Jews in the first century. Its literary form is that of a 'Vision-voice', which occurs several times in the Palestinian Targum (Neofiti).[25]

---

24. So for example de la Potterie, 'La verité de la Sainte Écriture', 166-7.
25. For full details and other examples, see Fritzleo Lentzen-Deis, *Die Taufe Jesu nach den Synoptikern. Literarkritische und gattungsgeschichtliche Untersuchungen* (Frankfurter Theologische Studien, 4; Frankfurt: Knecht, 1970).

A targum is an Aramaic translation of the Hebrew Old Testament for use in the synagogue, which also embodied (as expansions) traditional interpretations. The similarity becomes visible when the texts are set in parallel.

Gen 22:10 in Hebrew	Gen 22:10 in Targum[1]	Mark 1:10–11
Abraham put forth his hand	Abraham stretched out his hand	
and took the knife	and took the knife	
to slay his son	to slay his son, Isaac	
	Isaac answered and said to his	
	father Abraham, 'Father tie me	
	well lest I kick you and your	
	sacrifice be made unlean, and	
	we be pushed down into the pit	
	of destruction in the world to	
	come'	
	The eyes of Abraham were on	
	the eyes of Isaac, and **the eyes**	
	of Isacca were seeing the	**He saw the heavens opened**
	angels on high.	and the spirit descending upon
		him like a dove.

	Abraham did not see	
	them.	
	In that hour **a voice came forth**	And **a voice came from heaven**
	from the heavens and said.	
	'Come see two just people who	'You are my beloved Son, with
	are in my world. One sacrifices	you I am well pleased'.
	and the other is sacrificed. He	
	who sacrificed does not hesitate,	
	and he who is sacrificed	
	streches out his neck.'	
The angel of the Lord	The angel of the Lord	
called to him from heaven,	called to him from heaven,	
and said, 'Abraham Abraham'.	and said, 'Abraham Abraham'.	
and he said, 'Here I am'.	and he said, 'Here I am'.	

1. Translation from Martin McNamara, *Targum Neofiti 1: Genesis* (The Aramaic Bible: The Targums, 1A; Collegeville, MI: Liturgical Press, 1992), 117–118. A slightly different form of the interpretation appears in Pseudo-Jonathan; see Michael Maher, *Targum Pseudo-Jonathan: Genesis* (The Aramaic Bible: The Targums, 1B; Collegeville, MI: Liturgical Press, 1992), 79–80. The interpretation is entirely lacking in Onkolos.

Since the events are different (the sacrifice of Isaac and the baptism of Jesus are completely different), one would expect the content of their respective interpretations to differ. Thus what is important are the two key structural elements, a vision of heaven and a voice from heaven (both in bold in the synopsis). These unambiguously betray the presence of the literary form of the 'Vision-voice'. In using this form the editor did not intend to write history in the sense of recounting facts. It was designed to suggest a meaning, to explain the significance of the event, whose historicity, on the other hand, is taken entirely for granted. Something must exist in order to demand an explanation.

What was Mark's 'explanation' of the baptism of Jesus? He saw it as the anwer to the great prayer of the Jewish exiles in Babylon in Isaiah 63:7–64:11. There is no space here to develop this dimension in detail but the many verbal connections are significant, for example the plea 'O, that you would open the heavens' (Isa 64:1) is answered by 'He saw the heavens opened' (Mark 1:10); the agonised question 'Can you remain silent?' (Isa 64:11) is answered by 'A voice came from heaven' (Mark 1:11). In his baptism, the first act of his public ministry, Jesus is shown as having been sent by God to once again manifest His saving presence to His people.

Thus the two facets of Mark's baptismal narrative reveal different aspects of truth. Both are true but not in the same way. One is historical in the sense that it really happened as written down. The other is historical only in the sense that it was the thought of a real person at a given moment in time. The factual truth of the event is complemented by the subsequent inspired interpretative truth of that event. It would be difficult to find a more vivid example of the importance of the literary form of a narrative, or of the various literary forms within a single narrative, for the correct interpretation of a passage.

After Vatican II

The highest authority in the church has consistently followed the lead of *DV* by affirming its confidence in biblical scholars and their use of the historical-critical method. In 1971 Pope Paul VI completely reformed the PBC. Those who previously had been mere 'consulters', that is, qualified experts, were promoted to full 'members', a rank hitherto reserved to cardinals, who in most cases lacked the appropriate qualifications. Its mission was not to act as a watch-dog but to apply its collective resources to the study of questions raised by a wide range of institutions ranging from the Pope to national biblical societies.[26] Three years later Paul VI gave an audience to the renewed PBC in which he proposed as their role model 'a masterful exegete who displayed exceptional critical sagacity, deep faith, and profound devotion to the Church'. The reference is to Marie-Joseph Lagrange OP, who during the Modernist crisis epitomised everything that Rome thought wrong in biblical studies![27] Graphic evidence of how completely the wheel had turned is provided by Pope Benedict XVI's use of the historical-critical method to write a life of Jesus that was well received in academic circles.[28]

The new role of the PBC has found expression in a series of documents, whose fidelity to the insights of *DV* when combined with their thoroughness and moderation have inspired scholars: *On Sacred Scripture and Theology* (1984), *Unity and Diversity in the Church* (1988), *The Interpretation of the Bible in the Church* (1993), *The Jewish People and their Sacred Scriptures in the Christian Bible* (2001), *The Bible and Morality. Biblical Roots of Christian Conduct* (2008).

Apparently the PBC was also requested to report on the question of the ordination of women. The two-years of sessions were intended to be confidential but it leaked out that the members voted 17–0 that the New Testament does not clearly decide the issue. Nonetheless the majority in a 12–5 vote insisted that nothing excluded the ordination of women.[29] No document was ever published.

A task-force was created by the Executive Board of the Catholic Biblical Association of America (CBA) in 1976 to research the same topic. Their report was published as 'Women and Priestly Ministry: The New Testament Evidence' and concluded that, far from excluding

---

26. The full text of *Sedula cura* is given in Béchard, *The Scripture Documents*, 147–50.
27. For the Pope's discourse, see Béchard, *The Scripture Documents*, 151–6. On Lagrange, see Bernard Montagnes, *The Story of Father Marie-Joseph Lagrange. Founder of Modern Catholic Biblical Study* (New York/Mahwah, NJ: Paulist Press, 2006).
28. *Jesus of Nazareth* (San Francisco, CA; Ignatius Press, 2011).
29. *Women Priests. A Catholic Commentary on the Vatican Declaration*, edited by Leonard and Arlene Swidler (New York: Paulist, 1977) 25–34, 338–46.

women, 'the NT evidence, while not decisive by itself, points towards the admission of women to priestly ministry'.[30]

The PBC was notified and in response merely requested to be kept informed. The final document was sent to Rome—and there was no official reaction.[31] However, just before the CBA report was finalised one of the members of the tast-force, Richard J Sklba, was named Auxilary Bishop of Milwaukee, USA. On publication of the report Rome withdrew the nomination. Rembrant Weakland, OSB, the Archbishop of Milwaukee, immediately brought Father Sklba to Rome, where the vicious little attempt at subversion was crushed from the top. On 19 December 1979 Sklba became America's youngest bishop, but he was never permitted to move up beyond Auxilary of Milwaukee.

The principal consequence of *DV* for exegetes was the gradual abandonment of the self-censorship that had become a way of life. The first edition of *The Jerome Biblical Commentary* appeared in 1968. It contained no article on 'Jesus'. Realising that what would be acceptable in the world of critical scholarship would be condemned by Rome, the editors opted for prudent silence.[32] Thirty-two years later it was re-edited as *The New Jerome Biblical Commentary* (1990). This time the same editors included a long critical article on the life of the historical Jesus by John P Meier, in which history has to be demonstrated, not taken for granted.[33]

Without the fear of facile condemnation, biblical scholarship flourished in areas where it had never done so before, notably the USA, Ireland and Australia, which produced prolific scholars who have gained the respect of their professional peers throughout the

---

30. *Catholic Biblical Quarterly,* 41 (1979): 608–13, here 612–13.
31. Personal communication from Joseph Jensen, OSB, Executive Secretary of the CBA, 14 June 2012.
32. The predecessor of the *Jerome Biblical Commentary* had been the *Catholic Commentary on Holy Scripture* (1955). It entrusted the article on 'The Person and Teaching of Our Lord Jesus Christ' to A Graham, a dogmatic theologian, who was fully aware of the implicit demands of Rome and, as one might have expected, produced a travesty of critical scholarship.
33. Subsequently this article has been developed by Meier into a multi-volume work, John P Meier, *A Marginal Jew: Rethinking the Historical Jesus* (ABRL; New York: Doubleday, 1991–2009), which, according to Benedict XVI, 'is in many respects a model of historical-critical exegesis' in *Jesus of Nazareth* (San Francisco, CA: Ignatius Press, 2011), Part 2, 296.

world. They made original contributions to scholarship while at the same time exhibiting a pastoral concern for the dissemination of the Good News.

If official criticism of biblical scholars has effectively ceased to exist, there remains a groundswell of opposition to the critical treatment of the New Testament. The type of exegesis made mandatory for Catholics by the *Instruction on the Historical Truth of the Gospels* is highly sophisticated. There are those who do not have the tools, the training, or the mental agility. Unfortunately such individuals often do not have the humility to refrain from asserting their interpretation of the Gospels as the criterion by which the work of professional exegetes should be judged. What is the root of such opposition? The best analysis is that of Pope John Paul II.

The occasion was his presentation of *The Interpretation of the Bible in the Church* to the cardinals and diplomatic corps. He begins by comparing and contrasting the biblical encyclicals *PD* (1883) and *DAS* (1943); they differ because they are historically conditioned. Papal documents, therefore, are subject to the same critical exegesis as biblical texts! The Pope went on to insist again on the importance of 'literary-forms' in Catholic exegesis, and continues,

> A false idea of God and the incarnation presses a certain number of Christians to take the opposite approach. They tend to believe that, since God is the absolute Being, each of his words has an absolute value, independent of all the conditions of human language. Thus, according to them, there is no room for studying these conditions in order to make distinctions that would relativise the significance of the words. However, that is where the illusion occurs and the mysteries of scriptural inspiration and the incarnation are really rejected, by clinging to a false notion of the Absolute. . . . Although he [God] expresses himself in human language, he does not give each expression a uniform value, but uses its possible nuances with extreme flexibility and likewise accepts its limitations. That is what makes the task of exegetes so complex, so necessary, and so fascinating.[34]

---

34. *The Interpretation of the Bible in the Church. Address of His Holiness Pope John*

The ignorant opposition criticised by the pope had its partisans in France,³⁵ but was particularly virulent in the USA, where its attention focused almost exclusively on Raymond E Brown, SS. In reality he was but a particularly well qualified representative of those who practiced the historical-critical method, but in 1977 he had published a major study entitled *The Birth of the Messiah. A Commentary on the Infancy Narratives in Matthew and Luke* (New York: Doubleday). In it he had to deal with a host of particularly tricky historical questions, for example the virgin birth. The mind-set of his critics was such that only a formal statement that everything in Matthw 1 – 2 and Luke 1 – 2 was strictly factual was acceptable. From that perspective a nuanced judgment that attempted to do justice to all the evidence was tantmount to a denial of historicity.

In the revised version of *The Birth of the Messiah* (1993) Brown dialogues with the some 500 books and articles that subsequently appeared on the topic.³⁶ With utter weariness he draws attention to the great number of occasions where he has been misunderstood and/or misrepresented.³⁷ None of his critics had given him his due of a close reading with an open mind, and a sophisticated understanding of the nuanced formulations of his judgments. This, unfortunately, is typical of current criticism of what is believed to be the pernicious influence of biblical scholarship in the church.

The epitome of criticism of the historical-critical method came from a priest-sociologist Msgr George A Kelly, *The New Biblical Theorists: Raymond E. Brown and Beyond* (Ann Arbor, MI: Servant Publications, 1983). His criticisms, as one might have expected, focus on their approach to historicity, but his real concern is that those complaints have not been listened to by those in authority. Hence, a vast conspiracy theory. Bishops who disagree with Brown are true servants of the Church. Others in the hierarchy, who speak out on his

---

Paul II and Document of the Pontifical Biblical Commission (Rome: Libreria editrice Vaticana, 1993), 13–14.

35. For example René Laurentin, *Les Évangiles de l'Enfance du Christ. Verité de Noël au delà des mythes d'exégèse et sémiotique historicité et théologie* (second edition; Paris: Desclée, 1982), *The Truth of Christmas. Beyond the Myths* (Petersham, MA: St. Bede's, 1986).
36. Raymond E Brown, *The Birth of the Messiah* (ABRL; new updated edition; New York: Doubleday, 1993), 9.
37. Brown, *Birth of the Messiah* (updated edition), 574–7.

behalf, are either 'overprotective' or do not understand what Brown is really saying. Scholars of the same persuasion as Brown protect him by abstaining from public criticism, and do not permit such criticism to appear in the periodicals that they control.

It was not the role of the hierarchy to protect Brown from serious argument. There can be little doubt, however, that hierarchies around the world have not done their duty by biblical scholars. Bishops refrain from criticism because they know perfectly well that they would not be backed up by Rome. The days of Cardinal Merry del Val are long past. But they do not do enough to bring home to *everyone* in their dioceses the entirely positive official attitude of the modern Church towards Gospel studies as embodied in *Dei Verbum*. Nor do they reprimand Catholics who impugn the integrity of critical scholars. This is a blatant breach of the fundamental commandment of charity, and the enforcement of morality is the duty of a bishop. Were the same individuals to preach abortion or gay marriage, they certainly would be censured (and have been) in the most public way. Without such episcopal action ignorant underground criticism of biblical scholars will continue to fester, and gravely endanger the health of the Church.

9

Breaking Open the Word: The Legacy of *Dei Verbum*

Elizabeth Dowling RSM

If it were not for *Dei Verbum* (*DV*), I would not be here now writing this article. On the one hand, that is patently obvious as I would not be writing for a volume marking the fiftieth anniversary of *DV* if the document did not exist. The reason for my comment, however, relates to an aspect of the legacy of *DV*. Prior to Vatican II, within the Catholic tradition, study of the Bible was principally undertaken in seminaries. Except for priests and seminarians, Catholics had little, if any, opportunity for formal biblical study. *DV* encouraged and authorised changes which led to the opening up of the Bible to the general Catholic public. As a Catholic woman, I have enjoyed the benefits of these changes and have taken the opportunity for ongoing biblical study and engagement. Thus, I am now in a position to be writing this article on the development of newer approaches to biblical interpretation in the wake of *DV*.

The final form of *DV* was accepted by the Council of Vatican II in 1965. Following on from the insights expressed by Pius XII in *Divino Afflante Spiritu (DAS)* in 1943, *DV* affirmed that the biblical books were composed by human authors who were inspired by God. Biblical interpreters, in order 'to ascertain what God has wished to communicate to us, should carefully search out the meaning which the sacred writers really had in mind'.[1] A publication by The Pontifical Biblical Commission (PBC) in 1964, entitled *Instruction Concerning*

---

1. Vatican II Council, *Dei Verbum*, *Dogmatic Constitution on Divine Revelation*, *DV* 12, in *Vatican Council II: The Conciliar and Post Conciliar Documents*, edited by A Flannery, revised edition (Northport, NY: Costello Publishing Company, 1988), 757.

the Historical Truth of the Gospels', was another important forerunner to *DV*. The PBC here affirmed the historical method, with its use of biblical languages, as well as textual, redaction and form criticism, although a word of caution regarding form criticism was also given. While some Catholic scholars were already employing such methods, this PBC statement was the first official endorsement of historical criticism for use by Catholic scholars, bringing Catholic biblical scholarship more into line with the methodology of its Protestant counterpart.

Presented in the year following the PBC statement and continuing some of the PBC's insights, *DV* highlights the understanding of literary forms within their particular historical and cultural contexts as essential to understanding the writer's intention (*DV* 12). As such, *DV* promotes elements of the historical critical method of biblical interpretation, although it does not use the term 'historical method' or 'criticism'. Hence, *DV's* endorsement of the historical critical method is less explicit than that in *Instruction Concerning the Historical Truth of the Gospels.* Nevertheless, *DV's* comments articulate the essential nature of critical biblical methodology in Catholic biblical scholarship.

That elements of historical criticism were raised in *DV* is not surprising, since historical criticism was the focus of critical biblical methodology prior to and at the time of Vatican II. This was particularly the case amongst Protestant biblical scholars who had been using this method well before it was sanctioned for use by Catholic scholars. Along with its non-inclusive language, *DV's* promotion of the study of literary form and authorial intention is an indication that the document is a product of its time.

Several of its statements, however, particularly in the final chapter, 'Sacred Scripture in the Life of the Church', show that *DV* was also a catalyst for changes that were to shape post-conciliar Catholic biblical studies:

> i. 'Access to sacred Scripture ought to be open wide to the Christian faithful' (*DV* 22).
> ii. 'The sacred Synod encourages those sons of the Church who are engaged in biblical studies *constantly to renew* their efforts, in order to carry on the work

they have so happily begun, with complete dedication and in accordance with the mind of the Church' (*DV* 23). (Italics mine).
iii. 'the sacred Synod forcefully and specifically exhorts *all the Christian faithful*, especially those who live the religious life, to learn "the surpassing knowledge of Jesus Christ" (Phil. 3:8) by frequent reading of the divine Scriptures' (*DV* 25) (Italics mine).[2]

DV placed the Bible at the centre of the life of the Church, calling on 'Catholic exegetes' to examine and explain the biblical texts 'using appropriate techniques' so that all the Church may be nourished (*DV* 23). While access to the Bible is to be given to all the Church, the language of *DV* presupposes that those who are engaged in Catholic biblical studies are male, referring to them as 'sons of the Church'. Indeed, at the time of *DV*'s production, Catholic biblical scholars were almost exclusively a male clerical group since the seminary was the home of Catholic biblical studies.

There is no indication in *DV* that its creators expected any great change to the characteristic composition of the community of Catholic biblical scholars. Yet, over time, some of the implications of living out *DV*'s exhortations have been the opening up of Catholic biblical study beyond the seminary and the clergy, as well as the resultant involvement of Catholic biblical scholars in the development of newer methods of critical biblical interpretation. While the authors of *DV* could not have been aware of the extent of the changes that were to come in the field of biblical interpretation in the decades to follow, one of the legacies of this document was that Catholic biblical scholarship was in a position to contribute to the ongoing evolution of biblical interpretation.

Contemporary biblical scholarship speaks of three different 'worlds' of the biblical text: the world behind the text, the world of the text, and the world in front of or before the text. The world behind the text is concerned with the ancient world of the author out of which

---

2. While such an exhortation encourages a more inclusive engagement with the biblical text, there is an especial mention of 'those who live the religious life'. Though the words 'all the Christian faithful' open a space for the laity in biblical engagement, it would appear that the laity is not the main focus of the exhortation.

the text emerged. The world of the text focuses on the biblical text itself and the world generated by this text, while the world in front of the text is concerned with the world of the present-day reader.³ When *DV* appeared in 1965, biblical criticism was essentially historical criticism. Until the 1970s, historical criticism was the dominant, if not exclusive, critical method of twentieth century biblical interpretation. Thus, the focus was on the world behind the text and on establishing the author's original meaning and intention in writing.

With the development of new literary theory in the wider literary world, it was only a matter of time before the insights coming out of this movement began to influence the interpretation of biblical literature. In particular, literary theory started to shift the focus of attention from the author to the text itself, and then eventually to the reader.⁴ As a result, the 1970s and 1980s saw the emergence of new literary criticism as a method of biblical interpretation. Like 'historical criticism', the term 'literary criticism' covers a range of methodologies. With literary criticism, however, the focus is more on the world of the text or on the world in front of the text. Initially, literary criticism focussed primarily on the text itself and its literary and rhetorical features. Over time, literary criticism expanded to analyse the reader and the reader's role in the production of meaning. This led to the possibility of multiple interpretations of a given text.⁵ The significance of the reader's role will be discussed further below.

As in the case of historical critics, literary critics can approach their task of biblical interpretation from differing positions. It is possible to treat the Bible as literature like any other literary corpus, ignoring any theological dimension of the text in the process of interpretation. One can confidently assume that is not what *DV* had in mind when it exhorted Christians 'to learn "the surpassing knowledge of Jesus Christ" (Phil 3:8) by frequent reading of the divine Scriptures' (*DV*

---

3. See Sandra M Schneiders, *The Revelatory Text: Interpreting the New Testament as Sacred Scripture* (San Francisco, CA: HarperCollins, 1991), 113.
4. This shift in focus is outlined in Roger Webster, *Studying Literary Theory: An Introduction*, second edition (London: Arnold, 1996), 16–30.
5. See Fernando F Segovia, "'And They Began to Speak in Other Tongues": Competing Modes of Discourse in Contemporary Biblical Criticism', in *Reading from This Place, Volume 1: Social Location and Biblical Interpretation in the United States*, edited by Fernando F Segovia and Mary Ann Tolbert (Minneapolis, MN: Fortress, 1995), 1–32, 15–20.

25). There is another position from which to undertake literary criticism, however, one that fits well with *DV*'s call to renewal of efforts in biblical interpretation. Fernando Segovia's comment on the emergence and influence of biblical literary criticism reflects this:

> . . . such a newfound interest in the formal features of the text could also be invested with a more explicit theological function. It could be argued that by bringing such features to the surface, literary criticism made possible not only a better appreciation of the craft and beauty of the Word of God but also a better feel for its power and hold upon readers.[6]

It is important to note here that a biblical interpreter can similarly choose to employ historical critical method or any other methodology without engaging the text from a faith perspective.

Another method of biblical interpretation that developed more or less parallel with literary criticism was social-scientific criticism, sometimes called cultural criticism. The focus here is on the socio-cultural context out of which the text emerged and how the text reflects this context. Hence, cultural codes of the ancient world of the text are studied, as well as the ways in which these codes are inscribed in the text.[7] This emphasis on the social and cultural context would appear to sit well with the exhortation in *DV* for interpreters to pay attention to 'the conventions which the people of [the sacred writer's] time followed in their dealings with one another' (*DV* 12).

As both literary and cultural criticism took hold, the significance of the reader and the reader's context in the production of meaning became more of a focus of biblical scholarship. Whereas historical criticism prized objectivity and the neutrality of the interpreter, the understanding grew amongst literary critics that such an objective reading was not possible to attain. This realisation provided a challenge to the validity of this aspect of the historical critical method. The real reader is 'always positioned and interested; socially and historically

---

6. Segovia, 'Competing Modes of Discourse', 19.
7. See Segovia, 'Competing Modes of Discourse', 21–3. Segovia is one who calls the method 'cultural criticism'.

conditioned and unable to transcend such conditions.'[8] This means that readers from different social locations interpret the same text in different ways.

When Catholic biblical interpretation was the exclusive domain of the clergy, the readings considered 'objective' were in reality readings from a predominantly white, male, Eurocentric, imperialist, anthropocentric social location. A problem, however, was that this particular position was generally considered to be the ideologically neutral position. Few perceived the inherent ideology in the interpretation. As Gale A Yee notes, 'The real danger in espousing a "value-neutral" perspective in reading is having an ideological agenda without acknowledging it.'[9] We each need someone from outside our own social location to introduce us to the biases of our location, to enable us to see that no one of us holds all the truth. Once the exhortations (if not the expectations) of *DV* moved into lived experience and access to biblical study was opened to 'all the Christian faithful', the social locations of Catholic biblical interpreters exhibited a wider range of characteristics. Catholic interpreters joined their colleagues in the wider biblical world to participate in and contribute to the development of newer approaches to the biblical text that recognised the import of the context of the reader in the act of interpretation.

Before I explore some of these approaches, it is important to recognise that many biblical scholars in the 1980s and 1990s began to use a combination of methods in their biblical research. The relative strengths and relevant features of historical, literary and cultural criticisms were combined to address the questions of an interpreter. Each of the elements—text, reader and context—and their interaction began to be understood as integral to interpretation.[10]

---

8. Segovia, 'Competing Modes of Discourse', 28-9.
9. Gale A Yee, 'The Author/Text/Reader and Power: Suggestions for a Critical Framework for Biblical Studies', in *Reading from This Place, Volume 1: Social Location and Biblical Interpretation in the United States*, edited by Fernando F Segovia and Mary Ann Tolbert (Minneapolis, MN: Fortress, 1995), 109-18, 116.
10. See, for instance, Yee, 'The Author/Text/Reader', 109-118; and Elaine M Wainwright, *Shall We Look For Another? A Feminist Rereading of the Matthean Jesus* (Maryknoll, NY: Orbis, 1998), 19-32.

Feminist Biblical Interpretation

With *DV*'s exhortation to open up access to the Bible, Catholic women were more able to engage in biblical study and were, therefore, in a position to join with other women in contributing to the ongoing evolution of biblical interpretation. One of the first fruits of women's subsequent contribution to biblical scholarship was the development of feminist approaches to reading the biblical text.[11] This did not constitute a new method as such but rather a new hermeneutical framework within which any method(s) of biblical interpretation could be employed, a framework which requires a particular shift in consciousness on the part of the interpreter.

Feminist biblical interpretation is grounded in a hermeneutics of suspicion. The feminist interpreter is aware that the biblical text emerged within patriarchal cultures and may reinforce a patriarchal mindset. Hence, the feminist interpreter is alert to the ways in which the biblical text itself or, indeed, an interpretation of the text may serve to oppress women. An early model of feminist biblical interpretation was articulated by Elisabeth Schüssler Fiorenza who proposed that a hermeneutics of suspicion be combined with a hermeneutics of proclamation, remembrance and creative actualisation.[12] Other feminist scholars have developed variations on this theme but they share the elements of critique and restoration or affirmation.

As feminist biblical interpretation developed, one of the criticisms levelled at it was that it carries a particular bias: 'Feminist exegesis, to the extent that it proceeds from a preconceived judgment, runs the risk of interpreting the biblical texts in a tendentious and thus debatable manner.'[13] Feminist interpreters are explicit about their

---

11. Groundbreaking feminist biblical works in this period include Phyllis Trible, *God and the Rhetoric of Sexuality* (Philadelphia: Fortress Press, 1978) and Elisabeth Schüssler Fiorenza, *In Memory of Her: A Feminist Theological Reconstruction of Christian Origins* (New York: Crossroad, 1983). Significant early feminist biblical collaborations between women include *The Women's Bible Commentary*, edited by Carol A Newsom and Sharon H Ringe (London: SPCK, 1992); and *Searching the Scriptures*, edited by Elisabeth Schüssler Fiorenza, 2 Volumes (New York: Crossroad, 1993-4).
12. Fiorenza, *Bread Not Stone: The Challenge of Feminist Biblical Interpretation* (Edinburgh: T&T Clark, 1990), 15-22. Schüssler Fiorenza has continued to develop her approach over the decades since the emergence of *In Memory of Her*.
13. See The Pontifical Biblical Commission, *The Interpretation of the Bible in the*

stance and social location, aware that their context will influence how they interpret biblical texts. The inherent irony in the above comment on feminist interpretation is that *every* biblical interpretation carries its own bias, as mentioned previously. The comment reflects the prizing of objectivity which is not practicable, while ignoring the bias inherent in its own stance.

Another challenge levelled at some feminist interpreters, particularly in the 1980s and early 1990s, reflected the fact that the majority of the feminist interpreters of that period were white, western, middle class women. Women biblical interpreters from other social locations challenged these western women, rightly highlighting the differences that exist among women.[14] Western women's interpretation reflects the circumstances of a particular social location not shared by all women. While women share the same gender, differences in ethnicity, class and many other categories produce differences in women's lived experiences.[15] Therefore, women will not all interpret a biblical text in the same way. This understanding has led to a far more nuanced approach by women biblical interpreters of more recent times. The term 'feminist' biblical interpretation is now one designation on a spectrum of terminologies relating to women's biblical scholarship, including womanist and *mujerista* interpretation. Asian, African, Pacific, and indigenous women are now also numbered among our biblical scholars. Again, an essential understanding which has emerged in biblical interpretation is that one needs to hear voices from outside one's specific location so that the inherent biases of one's own interpretation can be identified. This understanding leads into the next area for discussion, broadly designated a postcolonial approach.

Church: Address of His Holiness John Paul II and Document of the Pontifical Biblical Commission (Boston, MA: St Paul Books and Media, 1993), 71.

14. For a critique of white Australian women's assumption of commonality between the experience of white and Aboriginal women, see Anne Pattel-Gray, 'Not Yet Tiddas: An Aboriginal Womanist Critique of Australian Church Feminism', in *Freedom and Entrapment: Women Thinking Theology*, edited by Maryanne Confoy, Dorothy A Lee and Joan Nowotny (Blackburn, Vic: Dove, 1995), 165–92.

15. For an excellent discussion of 'differences among women', see the chapter with this title in Gerda Lerner, *Why History Matters: Life and Thought* (New York: Oxford University Press, 1997), 131–45.

Postcolonial Biblical Interpretation

Once the voices of biblical interpreters from across the globe began to be heard, the imperialist overtones of some of the earlier biblical interpretation were recognised. Men and women who had experienced colonisation or postcolonial contexts were able to critique the colonialist perspective in the biblical text itself, as well as in the writing of male and female biblical interpreters from positions of imperialist power. In the 1990s, the particular postcolonial hermeneutical stance developed in response to this consciousness. Like feminist hermeneutics, postcolonial hermeneutics 'foreground relationships of domination and subordination, that is to say, uneven relationships of power.'[16] While gender relationships are at the forefront of feminist studies, the relationship between imperial power and colonised peoples are highlighted in postcolonial studies. It is important to note, however, that interpreters grounded in these approaches are not only concerned with the relationship which they foreground but can be attuned to imbalance of power across a range of categories.[17] Musa W Dube, for instance, explicitly combines postcolonial and feminist approaches.[18] Various categories of subordination are not mutually exclusive. Rather, they are intersecting and interrelated.[19]

Postcolonial biblical studies are grounded in the experience of indigenous peoples at the time of colonisation by a ruling empire and/or the experience of these people in the postcolonial period. Like feminist biblical interpretations, postcolonial biblical interpretations are concerned with elements of critique and restoration. Postcolonial studies critique aspects of the biblical text and biblical interpretations that reinforce and thus contribute to the continuation of imperialist structures and thinking. They also affirm the voice of the colonised peoples and the subversion of imperialist thinking. As in the case of

---

16. Fernando Segovia and Stephen D Moore, 'Postcolonial Biblical Criticism: Beginnings, Trajectories, Intersections', in *Postcolonial Biblical Criticism: Interdisciplinary Intersections*, edited by Fernando Segovia and Stephen D Moore (London: Continuum, 2006), 1–22, 10.
17. Segovia and Moore, 'Postcolonial Biblical Criticism', 10.
18. See Musa W Dube, *Postcolonial Feminist Interpretation of the Bible* (St Louis, MO: Chalice Press, 2000).
19. Fiorenza refers to the pyramidal system of oppression, with its intersecting facets as 'kyriarchy'. See Fiorenza, *But She Said: Feminist Practices of Biblical Interpretation* (Boston, MA: Beacon Press, 1992), 114–20.

feminist interpreters, post-colonialist interpreters are aware that their own context informs their interpretation and they are explicit about their stance.

Ecological Biblical Interpretation

A relative newcomer in the field of biblical interpretation is ecological interpretation of the biblical text. Again the context of biblical interpreters has been the catalyst for this development:

> Those of us who stand in the midst of today's reality as humanity and our planet enters a new millennium cannot be immune to the challenges of climate change and ecological degradation, their threat to food supplies on planet Earth and the growing shortage of water. They threaten not only the human community whose numbers are growing as never before, but ecological systems and all Earth species and constituents, indeed the very planet itself and its future.[20]

It is the consciousness of human domination over the rest of the Earth community and the subsequent disastrous effects of this domination that has led to the development of an ecological hermeneutical approach to biblical interpretation. Ecological interpreters are alert to the anthropocentric nature of some biblical texts and biblical interpretations. A key understanding in this approach is the interrelationship between humans and all Earth creatures and elements, and indeed, the Earth itself. With the effects of climate change becoming increasingly evident, more and more people are recognising this interconnectedness and consequently a growing number of biblical scholars are utilising an ecological hermeneutic in their biblical interpretation.

An early and influential outcome from an ecological reading of the biblical text is The Earth Bible series.[21] Six ecojustice principles lie

---

20. Elaine M Wainwright, 'Reading Matt 21:1–22 Ecologically', in *Australian Biblical Review,* 60 (2012): 67–79, 68.
21. The first volume in this series is *Readings from the Perspective of Earth,* edited by Norman C Habel, The Earth Bible 1 (Sheffield: Sheffield Academic Press, 2000). In all, five volumes have been published in the series. For a more recent development

behind this work: intrinsic worth, interconnectedness, voice, purpose, mutual custodianship and resistance.[22] The aim of these principles for biblical interpretation is to promote justice for Earth and the entire Earth community. A hermeneutic of suspicion alerts the reader to the anthropocentric nature of much of the biblical text and/or its interpretation. Like feminist and postcolonial interpretations, such ecological readings are concerned with critique and retrieval.[23] As Elaine Wainwright points out, an ecological reading 'entails more, however, than simply adding ecology to such epistemologies for these often do not address the significant and critical shifts in thinking necessary to confront the profound anthropocentrism that has developed in at least most western but also many other human and cultural understandings of planet Earth and its more-than-human constituents.'[24]

Biblical interpreters engaged with an ecological hermeneutic, as with other contextual hermeneutics, employ combinations of critical biblical methods which allow the particular issues highlighted by their hermeneutical stance to be addressed.[25] Such contextual readings which explicitly identify their hermeneutical approaches, are no less critically rigorous than those readings where the ideological agenda is not identified but is nevertheless present, perhaps even unconsciously.

---

and articulation of this ecological approach, see Habel, 'Introducing Ecological Hermeneutics', in *Exploring Ecological Hermeneutics*, edited by Norman C Habel and Peter Trudinger, SBL Symposium series 46 (Atlanta, GA: Society of Biblical Literature, 2008), 1–8.

22. See The Earth Bible Team, 'Guiding Ecojustice Principles', in *Readings from the Perspective of Earth*, 38–53.
23. The Earth Bible Team, 'Guiding Ecojustice Principles', 39–40.
24. Wainwright, 'Reading Matt 21:1–22 Ecologically', 71.
25. Wainwright names her approach 'ecological reading' and analyses the text's inner texture, intertexture, and social and cultural texture which she names 'ecological texture'. See Wainwright, 'Reading Matt 21:1–22 Ecologically', 71–2. Anne Elvey attends to the materiality of the biblical text in her approach which she names 'eco-materialist'. See Anne F Elvey, *The Matter of the Text: Material Engagements between Luke and the Five Senses*, The Bible in the Modern World 37 (Sheffield: Sheffield Phoenix Press, 2011), 24–25. A different ecological approach is taken by the Uses of the Bible in Environmental Ethics team, led by David Horrell, from the University of Exeter. Inspired by the theology of Ernst Conradie, this approach uses doctrinal lenses to focus the understanding of the text. This is explained in David Horrell, *The Bible and the Environment: Towards a Critical, Ecological Biblical Theology* (London: Equinox, 2010), 117–27.

The above discussion of some of the newer approaches to biblical interpretation does not reflect the complexity and richness of these approaches. The limits of this article preclude a detailed analysis. It is only possible to outline some of the important developments in biblical interpretation since the appearance of *DV* in 1965. An important point to remember, however, is that many biblical interpreters now employ a combination of methodologies, and their interpretations emerge from a blend of hermeneutical approaches. Furthermore, biblical scholars today often also engage with a range of interdisciplinary influences in developing their approach. Philosophical theory, archaeology, science, art and poetry are amongst the diverse strands that can add to the tapestry of biblical interpretation.

Dei Verbum's Legacy

I return now to two key exhortations *of DV* highlighted earlier. The first is to open up access to the Bible so that all the Christian faithful can participate in biblical learning (*DV* 22). The second exhortation is for those 'sons of the Church who are engaged in biblical studies constantly to renew their efforts' (*DV* 23). I have already commented that the language of *DV* which identifies those engaged in biblical studies as 'sons of the Church' suggests that the authors of the document did not envisage Catholic women as biblical scholars. Nevertheless, the changes that ensued once the Bible was made more accessible to the general Catholic population led to both female and male religious and laity joining the male ordained clergy in the ranks of Catholic biblical scholars.

At the first meeting of the Australian Catholic Biblical Association (ACBA) in 1964, the attendees were an all-male clerical group.[26] At the meeting in 1965, five women from religious orders were present, although they were not listed as members. Several women were also present in 1966 and one in 1972, though again they were not listed as members. It was 1981 before women members were listed in the records, although there was at least one woman who was a member

---

26. All the information here on the early ACBA membership and participants at the early ACBA meetings was obtained from Elaine Wainwright, 'In Fear and Great Joy: Forty Years of Feminist Biblical Scholarship', *Compass: A Review of Topical Theology*, 39/1 (Autumn 2005), accessed 19 April 2013, http://compassreview.org/autumn05/7.html.

before this.[27] While it was initially members of religious orders who were more able to take up the opportunities for biblical education that were being opened up beyond the male clergy, gradually opportunities were also grasped by the Catholic laity.

DV's exhortation to Catholic biblical scholars 'constantly to renew their efforts' is an endorsement of Catholic biblical scholars' engagement with the newer biblical methods and approaches which have developed since Vatican II. The document's implicit call to engage in critical biblical methodology represented a move away from a literal interpretation. The ongoing urge to constantly renew their engagement with critical biblical methodology was the impetus for Catholic scholars to eventually venture beyond the confines of historical criticism into other methods. Such Catholic scholars were able to both participate in and contribute to the development of biblical interpretation well beyond what could possibly have been envisaged at the time of *DV*.

Catholic biblical scholarship today is undertaken by men and women from various backgrounds bringing a diverse range of lived experience to their engagement with the biblical text. Such is the effect of *DV*. That biblical interpretation will continue to nuance its methods and approaches and that Catholic biblical scholars will continue to be part of this development is the ongoing legacy of *DV*.

I return now to my comments at the beginning of this paper. If it were not for *DV*, I would not be writing this. That a Catholic woman would have the possibility of engaging in critical biblical study was almost unheard of, at least in Australia, prior to Vatican II. The winds of change that have blown since that time have acted as a catalyst for the opportunities that I have eagerly taken to engage with the biblical text, using a number of the newer methods and approaches to biblical interpretation that I have here outlined. In this regard, my story matches the experience of so many other Catholic biblical scholars who have been inspired to engage with the biblical text and to constantly renew their efforts in interpretation.

---

27. See Wainwright, 'In Fear and Great Joy'.

10

Translating Biblical Texts Within an Ecclesial Context

Dale Launderville, OSB

Standardisation is necessary for coordinated group activity. There must be some fixed point or process that keeps the diverse members of the group acting in concert. With regard to the sacred text of the Bible, the translator is called to be faithful to the text. Yet as the Word of God, the message is communicated by God's speaking it and the members of the community hearing it. The letters on the page participate in this communicative act and facilitate it as a fixed point within the process of communication. The translation of God's Word via human words is more than a mechanical activity. Faithfulness to God's Word in a Roman Catholic liturgical assembly necessitates attention to its symbolic character where the triadic relation of biblical text (sign), Word of God (object), and interpreter (interpretant) can be viewed as parallel to the triad of biblical text, liturgical tradition, and ecclesial authority.[1] The communicative act cannot occur without the right amount of standardisation. The constructiveness of the instruction *Liturgiam Authenticam* (*LA*) will be contingent on its capacity to promote the tria-lectical tension between biblical text, Latin liturgical tradition, and ecclesial interpreters. To assess the positive or negative influence of *LA* on translators for promoting this tria-lectical tension, the following three pressure points will

---

1. Cf Karl Rahner, 'The Theology of Symbol', in *More Recent Writings*, translated by Kevin Smyth; volume 4 of *Theological Investigations* (Baltimore: Helicon Press, 1966), 221–52, 224; Stephen Fields, SJ, *Being as Symbol: On the Origins and Development of Karl Rahner's Metaphysics* (Washington: Georgetown University Press, 2000), 2–4; Andrew Robinson, *God and the World of Signs: Trinity, Evolution, and the Metaphysical Semiotics of C. S. Pierce* (Leiden: Brill, 2010), 133–40.

be examined: (1) standardisation as an act for promoting unity-in-diversity rather than uniformity, (2) the necessity of standardising a pluriform biblical text for religious use, and (3) standardising a biblical text for liturgical use versus standardising it for study.

Unity-in-Diversity Versus Uniformity: A Necessary Debate in Standardising Lectionary Texts

On 28 March 2001, the prefect of the Congregation for Divine Worship and the Discipline of the Sacraments, Jorge A Cardinal Medina Estévez, published the Instruction '*Liturgiam Authenticam*: On the Use of Vernacular Languages in the Publication of the Books of the Roman Liturgy' (*LA*). The goal of this Instruction is 'the right implementation of the Constitution of the Sacred Liturgy of the Second Vatican Council' (*Sancrosantum Concilium*, 36).[2] The instruction articulates 'general principles applicable to all translation' in paragraphs 19–33 and 'other norms pertaining to the translation of the Sacred Scriptures and the Preparation of Lectionaries' in paragraphs 34–44. On 13 August 2001, the executive board of the Catholic Biblical Association of America mailed a letter to the US Conference of Catholic Bishops expressing its serious concerns about 'the massive authority' given to the *Nova Vulgata* in paragraphs 24, 33, 37, 41a, and 43.[3] Cardinal Estévez responded in a letter on 5 November 2001.[4] This exchange between the hierarchy and biblical theologians illustrates a form of the 'tria-lectic' expressed by Irenaeus in the late second century in which Scripture, tradition, and episcopacy must be mutually engaged in order to discern the Word of God for the worshiping community.[5] The debate over the authority attributed to

---

2. *Liturgiam Authenticam: Fifth Instruction on Vernacular Translation of the Roman Liturgy* (Latin-English Edition) issued by the Congregation of Divine Worship and Sacraments (Washington, DC: United States Conference of Catholic Bishops, 2001), 47. Also published at <http://www.vatican.va/roman_curia/congregations/ccdds/documents/rc_con_ccdds_doc_20010507_liturgiam-authenticam_en.html>. Accessed 25 March 2013.
3. <http://www.bible-researcher.com/liturgiam-authenticam2.html>. Accessed 25 March 2013.
4. 'Litterae Congregationis', *Notitiae* 37(2001): 521–26.
5. On the term 'tria-lectic' as three perspectives of 'the perceived', 'the conceived', and 'the lived' that shape the worlds that we each create, see Christl Maier (*Daughter Zion, Mother Zion: Gender, Space, and the Sacred in Ancient Israel*

the *Nova Vulgata* by *LA* centers on how to standardise the biblical text within the liturgical life of the Latin rite.

The tria-lectical logic necessary for constructive standardisation of communal texts can be illustrated by a local example on pronouncing biblical names in lectionary readings. Because lectors often improvise in pronouncing Hebrew names in the Old Testament readings, publishers have created guides for the pronunciation of these Hebrew names according to English usage. In these published guides, authority is given to the compiler who has selected the English usage that seems to have predominated over the past two centuries in English-speaking lands.[6] Data can apparently be supplied to indicate that the proposed pronunciation has been in practice in many communities for many generations; nevertheless, the attempt to universalise this usage among English-speakers raises the question of how well this pronunciation reflects the Hebrew character of the names. The lector who uses the pronunciation guide to pronounce a relatively simple name like 'Ramah' will give voice to a name that will sound peculiar to a Semitic-speaker of the Middle East. Scholars trained in the Masoretic pronunciation of Hebrew will often find the English pronunciation standardised by the pronunciation guides to be 'falsely correct' or ungrounded in the Masoretic Hebrew text. Nevertheless, liturgists who promote the use of pronunciation guides have an important objective of increasing the listening comprehension and retention of the words of the text by the congregation. Should the standardisation of pronunciation of names come from a guide that may or may not be grounded in the biblical text? How much uniformity in pronunciation is required? Perhaps each local community could develop a consistent way of pronouncing the Hebrew names that would effectively communicate the texts. In terms of the English-speaking world of worshipers, there would then be a diversity of ways of pronouncing the same Hebrew names. The

---

[Minneapolis: Fortress, 2008], 12) who quotes Henri Lefebvre (*The Production of Space*, translated by D Nicholson-Smith [Malden, Mass: Blackwell, 1991], 170). On the 'corpus triforme' in Irenaeus' theology, see Kevin Mongrain, *The Systematic Thought of Hans Urs von Balthasar: An Irenaean Retrieval* (New York: Crossroad, 2002), 38–9.

6. William O Walker, Jr, 'Preface', in *The Harper Collins Bible Pronunciation Guide*, edited by William O Walker, Jr, Toni Craven, J Andrew Dearman (San Francisco: HarperSanFrancisco, 1989), ix–xi, x.

issue in standardisation is how to strike a balance between uniformity and diversity so as to produce a constructive unity-in-diversity. The dynamic producing proper pronunciation can be framed as follows: the Hebrew names (biblical text), the pattern of pronunciation in the community (tradition), and the published pronunciation guide (juridical authority) interact to form a 'tria-lectic' aiming to embody the Word of God in the worship of the community.

Standardising a Pluriform Biblical Text for Religious Use

LA's designation of the *Nova Vulgata* as normative for Roman Catholic Liturgy has seemed to many biblical scholars to promote uniformity at the expense of diversity in our current knowledge of the original biblical texts. Biblical scholars find the 'massive authority' given to the *Nova Vulgata* by *LA* to be in contradiction to the mandate of *Divino Afflante Spiritu* 17–22 and *DV* 22 to prepare translations based on the Hebrew, Aramaic, and Greek originals.[7] *LA* 37 states:

> If the biblical translation from which the Lectionary is composed exhibits readings that differ from those set forth in the Latin liturgical text, it should be borne in mind that the *Nova Vulgata Editio* is the point of reference as regards the delineation of the canonical text. Thus, in the translation of the deuterocanonical books and wherever else there may exist varying manuscript traditions, the liturgical translation must be prepared in accordance with the same manuscript tradition that the *Nova Vulgata* has followed.

How is the canonical text in particular passages of biblical books determined? Is it subject to the findings of text critics who make convincing arguments for the 'best text'? Or is the canonical text identified by the ecclesiastical authority? *LA* states that in those cases where the original texts do not provide an uncontested version, then the *Nova Vulgata* should be used to settle upon a text for liturgical use. Critics contend that such standardisation will result in an

---

7. Richard Clifford, SJ, 'The Authority of the *Nova Vulgata*: A Note on a recent Roman Document', in *Catholic Biblical Quarterly*, 63 (2001): 197–202, 199–201.

inferior text becoming the formator of the community. Do all text critics agree on the inadvisability of appealing to a text named by an ecclesiastical authority?

Emanuel Tov notes that, in contrast to scholarly communities, religious communities are justified in selecting a particular text-tradition as normative.[8] Tov makes this comment in the context of an article in which he has come to the conclusion that the Masoretic Text (MT) is no longer the central text for the study of the Hebrew Bible. The more he works with the Qumran biblical manuscripts and the Greek Septuagint, he sees that these texts often derive from a Hebrew text-type that is earlier than that of the MT. But the MT seems to draw the support of scholars because of its religious association.[9] He notes that the MT has been carefully preserved since the first century CE: medieval manuscripts preserve the proto-rabbinic texts and then Jacob ben Hayyim edited the *Second Biblia Rabbinica* in Venice in 1524–25 which became the *textus receptus* of the MT from that point on.[10] Tov notes that he finds himself agreeing more frequently with those scholars who 'claim that the Septuagint more often than the MT reflects the original text of the Hebrew bible'.[11] He has come to accept the assessment of Eugene Ulrich that there is no unified text-tradition before the turn of the era.[12] The more text-critics search for the earlier text, the more they find a diversity of text-witnesses rather than a single text from which other texts have diverged. The task of the text-critic has shifted from trying to find the Ur-text to that of mapping out the terrain which the diverse text-witnesses occupy so as to understand their interrelationships. The product then that text-critics should aim to produce will not be an eclectic text in which

---

8. Emanuel Tov, 'The Status of the Masoretic Text in Modern Text Editions of the Hebrew Bible: The Relevance of Canon', in *The Canon Debate*, edited by Lee Martin McDonald and James A Sanders (Peabody, Mass: Hendrickson, 2002), 234–51, 242, 250.
9. Tov, 'The Status of the Masoretic Text in Modern Text Editions of the Hebrew Bible', 234.
10. Tov, 'The Status of the Masoretic Text in Modern Text Editions of the Hebrew Bible', 235.
11. Tov, 'The Status of the Masoretic Text in Modern Text Editions of the Hebrew Bible', 238.
12. Tov, 'The Status of the Masoretic Text in Modern Text Editions of the Hebrew Bible', 249; Eugene Ulrich, *The Dead Sea Scrolls and the Origin of the Bible* (Grand Rapids, MI: Eerdmans, 1999), 114–15.

the best reading from the best manuscripts is placed in the main text and the variants are referenced in the footnotes. Instead, Tov recommends that an edition be prepared with parallel texts, much like Origen's *Hexapla*.[13] The advantage of such a parallel arrangement is that it would give equal voice to each text-tradition and encourage the development of a commentary on each text-tradition insofar as this would be possible. Such an approach promotes a responsible scholarly approach to a pluriform text-tradition but is hardly serviceable to a religious community that requires a biblical text for its lectionary. For this religious purpose, Tov endorses the MT as a text-tradition that has maintained its unity via many text-witnesses from the third century BCE to the Middle Ages rather than being passed on through 'a uniform textual unit'.[14] He claims that the Roman Catholic community turned from the Vulgate as its normative text to the MT with the directives in *Divino Afflante Spiritu* and *DV* to develop translations based on the original texts.

Cardinal Estévez notes in his response to the letter from the executive board of the Catholic Biblical Association that *LA* 24 makes explicit that the translations of texts for the liturgy must be made from original texts.[15] He goes on to state:

> The Instruction in fact provides a clearer statement on the use of the original biblical texts as the basis for liturgical translation than the norms previously published in the *Instruction Inter Oecumenici*, n. 40a, published on September 26, 1964 (*Acta Apostolicae Sedis* 56 [1964]: 885).[16]

He points out that *LA* identifies the *Nova Vulgata* as 'an auxiliary tool' used 'to maintain the tradition of interpretation that is proper to the Latin liturgy'.[17] *If the original text is seen to be pluriform,* then the directive of *Divino Afflante Spiritu* and *DV* to search for the original

---

13. Tov, 'The Status of the Masoretic Text in Modern Text Editions of the Hebrew Bible', 249–50.
14. Tov, 'The Status of the Masoretic Text in Modern Text Editions of the Hebrew Bible', 241.
15. 'Litterae Congregationis', in *Notitiae,* 37 (2001): 522.
16. 'Litterae Congregationis', 522.
17. 'Litterae Congregationis', 522.

text would present the translator with the dilemma as to which original should be selected. *LA* 24 directs that the translator should turn to the *Nova Vulgata*. If so, the Vulgate rather than the MT is the normative text for the Catholic community.

Catholic biblical scholars have protested that the *Nova Vulgata* is not Jerome's Vulgate nor the Clementine Vulgate. Instead, it is a text that originated from a directive from Pope Pius X to the monks of San Girolamo in Rome to revise Jerome's Vulgate in light of the Hebrew, Aramaic, and Greek originals.[18] Pope Paul VI, prior to the directive to prepare vernacular translations of liturgical texts, requested that a revised Latin translation be prepared for liturgical use.[19] This revised Latin text is the *Nova Vulgata*. As published in 1979,[20] it has no critical apparatus to indicate the judgments of the text critics on the best reading and to leave open the possibility of recommending alternative readings. Instead, the text as it stands gives the impression that it 'is set in concrete as of 1979'.[21] However, Cardinal Estévez emphasises that

> the Church has never claimed unalterable perfection for her own officially approved Latin edition of the Scriptures, and has sought to improve versions several times. It is not to be excluded, and indeed, it is to be expected, that such work continue in the future.[22]

He then invites biblical scholars to recommend improvements to the *Nova Vulgata* but counsels 'that their criteria for the "best" text or even the most "original" text may not in every instance coincide with the Church's criteria for the canonical text'.[23] This process implemented

---

18. Clifford, 'The Authority of the *Nova Vulgata*', 198–99; Tarcisio Stramara, 'Die Neo-*Vulgata*; Zur Gestaltung des Textes', in BZ 25 (1981): 67–81, 72.
19. Joseph Jensen, 'Liturgiam Authenticam and the New Vulgate', *America*, 13 August 2001. <http://americamagazine.org/issue/324/article/liturgiam-authenticam-and-new-vulgate>. Accessed 1 March 2013.
20. *Nova Vulgata: Bibliorum Sacrorum, Editio* (Rome: Libreria Editrice Vaticana, 1979). <http://www.vatican.va/archive/bible/nova_vulgata/documents/nova-vulgata_index_lt.html>. Accessed March 25 March 2013.
21. Jensen, 'Liturgiam Authenticam and the New Vulgate', in *America*, 13 August 2001.
22. 'Litterae Congregationis', in *Notitiae*, 37 (2001): 524–25.
23. 'Litterae Congregationis', 525.

by *LA* conforms to the scenario sketched out by Tov in which the early text tradition is pluriform and the religious tradition is justified in selecting the text that best fits its history and values.

An example of an emerging awareness of a pluriform text-tradition involves a text integral to the readings of Easter vigil: Ezekiel 36:16–17a, 18–28. A major part of this text is from a passage (Ezek 36:23c–38) that is missing from an early Greek manuscript P967. The striking theological message of this passage summarises key themes of the book of Ezekiel; therefore, the claim that this passage is secondary to the original book of Ezekiel has predictably generated much resistance from scholars who do not want to see this passage reduced in authority. Nevertheless, a series of articles by Johan Lust and a monograph by Ashley Crane have tipped the scales toward seeing the Hebrew *Vorlage* of P967 as earlier than the proto-MT.[24] Crane contends that earlier does not mean better and urges that the texts of each of these traditions be compared with equal attention given to each tradition.[25]

In light of *LA* 24, a translator of this text for the Roman Catholic lectionary would be assisted by the *Nova Vulgata*, which includes Ezekiel 36:23c–38. If further text critical work were to establish that Ezekiel 36:23c–38 was added to the Book of Ezekiel in the second century BCE by an editor in Hasmonean times who was trying to counter the apocalyptic flavor of the invasion of Gog (Ezek 38–39) followed by the rising to new life of the dry bones (Ezek 37:1–14),[26] then a text critical argument might be made for removing it from the *Nova Vulgata*. As unthinkable as this might seem to a Roman Catholic accustomed to the liturgy of the Easter Vigil, the argument would be based on the principle that the earliest text is the best text. But Crane, Lust, and Tov are in agreement that the earliest text should not merely replace the other text but rather each should stand over

---

24. Ashley S Crane, *Israel's Restoration: A Textual-Comparative Study of Ezekiel 36–39* (VTSup 122; Leiden/Boston: Brill, 2008), 207; Johan Lust, 'Ezekiel 36–40 in the Oldest Greek Manuscript', in *Catholic Biblical Quarterly*, 43 (1981): 517–31; idem, 'Textual Criticism of the Old Testament and of the New Testament: Stepbrothers?', in *New Testament Criticism and Exegesis: Major Omissions in P967 Ezekiel*, edited by Adelbert Denaux (BETL 161; Leuven: University Press/Peeters, 2002), 15–31, 24–25, 28–29.
25. Crane, *Israel's Restoration*, 220.
26. Lust, 'Ezekiel 36–40 in the Oldest Greek Manuscript', 531–32.

against the other and receive equal attention as a voice prior to the standardisation of the text in the first century BCE.[27] The recovery of the voice of P967 illustrates how the process of standardisation of the consonantal text in proto-MT circles in the second century BCE to the first century CE silenced an alternative viewpoint within the Judean communities of the early first millennium CE.[28] This fuller picture of the history of the transmission of the book of Ezekiel to the first century BCE will have a significant impact on the interpretation of Ezekiel 36–39. However, the version of Ezekiel 36 – 39 preserved in the MT has a well-established position, one that influenced both the Septuagint and Jerome's Vulgate. The appeal to the *Nova Vulgata* would silence any questions about the canonical status of Ezek 36:23c–38 for Roman Catholics and would facilitate the translation of the text for liturgical purposes, but the debate concerning the transmission of the Book of Ezekiel would be valuable for understanding the complexity surrounding the process of standardising a biblical text. Such understanding would contribute to an appreciation of the mystery of God's Word in our midst—a dialogue that cannot be contained within a static text.[29]

Standardising a Biblical Text for Liturgical Use Versus Standardising it for Study

LA 29 emphasises the importance of the homily and catechesis for contextualising liturgical texts. The particular concern of this section of the Instruction is to locate the responsibility for ecumenical and interreligious sensitivity as well as attentiveness to 'the dignity and equality of all' on the homilist and catechist when language in the text might prove offensive to the hearers. The Instruction directs that such

---

27. Crane, *Israel's Restoration*, 240; Lust, 'Ezekiel 36–40 in the Oldest Greek Manuscript', 517–31; Tov, 'The Status of the Masoretic Text in Modern Text Editions of the Hebrew Bible', 249–50.
28. Adrian Schenker, 'Der Ursprung des massoretischen Textes im Licht der literarischen Varianten im Bibeltext', in *Anfänge der Textgeschichte des Alten Testaments: Studien zu Entstehung und Verhältnis der frühesten Textformen* (BWANT 194; Stuttgart: Kohlhammer, 2011), 33–43, 42.
29. *Post-Synodal Apostolic Exhortation of Pope Benedict XVI: Verbum Domini*, 18. <http://www.vatican.va/holy_father/benedict_xvi/apost_exhortations/documents/hf_ben-xvi_exh_20100930_verbum-domini_en.html>. Accessed 25 March 2013.

concerns 'are not to be considered reasons for altering either a biblical text or a liturgical text that has been duly promulgated'. This directive increases the seriousness of homiletical and catechetical efforts to communicate the Word of God. *LA* 28 emphasises the importance of 'full and conscious participation in the liturgical celebration'. In those cases in which the linguistic expressions of the traditional biblical or liturgical translation do not communicate well with a particular audience, then much effort must be invested to explain why this traditional expression is maintained and what it means in the contemporary context. Critics will note that this philosophy of translation (*viz* formal correspondence) does not respect the structure and dynamics of the target language. An alternative philosophy of translation (*viz*, dynamic equivalence) prioritises the communication of the message of the source text in the idiom of the target language.[30] Proponents of the translation philosophy of dynamic equivalence argue that the text's potential to communicate is compromised if the translator does not recognise that each culture has distinctive forms that cannot be mechanically transferred by a word-for-word rendering of texts.[31]

LA 26–28 emphasises that biblical and liturgical texts communicate faith and morality on both conscious and unconscious levels. Translations are expected to communicate the linguistic form and meaning of the approved source text as closely as possible into the target language because the liturgical texts have the power not only to instill their truth in the hearer but also to shape the everyday language of the hearer. The rationale for keeping the expression of the target text as close as possible to the source text is that a larger measure of uniformity in the translation of the original text to the various vernacular languages will create stability and facilitate the memorization of biblical texts (no. 36). When these emphases upon staying close to the form and expression of the source language are paired with the expectation that the target text be 'easily understandable' (no. 25), the tension between the particular and the universal, the local and the global challenges the translator.

---

30. Eugene A Nida and Charles R Taber, *The Theory and Practice of Translation* (Leiden: Brill, 1969), 1–2.
31. Umberto Eco, *Experiences in Translation* (Toronto: University of Toronto Press, 2001), 8–9.

The tug-of-war between the preservation of the source-text and the communicability of the target-text call for a constructive balance. Otherwise, the process of standardisation will allow uniformity to stifle a necessary diversity in expression. *LA* 27 recognises that some 'expressions should be avoided which hinder comprehension because of their excessively unusual or awkward nature'. Nevertheless, it goes on to mystify the phenomenon of foreign-like expressions by referring to them 'as the voice of the Church at prayer, rather than of only particular congregations or individuals'.

The Latin liturgical tradition, which the formal correspondence philosophy of translation and the normative status of the *Nova Vulgata* are called upon to maintain, is one that shows development and diversity throughout its history.[32] Trent declared the Vulgate to be authentic insofar as it had served as the basis for the teaching authority of the Church for centuries.[33] If the Church Fathers could be shown to be unanimous on a particular doctrine contrary to a position held by the Vulgate, then their position would be followed. However, as Crehan notes,[34] the Fathers were rarely unanimous on interpretations of particular issues.

Trent did not address the question of whether or not the Vulgate was in need of revision. But under Pope Sixtus V in 1587, a new edition of the Septuagint was produced based on *Vaticanus*, which became the standard edition for more than three centuries. With this accomplishment Pope Sixtus moved to have the Vulgate revised. The process was completed by 1588, but Sixtus was not satisfied. He had incorporated readings familiar to the faithful but lacking in manuscript evidence. With the death of Sixtus in 1590, the new Pope Gregory XIV appointed a commission of theologians and cardinals to

---

32. Peter Jeffery (*Translation Tradition: A Chant Historian Reads Liturgiam Authenticam* [Collegeville: Liturgical Press, 2005], 39) notes 'that the traditional Roman liturgy resembles the canonical Scriptures in its capacity to hold competing models in creative tension . . . *LA*'s monochromatic invocations of Roman tradition seems completely unaware of this'.
33. Francis J Crehan, SJ, 'The Bible in the Roman Catholic Church from Trent to the Present Day', in *The Cambridge History of the Bible: The West from the Reformation to the Present Day* (Cambridge: Cambridge University Press, 1963), 199–237, 204.
34. Crehan, 'The Bible in the Roman Catholic Church from Trent to the Present Day', 204.

revise Sixtus's Vulgate. It was in 1592 under Pope Clement VIII that a new version of the Vulgate was issued. There were 4900 differences between the Vulgates of Clement and Sixtus.[35] The Clementine Vulgate was the normative Latin text of the Bible until 1962. But as Peter Jeffery notes: 'Clement's model was one of uniformity from above'.[36] While he promulgated his new edition of the Vulgate in 1592, he simultaneously restored non-Vulgate chant texts and traditional biblical passages to the Roman Missal as they had appeared in Sixtus's edition in 1570. There is a unity-in-diversity in the Latin liturgical tradition that is paradoxical in view of the claim that the Clementine Vulgate was the normative text.[37]

In the preface to the fourth edition of the Stuttgart Vulgate published by the Deutsche Bibelgesellschaft in 1994, Roger Gryson notes that the Clementine edition

> frequently deviates from the manuscript tradition, for literary or doctrinal reasons, and offers only a faint reflection of the original Vulgate, as read in the *pandecta* of the first millennium . . . The Clementine text is often supported only by the Paris University recension of the 13th century, which is already a simplifying text, far removed from the most ancient witnesses.[38]

Gryson goes on to note that the Stuttgart Vulgate aims to recover the original text and not be compromised by the need to produce a 'theologically authorised' text.

The presentation of the Psalms in the Stuttgart Vulgate parallels the Hebrew Psalter of Jerome with Jerome's earlier OL Psalter, known also as the *Gallican Psalter* because of its common use in Gaul in Alcuin's time. Jerome's Hebrew Psalter was in place in the Vulgate until the

---

35. Crehan, SJ, 'The Bible in the Roman Catholic Church from Trent to the Present Day', 205-11; Ernst Würthwein, *The Text of the Old Testament*, fourth edition; translated by Errol F Rhodes (Grand Rapids: Eerdmans, 1979), 94.
36. Jeffery, *Translation Tradition*, 51.
37. Jeffery, *Translation Tradition*, 50. Also to be noted is that the *Vetus Latina* continued to circulate and was never completely supplanted by the Vulgate.
38. Roger Gryson, 'Preface to the Fourth Edition', in *Biblia Sacra: Iuxta Vulgatam Versionem*, fourth edition (Stuttgart: Deutsche Bibelgesellschaft, 1994), xxxiv–xxxvi, xxxiv.

time of Alcuin and remained so in many Spanish Bibles thereafter.[39] But Alcuin's influence was so strong that the Gallican Psalter replaced the Hebrew Psalter in the Vulgate. The editors recognise the privileged place of the Gallican Psalter in the history of the Vulgate, but in their effort to provide a text that gives access to the original text of the Vulgate, they juxtaposed both versions.[40] Such a parallel presentation echoes the call of Tov for a similar presentation of competing text witnesses of the Hebrew Bible prior to its standardisation in the first century CE.

Cardinal Estévez has noted that *LA* does not view the *Nova Vulgata* as a perfect version that cannot be revised. Such revisions can arise not only from newly recovered Latin manuscripts but also from Hebrew, Aramaic, and Greek originals. The potential for parallel texts to open new insights in the understanding of the biblical texts indicates that teachers, homilists, and catechists will communicate the findings of biblical scholarship to the faithful in ways not open to translators of lectionary texts. These pastoral leaders will be faced with negotiating the tension between text, tradition, and ecclesiastical authority so that the liturgical and biblical texts speak to their contemporary audiences.

The standardisation of the biblical text for liturgical use can potentially direct interpreters to see the biblical text as a symbolic reality that unfolds through the generations. If the symbolic character of the biblical text calls for a corresponding symbolic interpretation of the text, then one might characterise this symbolic method as 'tria-lectic'. The deeper meaning of the text characterised by patristic and medieval exegesis as the allegorical, tropological, and anagogical senses are levels of meaning that can be evoked by ancient texts whose obvious meaning does not resonate with a contemporary audience. But if the interpreter stays with the obscure biblical text, the interpreter may see that his or her perceived experience may

---

39. Jeffery (*Translation Tradition*, 49) notes that many medieval manuscripts have triple Psalters: they parallel the Roman Psalter, the Gallican/Vulgate Psalter, and Jerome's *juxta Hebraeos*. Some manuscripts also have more columns *with* other versions of the Psalter, including Milanese, North African, and Hispanic text types.
40. 'Preface to the First Edition (1969)', in *Biblia Sacra: Iuxta Vulgatam Versionem*, edited by B Fischer and others, fourth edition (Stuttgart: Deutsche Bibelgesellschaft, 1994), xxix–xxxiii, xxx.

interact with the experience conceived in the text in order to create a new lived experience. This kind of creative engagement with the ancient text would not occur if the literal meaning of the text was not first addressed. It is the tension between the literal meaning of the text and one's own world that triggers the search for a deeper meaning that the valued text is believed to convey. The stability effected by standardisation of biblical texts for liturgical use bears fruit by bringing to light the potential of the biblical text to address the diversity of experience of its many audiences.

Conclusion

How standardisation of the biblical text for use in the liturgy is implemented will have a serious impact on full and conscious participation in the liturgy. The symbolic character of the biblical text requires the engagement of the interpreter if the text is to mediate the presence of God. Standardisation can assist in negotiating a pluriform biblical text, but it may also prematurely exclude the fruits of text-critical scholarship from the lectionary. Cardinal Estévez insists that *LA* puts more emphasis rather than less on using the original texts for biblical translations that will be included in the lectionary. The preference of *LA* for the translation philosophy of Jerome (formal correspondence) supports the priority of the sacred text over the adaptation of the text to contemporary culture. The key to the constructiveness of *LA*'s directives requires that theologians, translators, and bishops keep alive the tria-lectical tension between the sacred text, the liturgical tradition, and ecclesial authority. Stability of the text and socialisation into the world of the text can emerge in a more authentic way from this tria-lectical tension.

11

Dei Verbum, Communication and Media

Peter Malone MSC

Dei Verbum (*DV*), with its focus on the word, is a document about communication. While the title speaks of God's communication and implies our listening, it leads to understanding the human response to God's word as well as the realisation that it is a human mission to communicate that word. The first communication is speaking the word, speaking it out. Then comes the writing down of the word for people to 'hear' it by reading. But, we are in a different era in the twenty-first century with so many ways of communicating God's word, so many ways of 'hearing' it. As we were reminded by Tim Rice, in *Jesus Christ Superstar*, 'in 4 BC there was no mass communication'.

So, how do we read and respond to *DV* in a time of mass communication and of social, as well as traditional, media?

Before moving to answer this question, it is useful to compare the state of communication in 1965, when the Council voted on the Constitution, and the present day, almost half a century later. What a difference a day makes! What of fifty years?

The language of communication in the early 1960s, and, therefore, in the minds of the writers of the document, concerned individual communication and interpersonal communication. It was an era of theorising about communication and its reception, the nature of the message and the pre-dispositions of the receptor. One of the issues in these theories as it applied to the Scriptures, which the document took up, was awareness of the hearers of the word, the receptors of the word of God. There was concern about the ways in which this word was incarnated in its times, in the language of the times and in the 'literary forms' of the times. Receptors tend to be literal in their listening to the word—which still remains a challenge in biblical communities and churches which we call fundamentalist. That led on to studies in the post-conciliar church of a more communitarian response to the word. Much of the literature that followed Vatican II was geared to help faithful listeners immerse themselves more deeply in the world of Israel, in the world of Jesus and of the early Church. Listening was not merely listening but interpreting and responding accordingly, interpreting with more knowledge and depth the literature of salvation history.

But, in the early 1960s, at the time of the Second Vatican Council, a Canadian theorist (Catholic also) came up with the slogan that has been a powerful influence on communication theory. 'The medium is the message': the slogan of Marshall McLuhan. Yes, the dynamic word of God, proclaimed, was medium and message.

1965 Mass Media

Looking at 1965, where were we in terms of the medium, of the media? In terms of what was being called the 'Mass Media'?

There was the traditional (at least from the fifteenth and sixteenth centuries) print media, newspapers and magazines. The world took them for granted in 1965, so did the Council members—as they read instantly the newspaper reports of debates, of behind the scenes deals and manoeuvres. Insider insight books were quick to follow and read with avid curiosity (both for and against Council activities).

Public screenings of cinema began in 1895. Amongst the earliest of the short films were many biblical stories, many Gospel stories, which were prominent in feature length films within twenty years, *From the Manger to the Cross* (1913), *Christus*, from Italy (1916), DW Griffith's *Intolerance* (1916). They were followed by Cecil B de Mille and *The Ten Commandments* (1923) and *The King of Kings* (1927). Biblical epics began to appear again in the late 1940s, early 1950s: *Samson and Delilah* (1949), *David and Bathsheba* (1951), *Quo Vadis* (1951) and *The Robe* (1953). Six years before the opening of Vatican II, world audiences responded to de Mille's spectacular re-make of *The Ten Commandments* (1956). The first commercial Jesus film since de Mille was *King of Kings* (1961). During the Council, Pasolini's *Vangelo Secondo Matteo/The Gospel According to St Matthew* (1964) was released. Images and stories about the word of God were popular.

Television had been available for almost thirty years, but was not yet common in most countries. Australia, for instance, did not have television until January 1957. Some Pacific nations, like Fiji, were not to have television until the early 1990s. In 1965, most television was in black and white, colour becoming more widespread in the 1970s. And video cassettes did not become available until the early 1980s, and CDs and DVDs, much, much later. Men and women now in their forties, let alone under, might find this media-limited world hard to imagine.

It was radio that was the medium available to most people—and yet, radio broadcast began only in the 1920s. Vatican Radio was established merely thirty one years before the opening of Vatican II. But, it was the transistor radio at that time which offered opportunity for hearing news and information more instantly. Scarcely had the Mass in St Peter's Square for the dying John XXIII finished and the blind or curtain drawn in the papal apartment, than transistor listeners heard that the pope had died only minutes earlier.

In 1965, print media was dominant, with radio fast moving up on it. Television as well. No personal computers in view and the worldwide web decades away. But, there were always the biblical stories at the movies.

Which means that the proclamation of the word of God through the media was very limited. Newspapers had religious columns. Magazines could have feature articles. There were many theological periodicals for specialists. Radio had moved with the times in the 1920s and 1930s with some religious features, the broadcasting of ceremonies and didactic programs along the *Radio Replies* genre or *The Catholic Hour*. Some regulations would be introduced in many countries in the 1970s, requiring an allotment of time, again broadcast of ceremonies and Sunday Magazine shows.

Inter Mirifica (IM)

How had the Church responded to the Mass Media signs of the times?

In fact, though some find it hard to remember because of the more dramatic discussions on the *Constitution on the Liturgy*, the *Constitution on the Church*, on the *Constitution on the Church in the Modern World*, that the first topic of discussion in the Council in

October 1962 was on the means of social communication. It produced the comparatively brief document, *IM,* promulgated in 1963. This document should have been seen as the Church attempting to come to terms with the changing world, the world of media, the first response to John XXIII's talk about opening the windows. It was not without precedent as both Pius XI (*Vigilanti Cura* in 1936) and Pius XII (*Miranda Prorsus* in 1957) had both written media encyclicals on media, specifically cinema.

Whether the bishops and their advisers at Vatican II really appreciated the role of Mass Media makes for an interesting discussion. Despite the prolific developments over the decades, it is still true enough to generalise that so many bishops and their advisers do not appreciate, really underestimate and sometimes dismiss (in troubled and troublesome times) the media as the enemy.

But, here was the media in the 1960s, and media and the proclamation of the word of God, in *IM*:

> The most important of these inventions are those media which, such as the press, movies, radio, television and the like, can, of their very nature, reach and influence, not only individuals, but the very masses and the whole of human society, and thus can rightly be called the media of social communication (*IM 1*).
>
> The Church recognises that these media, if properly utilised, can be of great service to mankind, since they greatly contribute to men's entertainment and instruction as well as to the spread and support of the Kingdom of God (*IM 2*).
>
> The Catholic Church, since it was founded by Christ our Lord to bear salvation to all men and thus is obliged to preach the Gospel, considers it one of its duties to announce the Good News of salvation also with the help of the media of social communication and to instruct men in their proper use (*IM 3*).
>
> All the children of the Church should join, without delay and with the greatest effort in a common work to make effective use of the media of social communication in various apostolic endeavors, as circumstances and conditions demand (*IM 13*).

Communio et Progressio (CP)

In 1971, the Pontifical Council for Social Communications, which replaced the Pontifical Commission, produced a lengthy pastoral document on all aspects of mass media and the church, theoretical and practical. It also touched on the media and spreading the word of God:

The heading of Part 2 was: The use of the media for giving the good news.

> Christ commanded the Apostles and their successors to 'teach all nations', to be 'the light of the world' and to announce the Good News in all places at all times. During His life on earth, Christ showed himself to be the perfect Communicator, while the Apostles used what means of social communication were available in their time. It is now necessary that the same message be carried by the means of social communication that are available today. Indeed it would be difficult to suggest that Christ's command was being obeyed unless all the opportunities offered by the modern media to extend to vast numbers of people the announcement of his Good News were being used. Therefore the Second Vatican Council invited the people of God 'to use effectively and at once the means of social communication, zealously availing themselves of them for apostolic purposes'.
>
> In order to make the teaching of Christianity more interesting and effective the media should be used as much as possible. Every effort should be made to use the most appropriate technique and style in fitting a communication to its medium (*CP 131*).

And, as early as 1971, there was the wish, sometimes, often, reduced to a velleity:

> In view of the mounting importance of the means of social communication—to the life of mankind in general and of the Church in particular—the media should receive a great deal more emphasis than they

presently get in the overall plans for pastoral action made by episcopal conferences. These plans should make the necessary funds available for use in the areas under their jurisdiction. Funds should also be made available for international cooperation (*CP* 134).

Since 1971, with the establishment of World Communications Day, Papal statements from the Pontifical Council for Social Communications have offered four decades of reflection on the spiritual and pastoral dimensions of the media, an annual opportunity to recognise the signs of the times as well as to move with the times (recent statements, of course, focusing on social media).

Communication in *DV*

What are the emphases on communication of the word in *DV* itself?

Already in the introductory paragraph, the impact of the word for all people: 'by hearing the message of salvation the whole world may believe, by believing it may hope, and by hoping it may love' (*DV* 1). Then comes the important reminder that Jesus is not just the Word of God (John 1). Reading and preaching focused culture, the culture of authorities, has emphasised, even over-emphasised the word aspect. The opening of the Letter to the Hebrews (1:3) reminds us that God's revelation had been given in many and varied ways but, in Jesus, we have the radiant light of God's glory, the perfect copy of God's nature. Pauline tradition, Colossians 1:15, also highlights Jesus as the Image of God (which a more media-conscious culture welcomes). Word and image are the means for the Son (at the Father's side/nearest to God's heart, John 1:18)s, to communicate both grace and truth (*DV* 2).

Decades ago, Tony Kelly CSsR, reflected on image and word, combining them in communication by story. He pointed out that when the second person of the Trinity became incarnate, it was not in doctrine or dogma but in story, a human story, from birth to death (or one might say, from conception to resurrection).[1]

The opening to the *Letter to the Hebrews* reminds us that word is not the sole way of revelation, that Jesus, in the final times, communicated in his words and deeds (*DV* 4). 'And so the apostolic

---

1. See *Compass Theology Review*, 1974/2.

preaching, which is expressed in a special way in the inspired books, was to be preserved by an unending succession of preachers until the end of time.' This unending succession of preachers chooses all kinds of ways/media for communicating (*DV* 8). The following paragraph describes the formation of Tradition, linking it with communication of the word (*DV* 9).

In speaking about the inspiration of the scriptural writings, the document highlights the differing abilities (ways of communicating) of the different authors. While preachers throughout the centuries are not inspired in this biblical way, they are, by analogy, faith-responsive in their different media modes.

> In composing the sacred books, God chose men and while employed by Him they made use of their powers and abilities, so that with Him acting in them and through them, they, as true authors, consigned to writing everything and only those things which He wanted (*DV* 11).

When *DV* considers the importance of literary forms in the texts, it offers reasons why the many preachers need to find the language of their times to communicate the word:

> For the correct understanding of what the sacred author wanted to assert, due attention must be paid to the customary and characteristic styles of feeling, speaking and narrating which prevailed at the time of the sacred writer, and to the patterns men normally employed at that period in their everyday dealings with one another (*DV* 12).

Later, when speaking of the impact of the books, the document introduces a phrase which should apply as strongly to the different media communication, 'a lively sense of God' (*DV* 15).

Further exhortation is also relevant to preaching:

> The sacred authors wrote the four Gospels, selecting some things from the many which had been handed on by word of mouth or in writing, reducing some of them

> to a synthesis, explaining some things in view of the situation of their churches and preserving the form of proclamation but always in such fashion that they told us the honest truth about Jesus (*DV* 19).

And then to the ministry of the word: By the same word of Scripture the ministry of the word also, that is, pastoral preaching, catechetics and all Christian instruction, in which the liturgical homily must hold the foremost place, is nourished in a healthy way and flourishes in a holy way (*DV* 24). The faith commitment of the preacher ensures an authenticity in mediating the word of God, so that none of them will become 'an empty preacher of the word of God outwardly, who is not a listener to it inwardly' (*DV* 25).

That was how the writers of the document thought of communicating the word of God in 1965.

Evangelii Nuntiandi

The major continuations of the document and proclamation of the word were in the 1974 Synod on Evangelisation and the subsequent publication of the encyclical by Paul VI, *Evangelium Nuntiandi (EN)*, 8 December, 1975, the tenth anniversary of the close of Vatican II.

> the duty of confirming the brethren—a duty which with the office of being the Successor of Peter we have received from the Lord, and which is for us a 'daily preoccupation', a program of life and action, and a fundamental commitment of our Pontificate - seems to us all the more noble and necessary when it is a matter of encouraging our brethren in their mission as evangelizers, in order that, in this time of uncertainty and confusion, they may accomplish this task with ever increasing love, zeal and joy (*EN* 1).

The main thrust of the encyclical is on the theological and practical reflection on what evangelisation means and what can be expected of evangelisers. There is a great deal of consideration of differing cultures in the contemporary world and, towards the end, of basic Christian communities and their faith and witness. Despite *CP*, 1975 was not yet a time when more could be elaborated on evangelisation and the mass media (which is acknowledged).

The second paragraph, however, sets the aim: '... the Second Vatican Council, the objectives of which are definitively summed up in this single one: to make the Church of the twentieth century ever better fitted for proclaiming the Gospel to the people of the twentieth century' (*EN* 2). And, quoting from Paul VI's address to the 1974 Synod:

> The conditions of the society in which we live oblige all of us therefore to revise methods, to seek by every means to study how we can bring the Christian message to modern man. For it is only in the Christian message that modern man can find the answer to his questions and the energy for his commitment of human solidarity (*EN* 3); at this turning-point of history, does the Church or does she not find herself better equipped to proclaim the Gospel and to put it into people's hearts with conviction, freedom of spirit and effectiveness? (*EN* 4).

And the pope adds: 'We wish to confirm once more that the task of evangelizing all people constitutes the essential mission of the Church' (*EN* 4). There is a salutary caution that evangelising means evangelising ourselves first, conversion.

Culture also becomes a focus: 'Nevertheless, the kingdom which the Gospel proclaims is lived by men who are profoundly linked to a culture, and the building up of the kingdom cannot avoid borrowing the elements of human culture or cultures' (*EN* 20).

> But evangelization would not be complete if it did not take account of the unceasing interplay of the Gospel and of man's concrete life, both personal and social. This is why evangelization involves an explicit message, adapted to the different situations constantly being realized, about the rights and duties of every human being, about family life without which personal growth and development is hardly possible, about life in society, about international life, peace, justice and development,

a message especially energetic today about liberation (*EN* 29).

While the encyclical acknowledges different means (mediating rather than media), they are not explored.

The obvious importance of the content of evangelissation must not overshadow the importance of the ways and means.

> This question of 'how to evangelize' is permanently relevant, because the methods of evangelizing vary according to the different circumstances of time, place and culture, and because they thereby present a certain challenge to our capacity for discovery and adaptation.
>
> On us particularly, the pastors of the Church, rests the responsibility for reshaping with boldness and wisdom, but in complete fidelity to the content of evangelization, the means that are most suitable and effective for communicating the Gospel message to the men and women of our times (*EN* 40).

Then, rather suddenly, a comment on talk fatigue in the civilisation of the image:

> Preaching, the verbal proclamation of a message, is indeed always indispensable. We are well aware that modern man is sated by talk; he is obviously often tired of listening and, what is worse, impervious to words. We are also aware that many psychologists and sociologists express the view that modern man has passed beyond the civilization of the word, which is now ineffective and useless, and that today he lives in the civilization of the image. These facts should certainly impel us to employ, for the purpose of transmitting the Gospel message, the modern means which this civilization has produced. Very positive efforts have in fact already been made in this sphere. We cannot but praise them and encourage their further development. The fatigue produced these days by so much empty talk and the relevance of many

> other forms of communication must not however diminish the permanent power of the word, or cause a loss of confidence in it. The word remains ever relevant, especially when it is the bearer of the power of God. This is why St. Paul's axiom, 'Faith comes from what is heard', also retains its relevance: it is the Word that is heard which leads to belief (*EN* 42).

And catechists:

> The methods must be adapted to the age, culture and aptitude of the persons concerned, they must seek always to fix in the memory, intelligence and heart the essential truths that must impregnate all of life (*EN* 44).

Finally, the paragraph that media personnel would value:

> Our century is characterized by the mass media or means of social communication, and the first proclamation, catechesis or the further deepening of faith cannot do without these means, as we have already emphasized.
>
> When they are put at the service of the Gospel, they are capable of increasing almost indefinitely the area in which the Word of God is heard; they enable the Good News to reach millions of people. The Church would feel guilty before the Lord if she did not utilize these powerful means that human skill is daily rendering more perfect. It is through them that she proclaims 'from the housetops' [72] the message of which she is the depositary. In them she finds a modern and effective version of the pulpit. Thanks to them she succeeds in speaking to the multitudes.
>
> Nevertheless the use of the means of social communication for evangelization presents a challenge: through them the evangelical message should reach vast numbers of people, but with the capacity of piercing the conscience of each individual, of implanting itself in his heart as though he were the only person being addressed, with all his most individual and personal

qualities, and evoke an entirely personal adherence and commitment (*EN* 45).

But the encyclical moves to person-to-person communication and faith communities and witness. Nevertheless, *EN* reinforces the media thrusts of Vatican II and the links to contemporary evangelisation.

Since 1975

How has this changed since 1975?

In the first part of this article, we reached the landmark document, *CP* (1971, which was the Pontifical Council for Social Communications expanding in detail on the ideas in *IM* and *Gaudium et Spes*. There were developments in *EN*, but hindsight makes us realise that it was in the 1980s and 1990s that the consciousness of the diversity of mass media took hold.

It was John Paul II, actor and expert at the use of media, who moved the Church on to media and media/message. He constantly used the phrase, 'Media, gifts of God' (a phrase that was used by Pius XII in his media encyclical, *Miranda Prorsus* (1958)). He was to link this to another favourite phrase about the media, 'Media, the New Areopagus'. Which, of course, takes us back to the *Acts of the Apostles*, chapter 17.

In Athens, Paul was not preaching to the converted. In fact, Acts 17 is not exactly a success story for evangelisation. The people in the market place listened but said that they would like to listen another day. Conversion was not immediate. Perhaps, merely postponed. However, it was Paul's approach that interested John Paul II. While it was communication by word, it was also pitched as an appeal to the listeners' experience and their culture. Paul quoted poets his audience was familiar with. More words. But he also appealed to the images around them, the statues of the gods and, that hedging of bets, 'to the unknown god'. He appealed to their religious sense for the credibility of his preaching. He set a model for use of all aspects of culture in the new evangelisation.

Pope John Paul wrote many encyclicals and in his over twenty six years as pope issued twenty six statements for World Communications Day. In 7 December 1990 in his encyclical, *Redemptoris Missio* (henceforth *RM*), he cited the Areopagus and its significance:

> After preaching in a number of places, St. Paul arrived in Athens, where he went to the Areopagus and proclaimed the Gospel in language appropriate to and understandable in those surroundings (cf Acts 17:22–31). At that time the Areopagus represented the cultural center of the learned people of Athens, and today it can be taken as a symbol of the new sectors in which the Gospel must be proclaimed (*RM* 37).

His last document before going into hospital in 21 February 2005, was *Il Rapido Sviluppo/On the Rapid Development . . . of technology in the area of media*, an Apostolic Letter to those responsible for Social Communications. We might see them as 'famous last words' as the new social media were about to envelop the world. Benedict XVI and Francis had and have Twitter accounts. Best to quote John Paul's words as the fortieth anniversary of the end of Vatican II was coming:

> The first Areopagus of modern times is the *world of communications*, which is capable of unifying humanity and transforming it into . . . 'a global village'. The communications media have acquired such importance as to be the principal means of guidance and inspiration for many people in their personal, familial, and social behavior. We are dealing with a complex problem, because the culture itself, prescinding from its content, arises from the very existence of new ways to communicate with hitherto unknown techniques and vocabulary.

Medium and message becoming closer. The world had changed enormously in the forty years since Vatican II and the Constitution, *Dei Verbum*. New evangelisation means new means of communication, the new media.

So . . .

Were *DV* being written now, what would the background notes be in terms of its key points, especially communicating the word and for the final section of the Constitution on possibilities for people to study the Scriptures and learn about their background and their meaning?

The notes might remind readers (who were reading them in print or reading words on their computer screens, having Googled the text) that in the 1980s, a huge step in making words and images and moving images more available than by print, cinema and television, was the quick introduction of the videocassette, the video-camera and the video player. At the video store (which is now becoming part of ancient late twentieth century history for the younger generations), so much more was available. And not just available, able to be watched whenever the borrower wanted. Availability and accessibility were becoming instant in ways never before possible. This began to change so much of word-based and still-image-based, pictures and slides, teaching. Students could not just read more, they could watch more, absorb more. They could see dramatisations of biblical, Gospel stories. They could see Israel. And, something that happened in the 1990s as many churches began to make feature films for television and video distribution, individuals and groups could make their own biblical home-movie re-enactments—and with their own cultural interpretations. But videocassettes and players are now relegated to re-cycling companies and DVD and Blue-Ray copies, with an even more vast catalogue, have taken their place. Now digital players and screens. And, even on a whim, instant downloading. And this is not just for affluent countries, but becoming more and more prevalent in Africa, Asia and the Pacific islands.

Distance learning and on-line courses, including communicating the word, have become an education industry.

A powerful 2004 example of this power for evangelisation (whether one likes Mel Gibson's presentation or not) was the worldwide impact of *The Passion of the Christ*. In the first three days of its US DVD release, it sold 9,000,000 copies. American evangelical churches with the money to do so began to produce feature films with Gospel messages in contemporary stories.

While deregulation in many countries meant that there were no obligations for radio stations or television channels to broadcast religious material, broadcasting of ceremonies, documentaries and speakers and panels on religious themes have by no means disappeared. And there are radio networks like Radio Maria in Europe and beyond and EWTN (Eternal Word Television Network) from the US which are dedicated full-time to this media evangelisation ministry (whether one likes them or agrees with their content or not).

We can Google anything (as the present writer did for the papal texts quoted). We can Google You-Tube and find enough New Areopagus programs, features, clips to be occupied all day. We can be on Facebook to enter anything we like, anything that we really like and illustrate it. Facebook can bring to instant attention any information (useful or not) that promotes biblical studies or provides momentary inspiration. The same with Twitter but with the limit of 140 characters. Anybody can be an instant evangelist.

Of course, this brings its own problems of what is relevant, what is gossip, what is correct or erroneous.

Nobody in 1965 would have dreamed that half a century on this is how we would be speaking and reflecting. While the Word of God, the Dei Verbum, is our constant heritage, the media for communication, teaching and discussing, listening and sharing are up-to-date. And this commentary may seem, in fifty years time (or fewer), a touch antiquated as the Rapid Development becomes more rapid.

12

Dei Verbum and the Philosophy of Hans-Georg Gadamer

John F Owens SM

I

The relation between *Dei Verbum* (*DV*) and the philosophy of Hans-Georg Gadamer can be discerned in a contrast that is drawn in a key paragraph in which *DV* addresses the question of interpretation. The paragraph begins by endorsing use of the historical-critical method, recommending attention to what the authors of the sacred texts originally meant, the literary forms they used, customary patterns of expression which prevailed at the time of composition, and so on. But the Council fathers add a qualifying paragraph, insisting that the scholarly enterprise should keep in mind 'the content and unity of the whole of Scripture', and the 'living tradition of the whole church'.[1] They could scarcely have guessed that the tradition-based style of reading to which they refer in passing, mainly as a check on possible excesses of the historical-critical method, was about to become a topic of intense philosophical debate, and to give rise to a bewildering variety of possibilities. When the Pontifical Biblical Commission makes a list of interpretative styles some thirty years later, it records no fewer than a dozen major types, all of which, it readily concedes, have something to offer.[2]

This development beyond historical criticism alone, to acceptance of a more engaged style of reading, owes much to Gadamer's

---

1. 'Dogmatic Constitution on Divine Revelation' (*Dei Verbum*) 12, *The Documents of Vatican II* (London: Geoffrey Chapman, 1966), 111–28.
2. Gadamer's own approach is probably included as one of these 'methods'. Cf 'Approach by the History of the Influence of the Text (*Wirkungsgeschichte*)', in *The Interpretation Of The Bible In The Church* (Rome: Libreria Editrice Vaticana, 1993), 55.

influence. His best-known work, *Truth and Method*, appeared four years before the promulgation of *DV*.³ It signals a shift of focus beyond historical scholarship to a style of reading where ancient texts speak in the present to a contemporary reader. It is one of Gadamer's achievements to make this sort of reading academically respectable again. To the positivist eye of preceding generations, the circular, interest-based methods of human sciences like history or literary criticism, had looked impossibly subjective, falling far short of the standards of paradigmatic sciences like physics and chemistry. Dilthey had proposed a separate-but-equal status for the human sciences, claiming they had a respectable method of their own, that differed from the methods of the exact sciences. Gadamer claims not only that the circular procedures of the human sciences have their own validity, but that even the exact sciences rely in the end on similar procedures. *All* understanding ultimately works in the way that the human sciences do. The story of detached observation and hypothesis which the hard sciences tried to tell about themselves is in important respects illusory. This stunning reversal of the old positivist hierarchy caught seasoned defenders of the human sciences by surprise. Charles Taylor describes 'old-guard Diltheyans who suddenly pitch forward on their faces as all opposition ceases to the reign of universal hermeneutics'.⁴

In most respects, this development is very favourable to the interests expressed in *DV*. Historical-critical study becomes the background to an encounter with the text, and no longer dominates the reading process. If Catholics read the bible from within the life of the Church, learning to articulate and develop a tradition that has already formed them and their reading style, they are doing what everybody does who reads a text. So long as they allow the text to challenge them, and consent to be led beyond their starting-point, there is nothing necessarily 'subjective', or partisan in what they are doing. But alongside such areas of agreement, there are questions about how Gadamer's philosophy relates to wider interests of *DV*. Most obviously, the document insists on an authoritative Magisterium

---

3. Hans-Georg Gadamer, *Truth And Method*, translation revised by Joel Weinsheimer and Donald G Marshall, second revised edition (London: Continuum, 2004), henceforth *TM*.
4. Charles Taylor, 'Understanding In Human Science', *The Review of Metaphysics*, 34/1 (1980): 25–38, 26. Taylor thinks the view exaggerated.

that has the last word in the interpretative process. By contrast, universal hermeneutics seems to leave little room for anything *besides* hermeneutics. While the tensions here are real enough, I will suggest that they do not lie in the first place between ecclesiastical interests and those of contemporary philosophical hermeneutics. Rather they expose ambiguities and possible weaknesses within the hermeneutical approach itself.

II

The thought that revelation is in the first place *of* God, a kind of address where God speaks to us and we encounter him as a conversation partner, is now a commonplace. It was however not always so. In his influential 1967 commentary on *DV*, Joseph Ratzinger emphasises the size of the shift that has taken place in the document. He notes the abandonment of an earlier 'defensive' schema, one that viewed revelation as 'a store of mysterious supernatural teachings', in favour of a view that saw it as 'a true dialogue which touches man in his totality . . . addressing him as a partner . . .'[5] Gadamer's philosophy sets out to examine what is involved in seeing a text as addressing us in this way as if it were another person. His problem is not in the first place that of bridging the gap between a text and a person—though he is aware of this as a problem[6]—but rather of finding the right approach to *both* texts and persons. He is not concerned to recommend any novelty here, as if he were introducing a new method or procedure. Rather he tries to wake us up to what we already do when we come to understand, so that we see and describe it in a way that accurately expresses the phenomenon, and does not distort it. In this sense, his approach can be described as a 'phenomenology' (*TM* 513).

Among his preliminary moves is an attack on the positivist notion of an enquiry that has no presuppositions, and claims simply to register data and form testable hypotheses. For Gadamer, this can never be the most primitive description of how we come to know the world. He points out the role of our own expectations in enabling a meaningful world to appear, determining for example what is

---

5. Joseph Ratzinger, 'Dogmatic Constitution on Divine Revelation: Chapter 1', in *Commentary on the Documents of Vatican II*, Volume III, edited by Herbert Vorgrimler (New York: Herder and Herder, 1969), 170-80, 172.
6. Gadamer, *TM*, 370-71.

relegated to the background as we come to know something, and what stands out as new or surprising. Our pre-judgments enable an initial meaningful content to emerge at all. The objectivity of an enquiry does not come down to a passive reception of material, but rather to a readiness to revise both pre-judgments and the objects that appear in their light.

> the initial meaning emerges only because he (a person understanding a text) is reading the text with particular expectations in regard to a certain meaning. Working out this fore-projection, which is constantly revised in terms of what emerges as he penetrates into the meaning, is understanding what is there (*TM* 269).

When we come to understand a person or a text, there are three possible approaches to the process of projection and revision. At the first level, there is no revision to speak of. We simply measure data against our projections, without ever thinking that the latter might need fundamental revision. This illustrates 'method' as developed in early modernity, and as assumed by the exact sciences when pursuing their normal activities. No interpretation is needed here. Interpretation first looms as a topic when we take into account the fact that the object of enquiry itself has an opinion, or something like an opinion. At the second level, we recognise the opinion of the other, but fit it completely into our own perspective, implicitly assuming we know better. A convinced Freudian might read the letters of St Paul in this way, seeing Paul as recording experiences that are not properly identified until the arrival of Freud. St Paul could of course return the compliment, seeing Freud as a particularly unfortunate attempt at salvation through 'works'. Each of the partners can 'reflectively . . . outdo the other', as Gadamer puts it (*TM* 353). This second level characterises a historical approach to a text, which sees the opinion of the text as a primitive (perhaps erroneous) expression of what we know better. To take an example, we might see the disturbing story of Abraham's journey up Mount Moriah as reflecting a 'primitive understanding of religion', which has fortunately been overcome as understanding has developed. The utterance of the text, the implicit approval that it gives to Abraham's intent to sacrifice Isaac, is relativised so that it can be dismissed without really being heard. In approaching the text in this way, we never get beyond what we know already. Gadamer remarks that a reading at this level is really 'a form of self-relatedness' (*TM* 353). The other's view is never allowed to speak for itself. It does not occur to us, as we identify the historical limitations of the ancient statement, that we ourselves might be similarly limited, and that this has consequences for the way we proceed.

When we take our own historical contingency seriously, we enter the third level of interpretation. We allow the truth-claims of others to come into play as such. I see them as having 'something to say to me' (*TM* 355). To return to the example of Abraham on Moriah, we might allow into play the disturbing scriptural voice, which seems straightforwardly to approve Abraham's readiness to sacrifice. It might strike us how much we have domesticated our religious views, and suppressed their implicit danger. We wake up to ourselves and our own approach for the first time, entertaining the disturbing thought that the Moriah text might show us a side of every religious commitment, the absoluteness it brings to a life. Could our contemporaries have a point, when they depict religious belief as 'dangerous'? With this, we are grappling not just with a contrary or mistaken opinion that has strayed into our usual logical space. Rather, the space in which we began suddenly itself appears as limited—as just 'our' space. We realise that we too approach the world from a limited historical perspective, and are being called beyond it. In Gadamer's terms we wake up to the presence of our horizon, the particular vantage point that we inhabit, and its limited range of possible perceptions. Gadamer does not of course mean that we should simply take over the viewpoint of the alien horizon that confronts us. We are challenged rather to a process of growth, to let ourselves be taken beyond our own particular starting-point, so that we find ourselves 'rising to a higher universality' (*TM* 304). Understanding is not in the first place a process of assimilation, but a kind of journey on our part, where we come to inhabit a different horizon, and so come to understand the viewpoint of the other, even if we still do not agree with it. Gadamer refers to this as a 'fusion' of horizons (*TM* 305). It is an active process, which requires that our previous historical horizon is 'simultaneously superseded' (*TM* 306) even though it is always necessarily in play, if we are to proceed at all.

This description of the process of understanding as one where we begin with a perspective, are led to recognise its contingency, and are open to moving beyond it, helps resolve a good many questions. It explains the sides of life where people constantly explore other horizons—in conversation or fiction-reading for example. It fits with a view of scriptural reading that sees it not as acquisition of information but as gradual penetration into a mystery, involving a personal journey. Gadamer notes that the Gospel does not exist to be understood as 'a merely historical document', an information source about ancient beliefs, but is meant to be read so that 'it exercises its saving effect' (*TM* 307). He notes this, while also recognising that when properly interpreted, the Gospel retains the status of a canonical document, and acquires 'no new content' (*TM* 326).[7] To meet the Gospel word in the right way is like meeting a person in an encounter that changes our life, so that our reading is an 'event' as Gadamer calls it (*TM* 308). Understanding does not take place in an internal 'noetic' sphere that is purely theoretical, after which we decide how to act, but is itself the beginning of a response where we commit our lives in a certain direction. After such an encounter, we are not as we were before. Gadamer goes so far as to say that if it is to be understood properly, the Gospel text must be understood at every moment 'in a new and different way' (*TM* 308).

While this fits with the view expressed in *DV* 2 that reading of the scriptures is a kind of personal encounter, where readers hear the voice of God speaking 'so that He may invite and take them into fellowship with himself', Gadamer's emphasis on understanding as a process of change can seem exaggerated. His way of framing the question sees understanding as an advance that brings us into regions we had not previously entered. This means a preparedness to leave starting-points behind and move towards new possibilities. Insight always involves an escape from something that has 'held us captive' (*TM* 350). Every experience worthy of the name 'thwarts an expectation' (*TM* 350). This certainly captures a side of our encounters with others, whether in reading or conversation. We can feel a delight in encountering alien horizons that relativise and challenge our own, so that we are led in a kind of journey. Gadamer describes the aim of dialogue as reaching an understanding where we are 'transformed

---

7. It differs from the understanding of a legal text in this respect (*TM* 326).

into a communion in which we do not remain what we were' (*TM* 371).

But the universality of the claim can take us by surprise. Gadamer appears here as heir to a long tradition of German thought that centres around the notion of *Bildung*, the point that education is not in the first place a matter of coming to know new things, but rather of expanding the horizons in which we know them. *Bildung* belongs to the rise of 'historical' philosophy after Kant. While our knowledge is always caught up with particular historical categories, we also experience a drive that takes us beyond them, towards a greater universality. It involves 'keeping oneself open to . . . other, more universal points of view' (*TM* 15). For Herder, one of the founding figures of the ideal, this ascent is precisely a 'rising up to humanity' (*TM* 9). Such a view tends to regard everyday identification and manipulation of the things of the world as a secondary, technical affair. We discover reality at the moment when our whole horizon expands, and we see something for the first time, which had been hidden by the familiarity of everyday contact. This moment of discovery cannot be possessed in a straightforward manner, but requires a struggle against the flattening effects of the everyday. For Hegel, insight is always a function of this struggle, so that a moment of true experience invariably has the structure of a 'reversal of consciousness' (*TM* 349). This explains part of the appeal of Gadamer's approach—it is in touch with the historical sense that forms the contemporary world. It raises however the large question of how it ultimately stands to the Catholic tradition.

III

Gadamer's approach particularly raises the question of authoritative teaching in the form of doctrine or dogma, given that his model of understanding always involves a willingness to move beyond one's starting point. He says that the truly 'experienced' person is 'radically undogmatic' (*TM* 350). One who follows the historical interpretative path that he recommends does not find fulfilment in 'definitive knowledge', but rather in 'the openness of experience that is made possible by experience itself' (*TM* 350). Such statements seem to recommend an open-ended Socratic enquiry, and tell against positions that claim to be determined for all time in advance. Significantly, Gadamer describes his approach as fitting more naturally with Protestant rather than with Catholic traditions, and as being naturally antagonistic towards Catholic views of dogma. 'As a Protestant art of interpreting Scripture, modern hermeneutics is clearly related in a polemical way to the dogmatic tradition of the Catholic church' (*TM* 328). Gadamer does not deny that most of our beliefs must remain stable if a particular interpretation is to get off the ground. He says that 'only the support of familiar and common understanding makes possible the venture into the alien...'[8] But it is hard to see how any framework could be established as permanent within this approach. We cannot bind the interpretative future. This seems to follow an understanding that has taken hermeneutics from its limited beginnings as an interpretative aid or a methodology of the human sciences, and turned it into universal hermeneutics, with a claim to describe understanding as it always is. As Gadamer says: 'What I am describing is the mode of the whole human experience of the world. I call this experience hermeneutical...'[9]

DV seems to go against this in at least two ways. It reaffirms the creedal belief that Jesus is not just a part of the revelation, but its perfection and fulfilment. While different phases of interpretation come and go, and might be relativised by the arrival of a broader later viewpoint (as happened, in Christian view, to the covenant of the Old Testament), this will not happen to Jesus himself and the dispensation he brings. 'The Christian dispensation... will never pass away, and we now await no further public revelation...' (*DV* 4). If this view seems to speak for itself, it should not be forgotten that there have long been theological opinions that see Jesus as part of a larger historical process of education, and the New Testament as a kind of textbook that could conceivably be superseded in the future.[10] The question is whether views like this can ever be permanently excluded, by a statement that

---

8. Gadamer, 'The Universality of the Hermeneutical Problem', in *Philosophical Hermeneutics*, translated by David E Linge (Berkeley: University of California Press, 1977), 3–17, 15.
9. Gadamer, 'The Universality of the Hermeneutical Problem', 15.
10. The eighteenth-century German Enlightenment thinker Lessing holds, or hints at, both these opinions. Cf. 'The Education of the Human Race', numbers 64–72 in Gotthold Ephraim Lessing, *Philosophical and Theological Writings*, edited and translated by HB Nisbet (Cambridge, UK: Cambridge University Press, 2005), 217–40, 233–34.

claims to be able to bind future generations.[11] The second challenge to universal hermeneutics set down in *DV* 10 concerns authentic interpretation, which the document sees as entrusted 'exclusively to the living teaching office of the Church . . .'. However familiar such a claim might be in the Catholic tradition, it seems to take us outside the historical flux, claiming to have identified part of the permanent framework within which interpretation goes on, rather than being itself subject to interpretation. In an article written to commemorate the fortieth anniversary of the appearance of *DV*, the exegete Daniel Kosch raises the question of whether the document should not admit that the last word is always with the hermeneutical process:

> Unfortunately, *Dei Verbum* does not explicitly make the point that the enunciated principles apply in the first place to the magisterial teachings themselves, that official church teaching is always expressed in time-conditioned forms and that one can therefore 'rightly understand' the tradition and official church teachings only if one interprets them contextually. But what applies to the 'inspired authors' of Holy Scripture must first of all apply to those persons who 'authentically interpret' these (*DV* 10).[12]

Divino Afflante Spiritu offers a nice example of what Kosch refers to, in that it relativises earlier magisterial disciplinary decrees against the use of the historical-critical method and in favour of use of the Vulgate text, precisely seeing them as time-bound in important respects, and therefore able to be superseded or modified. It notes that the historical-critical method has come to develop necessary checks and balances, and points out that the decree in favour of the Vulgate text was preferring it to other *Latin* texts, and not to the Hebrew or Greek

---

11. Cf the statement of Kant: 'But would a society of pastors, perhaps a church assembly . . . not be justified in binding itself by oath to a certain unalterable symbol . . . and this for all time: I say that this is wholly impossible'. (Immanuel Kant, 'What Is Enlightenment?' in *Perpetual Peace and Other Essays*, translated by Ted Humphrey [Indianapolis: Hackett Publishing Company, 1983], 33–48, 35).
12. Daniel Kosch, 'Dei Verbum And Its Impact', translated by L Maluf, *Bulletin Dei Verbum*, 74/75 (2005), 13–16, 14–15.

originals.[13] Does hermeneutics ultimately rule, so that whatever a constituted authority says at a particular time should be explicitly recognised as time-conditioned, no more than the latest stage of a historical process whose future development could not be predicted or controlled? Some early commentators on *DV* express a wish for something like this, at least as regards the activities of scholars, that they must be 'free and unfettered' in pursuing their task, so that they can 'follow truth wherever it leads'.[14] While this can look like a tension between ecclesiastical authorities and hermeneutical philosophy or scholarship, I think this would be too simple a view. The tension is really deeper, and is to be found at the heart of the hermeneutical project itself.

IV

In responding to such concerns, Gadamer insists that he is not in fact interfering in the detailed ways in which different disciplines go about their business, and is not prescribing any 'open' or 'Socratic' method that should always be followed, as if hermeneutics were a method in competition with others. Rather it attempts to give an account of what all methods and procedures come down to in the end. Gadamer has a celebrated discussion on this point with the Italian legal historian Emilio Betti, who is concerned to develop a canon of hermeneutical principles that can be of direct use in the activity of interpretation, for example the principle that whenever we interpret a text, we should treat it as having an autonomy of meaning, or the principle that the objectivity of the content of a text must be grounded in an intention of the author (*TM* 511). Betti criticises Gadamer for not developing such principles, and therefore failing adequately to safeguard the scientific nature of interpretation. Gadamer protests that such criticism misunderstands his intentions. In an appendix to *TM* he reproduces part of a letter to Betti where he insists that 'fundamentally I am *not*

---

13. Cf. 'Pope Pius XII: Encyclical Letter Promoting Biblical Studies', numbers 13 and 14, in *The Scripture Documents,* edited and translated by Dean P Bechard (Collegeville, MN: The Liturgical Press, 2001), 115–39, 123 and 124.
14. Frederick C Grant, 'A Response' (to 'Dogmatic Constitution on Divine Revelation') in *The Documents of Vatican II,* edited by Walter M Abbott SJ and Very Rev. Msgr. Joseph Gallagher (London: Geoffrey Chapman, 1966), 129–32, 131.

proposing a method, but I am describing *what is the case...*' (*TM* 512). In other words he is not prescribing rules for how our understanding should proceed, but describing what we in fact do when, in various disciplines with different methods, we enquire systematically into a topic and come to understand it. For Betti, such a project is not satisfactory. It proceeds as if all historical interpretative processes were equal, and offers no criteria for judging whether they are right or wrong, or better or worse. The hermeneutical problem remains at the level of phenomenological description (*TM* 513), which is to say that it leaves all existing methods in place, apparently delivering us over to the relativism of history.

If Betti were right, and Gadamer's approach did renounce any attempt to reform existing modes of interpretation, we could imagine a quick way to harmonise Gadamer's approach with that of *DV*. There would be a recognition that the principles laid down in *DV* simply show us what Catholic interpretation of scripture ultimately *is*. 'The game is played', as Wittgenstein might have said, and there is no suggestion that it needs reforming in light of any external standard. I do not think however that Betti is right about Gadamer, at least as he has been taken up and interpreted. While Gadamer does not promote a particular method as such, his work almost invariably strikes the reader as *normative*, offering standards to which particular interpretations should conform. As noted above, he seems to recommend a kind of openness, where we are always prepared to call our current interpretation in question. If we refuse to do this, we have fallen into dogmatism, mistakenly privileging our own views, as if they are more than just an interpretation that has been tested in conversation. The Gadamer interpreter and commentator Georgia Warnke reflects this view in lamenting the 'lack of hermeneutic sensitivity and openness' which bedevils public discussions of controversial ethical issues like euthanasia or abortion. She recommends the kind of discussion that Gadamer seems to recommend, where participants acknowledge the 'legitimacy' of viewpoints other than their own, and form a kind of 'deliberative democracy'. 'Rather than holding dogmatically to their own interpretations, participants are open to developing them through the interpretations of others...'[15]

---

15. Georgia Warnke, 'Hermeneutics, Ethics and Politics', in *The Cambridge Companion to Gadamer*, edited by Robert J Dostal (Cambridge, UK: Cambridge

This is clearly a normative ideal, which sets out what people should be doing. It also highlights a striking lack in Gadamer's approach, given that at least some of the time, it is surely wrong for us to be 'open' like this. Gadamer does not seem to offer any clue for when we should *refuse* a conversation. Warnke is aware that this could lead to a relativist lack of standards or even 'a deference to any interpretive understanding different from our own'.[16] She herself puts her trust in the ultimate coherence of the views we already hold, believing that as long as we remain open to the logical consequences of our current best views, we will be led to alter views that are distorted or prejudiced. She cites legal decisions that eventually led to the abandonment of racial segregation in the United States, quoting Gadamer: 'Is it so perverse to think that in reality the irrational cannot hold out in the long run?'[17] But her example takes a popular issue whose outcome is now accepted more or less by everybody, and directs recommendations to those who need to *change* their views (so that dogma and doctrine again appear simply as possible hindrances to progress). Surely there are cases where we should hold on to our views, and even, at the extreme, *refuse* to listen to those who want to persuade us otherwise? One is reminded of the famous statement of Elizabeth Anscombe that we should not even argue with people who want us to consider certain moral positions, for example whether an innocent person should in a particular situation be judicially executed in order to achieve a greater good. One who argues like this simply 'shows a corrupt mind', and we should not enter into discussion with them.[18] Gadamer does not seem to consider cases like this. Ingrid Scheibler notes his encouragement that we take up a 'living relation' to tradition, and avoid the move where we reflect ourselves out of such a living relation by relativising an objection, and *a priori* refuse to consider it as a possible challenge to our position. Anscombe

---

University Press, 2002), 79–101, 97.
16. Warnke, 'Hermeneutics, Ethics and Politics', 98.
17. Warnke, 'Hermeneutics, Ethics and Politics', 100. The quote is from 'Hegel's Philosophy and Its Aftereffects Until Today' in Hans-Georg Gadamer, *Reason in the Age of Science*, translated by Frederick G Lawrence (Cambridge, MA: The MIT Press, 1983), 21–37, 36.
18. Gertrude Elizabeth Margaret Anscombe, 'Modern Moral Philosophy', in *Ethics, Religion and Politics, Collected Philosophical Papers Volume III* (Minneapolis: University of Minnesota Press, 1981), 26–42, 40.

recommends just such a reflection, seeing the view expressed above as the product of a 'corrupt mind'. By contrast, Gadamer seems to think we ought always to choose the living relation, and enter into conversation with the alternative view. Scheibler goes on:

> Gadamer ... never specifically addresses the *prescriptive* tone of his account ... Are there cases in which, once one *does* begin to view the relation to tradition as a living one ... one would 'reflectively'—that is, actively— opt out of the 'living relation' to tradition?[19]

This reveals perhaps that Gadamer smuggles into his approach more of a historical metaphysics, a view of 'how it always is', than he thinks. For him the task tends to be conceived as a slow breakout from encrusted prejudice into open dialogue with others. But this is itself a view that characterises a particular time. Geoff Waite makes a telling remark in commenting on the appearance of a volume called *Gadamer's Century*: 'as for "Gadamer's century", I'd prefer the term "current period of the globalizing tendency of liberal-parliamentarian free-market capitalism", though perhaps they amount to much the same thing—both promoting "moderation", "dialogue", and the like.'[20] Waite's remark effectively relativises Gadamer's whole approach, and raises the question again of what lies outside it. However this question is addressed, the Catholic tradition generally resists the move that might draw everything back into the process of interpretation itself, the programme of 'universal hermeneutics'. It maintains its unfashionable insistence that there are things we must hold on to through thick and thin, pointing beyond history to difficult questions of metaphysics. This seems to show that for all the coincidence of interest that obtains between *DV* and parts of Gadamer's philosophy, there are important aspects from which it remains resolutely aloof.

---

19. Ingrid Scheibler, *Gadamer, Between Heidegger and Habermas* (Lanham, MD: Rowan and Littlefield Publishers, Inc., 2000), 68.
20. Geoff Waite, 'Radio Nietzsche, or, How to Fall Short of Philosophy', in *Gadamer's Repercussions: Reconsidering Philosophical Hermeneutics*, edited by Bruce Krajewski (Berkeley: University of California Press, 2004), 169–211, 169.

13

Where do we Go From Here? The Future of Catholic Biblical Studies in the Wake of Vatican II

Donald Senior CP

The fiftieth anniversary of the Second Vatican Council has offered the opportunity to remember and re-appropriate the new life that the Council brought to the Church. Perhaps nowhere has that been more evident than in the biblical renewal the Catholic Church has experienced over the past fifty years, a renewal whose roots go back over most of the twentieth century. The editors have asked me to reflect on the future of the Catholic biblical studies in the wake of the Council. Although writing primarily from a Catholic perspective, I hope that my reflections might be of some worth for all Christian scholars who are pondering how biblical studies should affect the life of a faith community.

Vatican II as the Culmination of a Profound Biblical Renewal in the Life of the Catholic Church.

Although this ground has been charted by a number of recent publications, it is useful to trace at least in general terms the development of Catholic biblical renewal as an essential backdrop for any speculation about the future.[1] At the beginning of the twentieth century, the official Catholic Church had a wary view of a historical critical or 'scientific' approach to biblical research. The heroic patience and strong integrity of a scholar such as Marie Joseph Lagrange OP, founder of Jerusalem's École Biblique,[2] had helped blunt

---

1. See, for example, Ronald D Witherup, *Scripture: Rediscovering Vatican II* (New York: Paulist Press, 2006); James Chukwuma Okoye, *Scripture in the Church: The Synod on the Word of God* (Collegeville MN: Liturgical Press, 2011).
2. Bernard Montagnes, *The Story of Father Marie-Joseph Lagrange: Founder of*

an aggressive effort to suppress such studies among Catholic Scholars but the establishment of the Pontifical Biblical Commission in 1902 by Pope Leo XIII was intended to be a vigilant monitor of and check on Catholic biblical scholarship.

The breakthrough to a more peaceful acceptance of the validity of modern biblical scholarship came with Pope Pius XII's *Divino Afflante Spiritu* (*DAS*) of 1943, which stands as a kind of *Magna Carta* for Catholic biblical scholarship. His encyclical acknowledged the importance of studying the historical and literary contexts of the Bible and encouraged Catholic biblical scholars to employ the best of linguistic, historical and literary analysis in their exposition of the biblical text.

The impact of Pius XII's liberating text and the resurgence on a popular level in study and reflection on the Bible over the next several decades provide the backdrop for the conciliar text, *Dei Verbum* (*DV*), with its rich reflection on the Scriptures as the revealed Word of God, its detailed pastoral encouragement on making the Bible an integral part of the Church's life, and its call for a renewal of biblical scholarship in the Church. The doctrinal part of the declaration was not innovative as such but its tone and emphasis moved the question of the role of the Bible in the Church to a rich level of biblically grounded discourse. The source of the Word of God, it affirmed, is in the very life of the Trinity. God is self-communicating; wishing to reveal himself in love to his creatures and even to be reflected in the beauty and harmony of the created universe. Revelation, therefore, is not first of all a body of propositions but a personal relationship between the creative and loving God and the human person, the summit of creation. The culmination of God's self-revelation is found in the person of Jesus Christ and the harmony of the revealed Word with creation itself. That revelation of God is made manifest both in Tradition and in Scripture, with the Church to whom the Word of God is entrusted in a special way as authentic interpreter of revelation.

Because the Scriptures express the Word of God and find their origin in God, they are both inspired and inerrant. Yet the Scriptures, like the Incarnate Word of God himself, are God's Word in human words. *DV* did not expansively define the meaning of inspiration and inerrancy beyond the traditional assertions (a task that Pope Benedict

---

Modern Catholic Bible Study (New York: Paulist Press, 2006).

XVI requested the Pontifical Biblical Commission to address). The literary, historical and cultural limitations of the Scriptures as the Word of God temper any literal assertion of inerrancy and, as *DV* itself did, affirms that the 'truth' of the Scriptures applies in a unique way to those truths revealed in the Scriptures that are necessary for salvation.

DV also reaffirmed a venerable Catholic tradition that holds that both Testaments, Old and New, are truly and validly part of the inspired Word of God and the Old Testament has its own integrity and salvific message, even as it is also a preparation and anticipation of the fullness of the Word revealed in Jesus Christ.

Its final chapter, entitled 'Sacred Scripture in the Life of the Church,' recommended a series of initiatives for implementing the council's reforms: 'wide open access' to the Scriptures for all the faithful; new translations based on the original languages, including joint efforts with 'separated brethren'; encouragement of more scholars to take up biblical studies; encouragement of theologians and catechists to use Scripture in their materials; encouragement of priests, deacons and catechists 'to immerse themselves in the Scriptures by constant sacred reading and diligent study'; encouragement of bishops to provide the faithful with editions of the Bible that include explanatory notes. Coupled with these recommendations was the introduction of the three year lectionary as part of the liturgical renewal that for the first time ever gave Catholic congregations the opportunity to hear wide expanses of the Old and New Testaments on a regular basis at their Sunday (and daily) eucharist.

The Continuing Impact of *Dei Verbum*

The formulation of *DV* stretched out for almost the entire length of the Council before it was finally approved on October 29, 1965.[3] Its impact would continue well beyond the Council itself. Even before the Council had concluded its work, the Pontifical Biblical Commission issued a statement entitled, *Instruction Concerning the Historical Truth of the Gospels* in 1964 which amplified what would be stated in the final version of *DV* itself—namely that the gospels emerged from the life of the Church in various stages and that along with the

---

3. See Witherup, *Scripture*, for detailed description of formulation; 1–31.

historical nucleus of the gospel tradition there was also evidence of the Spirit—prompted theological interpretation of the Church itself evident in the gospel narratives.

Over the next decades following the Council, the Pontifical Biblical Commission (PBC), which under the reorganisation initiated by Pope Paul VI was now located within the Congregation of the Doctrine of the Faith, issued a number of major statements that would have been inconceivable prior to the biblical renewal championed by the Council. For example, on the occasion of the fiftieth anniversary of *DAS* in 1993, the PBC issued a comprehensive document on *The Interpretation of the Bible in the Church* which affirmed that the historical critical method and the literal sense of Scripture were fundamental, while at the same time acknowledging that a variety of methodologies could complement this method, taking into account various perspectives and disciplines such as historical, social, psychological, cultural, feminist and so on. The document also laid down some fundamental principles for what it considered a proper Catholic mode of interpreting the Scriptures. It should be noted that the laudatory preface to this document was written by the then Secretary of the Congregation of the Doctrine of the Faith, one Joseph Cardinal Ratzinger!

This remarkable text was followed by several other major statements, each of which employed historical critical approaches along with other methodologies. In 2002, at the direct request of then Pope John Paul II, the PBC published an extensive study on *The Jewish People and their Sacred Scriptures in the Christian Bible*. This text acknowledged in detail the debt Christianity owed to Judaism, affirmed the proper role of the Old Testament as integral to the Christian Bible, noted the differing and yet valid perspectives brought to the Scriptures by both Jewish and Christian faith, provided a frank assessment of the anti-Jewish potential of some New Testament texts, and concluded with an impassioned defense of the validity of Jewish faith and a sharp criticism of Christian anti-Semitism.

In 2008 the PBC produced another major statement entitled, *The Bible and Morality: The Biblical Roots of Christian Conduct.* The central concern of this text was how to properly bridge the gap between modern ethical concerns and an ancient text such as the Bible. Again using an array of biblical methodologies grounded in the historical critical perspective, the PBC scanned the moral horizon provided by the ensemble of biblical traditions and enunciated a series of principles for the use of the Bible in addressing moral concerns.

Currently, the PBC is working on a text on Biblical inspiration and inerrancy—an assignment given to the Commission by Pope Benedict XVI in response to the pastoral concerns stated by many bishops in the 2008 General Synod on the Scriptures in the Life and Ministry of the Church that there was not yet an adequate Catholic stance on these issues.

Another milestone on an official level that demonstrated the vitality of the Catholic Biblical Renewal was the 2008 General Synod mentioned previously. This synod focused on the 'The Scriptures in the Life and Ministry of the Church.' Among the many propositions formulated by the Synod and presented to the Holy Father were several decrying the inroads being made among Catholics, particularly in Latin America and Africa, by fundamentalistic Evangelical perspectives about the Scriptures. In accord with the normal protocol guiding the general synods, Pope Benedict would ultimately respond by means of a 'post-synodal exhortation'. This took the form of a major statement by Pope Benedict XVI on the Scriptures in the life of the Church, entitled *Verbum Domini* (*VD*) and published in September 2011. Pope Benedict's extensive 'exhortation' was divided into three parts: 1. On the interpretation of Scripture; 2. On the role of the Scriptures in the life of the Church; and 3. On the role of the Scriptures in the mission of the Church. It is the material in part I on interpretation that has the most significance for our topic here. More extensively than any other place in his writings, Pope Benedict laid out his own perspective on the nature of the Scriptures and the vital principles of interpretation of Scripture within a community of faith. The methodology he discusses is reflected in his own work of biblical exposition, his three volume work on *Jesus of Nazareth*.[4]

Verbum Domini and the Future of Catholic Biblical Studies

In many ways, *VD* represents the culmination of nearly fifty years of reflection and development in official Catholic teaching on the role

---

4. Joseph Ratzinger, *Jesus of Nazareth. From the Baptism in the Jordan to the Transfiguration* (New York: Doubleday, 2007); see particularly xv–xxiv.

of the Scriptures in the Church and their proper interpretation within a living community of faith. It is also, I believe, the proper starting point for reflecting on the future of Catholic biblical scholarship.

In Pope Benedict XVI the Catholic Church was blessed with a leader who has an exceptional knowledge and love of the Scriptures. This love affair with Scripture has been characteristic of his writings as the theologian Joseph Ratzinger and continued in the numerous pastoral letters, exhortations and homilies he produced as Pope. This deft knowledge of the Bible and love for it are on clear display in *VD*. As noted, I will concentrate on the first major section of Pope Benedict's exhortation. Every page of the text is filled with beautiful and substantive reflections on the role of Scripture in the life of Catholic faith and recommends itself as solid spiritual reading, including for readers who do not have a technical background in biblical studies.

Among the various topics covered in this major section (nearly ninety pages in length!), I would like to concentrate on one key issue—the Pope's reflections on the study and interpretation of the Bible from a Catholic perspective. Although this has been touched on in various other writings of Pope Benedict this strikes me as his most comprehensive reflection on the topic. This subject is not without controversy: some on the left are leery that he is opposed to a scientific, historical critical approach to biblical study; while some on the right assume he is their ally in opposing modern biblical interpretation as incompatible with authentic Christian faith. Both groups are dead wrong, as his clear statements in this document demonstrate.

Pope Benedict stresses that his teaching on the interpretation of Scripture in this latest text is in full continuity with a long line of official Catholic affirmations of modern biblical studies, that we have cited above, including Pius XII's *Magna Carta* of modern biblical studies in his ground-breaking encyclical, *DAS* (1943), on through the Second Vatican Council's Constitution on Divine Revelation, *DV*, and continuing with the official documents of the Pontifical Biblical Commission.

One of the keys to the entire document *VD* is the fundamental Christian doctrine of the incarnation. Pope Benedict reflects on the entire span of biblical revelation from the opening chapter of Genesis to the prologue of John's Gospel and find there the overarching theme that God speaks—through his Word which creates the world and the human person, and with that same Word of God continuing to be revealed in the unfolding of human history, reaching the culmination of this divine revelation in the person of Jesus, the 'Word made Flesh' (John 1:14). This foundational Christian belief is stated over and over in the pope's reflections as the key to the Christian view of the world and of history as well as the Christian understanding of human dignity and human destiny. It is also the fundamental key to understanding the nature of Scripture from a Christian and Catholic point of view.

Pope Benedict notes that this understanding of God's Word helps us to realize that, although we have a profound reverence for the Scriptures, 'Christianity is not a "religion of the book"; Christianity is the "religion of the word of God", not of "a written and mute word, but of the incarnate and living Word"' (*VD* 7). This one Word of God is expressed in multiple ways, preeminently, of course, in the person of Jesus Christ, but also in creation which is made in the pattern of God's Word, in the human person who is also created in the image of God, in the living and authentic tradition of the Church imbued with the Spirit of God's Word, and, in a privileged way, in the inspired Scriptures. Citing Saint Ambrose and the Vatican II Constitution *DV*, Pope Benedict notes that just as the Word of God became flesh in Jesus, so, too, the Word of God is revealed in the human words of the Scriptures (*VD* 18). Although he urges biblical scholars and theologians to give more attention to an understanding of the precise nature of biblical inspiration, yet this conviction about the sacred and unique character of the Scriptures as the Word of God remains fundamental.

This acknowledgement of both a human and divine dimension in the Scriptures lays the ground work both for a profound reverence and respect for the Bible as well as an endorsement of the various methods of interpreting the biblical text appropriate to an analysis of any human literature.

Throughout this first major section of the document, Pope Benedict notes several central principles or assumptions that should characterise an authentic Catholic interpretation of the Scriptures.

The Study and Interpretation of the Scriptures should be within the Context of a Living Community of Faith.

Pope Benedict stresses that authentic and complete biblical interpretation can take place only within the context of the Church as a community of faith. As he notes:

> Here we can point to a fundament criterion of biblical hermeneutics: *the primary setting for scriptural interpretation is the life of the Church* (italics original). This is not to uphold the ecclesial context as an extrinsic rule to which exegetes must submit, but rather is something demanded by the very nature of the Scriptures and the way they gradually came into being.

Pope Benedict goes on to say: 'The Bible is the Church's book, and its essential place in the Church's life gives rise to its genuine interpretation' (*VD* 29).

This is an extremely important point and needs to be properly understood. Pope Benedict does not mean to deride or dismiss the work of scholars who might approach a study of the Bible as an important literary text or a cultural artifact that has had a profound influence on human civilisation and history—but for whom the biblical text may have no personal religious claim or value. As he notes, 'Approaches to the sacred text that prescind from faith might suggest interesting elements on the level of textual structure and form, but would inevitably prove merely preliminary and structurally incomplete efforts' (*VD* 30).

From a perspective of Christian faith, the Scriptures do not have simply historical or literary or cultural meaning but have an intrinsic spiritual and revealed meaning that springs from their nature as the Word of God. Thus any approach to the Bible that stops short of considering the meaning of the biblical text for faith, may have great value but is essentially incomplete from the vantage point of the community of faith. In other words, studies that may explore the historical background or literature features of the Bible have value, but from the point of view of Christian interpretation such approaches are preliminary or incomplete until such interpretation engages the authentic meaning of the Scriptures within the Christian community of faith. This also does not mean that in every article or study a Catholic biblical scholar must conclude with some reflection on the ultimate meaning of this or that biblical text for Christian life. In some instances, for example, a study of the historical background of a particular text or an analysis of a point of grammar or language or a consideration of the literary form of a biblical passage may not immediately lead to a consideration of its meaning for the community of faith. But, on the part of the Christian scholar at the service of the community of faith, the ultimate sacred character of the biblical text is an underlying conviction and the potential and decisive meaning of Scripture for Christian life is not denied.

The Intrinsic Value of a Scientific and Historical study of the Scriptures.

In a strong section of the document, Pope Benedict stresses the importance and value of historical-critical exegesis, that is, an approach which considers the historical and social context of the biblical text, using literary, historical and social scientific methodologies appropriate to that task. As he notes:

> Before all else, we need to acknowledge the benefits that historical-critical exegesis and other recently-developed methods of textual analysis have brought to the life of the Church. *For the Catholic understanding of sacred Scripture, attention to such methods is indispensible, linked as it is to the realism of the Incarnation . . .* (italics mine; *VD* 32).

Here the importance of the Incarnation is once again the key factor in Pope Benedict's reflection. Just as Jesus, the Word made Flesh, is authentically, completely human as well as divine, so, too, the Scriptures are authentically, completely human as well as inspired. Therefore any rational method that has integrity from a scientific point of view can be properly used in a study of the Scriptures.

As has been affirmed in much of recent biblical scholarship, Pope Benedict also notes that, while fully valid, the historical-critical approach is not the sole method for studying the Scriptures. Here he also refers to renewed interest in patristic tradition which appreciated the various levels of the text, from the literal through to the allegorical, moral and 'anagogical' (that is, reflecting on the Scriptures to understand human destiny before God) approaches (*VD* 37).

Avoiding Dualism: Uniting the Rational and the Spiritual.

The Christian mystery of the Incarnation is also the key to a deep current of Pope Benedict's thought—a current apparent in many of his writings on other topics as well. Pope Benedict refuses to drive a wedge between the rational and the spiritual, between reason and faith. The kind of 'dualism' that separates these is too often characteristic of modern western civilisation in particular. Reason without faith, that is, a stance that *apriori* excludes the transcendent, Pope Benedict contends, leaves the interpreter with a truncated understanding of reality. At the same time, faith without reason can lead to unbridled ideology and extremism. In the world of biblical interpretation the cleavage between faith and reason can result in either of two types of distortion. One is a study of the Scriptures from a purely rationalistic or reductionist point of view with no interest in its meaning for the community of faith. This can go so far as to be convinced that the notion of the transcendent or spiritual dimension of life does not exist and is meaningless so that a study of the Bible is, by definition, an exercise in pure literary criticism or historical and cultural enquiry without any value beyond that. The Bible is reduced to being an interesting historical artifact with no real significance for today (*VD* 35).

At the same time, a radical dualism or separation of the spiritual and the human and rational can also lead to a kind of 'fideism' that treats the biblical text as a purely divine entity, dictated in its every word by God without any human mediation. Following a consistent trend in official Catholic teaching, Pope Benedict rejects a 'fundamentalist' approach which denies human instrumentality in the creation of the biblical text and promotes a kind of rigid 'literalism' which, the pope notes, 'is a betrayal of both the literal and the spiritual sense, and opens the ways to various forms of manipulation . . .' (*VD* 44). Quoting the Pontifical Biblical Commission's document, *The Interpretation of the Bible in the Church*, Pope Benedict observes that such fundamentalism by 'refusing to take into account the historical character of biblical revelation . . . makes itself incapable of accepting the full truth of the incarnation itself' (*VD* 44).

Other Ecclesial Principles for Catholic Interpretation.

Pope Benedict concludes this remarkable reflection on a Catholic approach to the interpretation of Scripture by citing a number of other principles, most of them already discussed in the Biblical Commission's 1983 document. Space permits only a brief mention of them here:

a) In interpreting a particular passage of Scripture the exegete should keep in mind the entirety of Scripture which is viewed from the perspective of faith as a unity even though composed through the span of history of many individual and diverse books.

b) The Christian interpreter also views the Scriptures from the vantage point of faith in Jesus Christ. This does not mean that every passage of the Old Testament was intended as an explicit preparation for the coming of Jesus but now, from the perspective of faith, it makes sense to understand the biblical message in the context of faith in Jesus as God's ultimate Word.

c) Since through the power of the Spirit, the one Word of God is expressed in the authoritative teaching and tradition of the Church as well as in the revealed biblical word, authentic interpretation of Scripture must be in harmony with the Church's Magisterium.

d) The Christian interpreter affirms the fundamental harmony of the Old and New Testaments and refuses to drive a wedge between them. At the same time, it is clear even within the body of Scripture itself there is a certain progression and development, and the New Testament is seen both as in continuity with the Old Testament and moving forward in other dimensions beyond the Old Testament perspective (these issues are taken up in detail in the Biblical Commission's texts, *The Jewish People and Their Scriptures in the Christian Bible* [2001] and *The Bible and Morality* [2008]).

e) The affirmation that interpretation of the Bible has important consequences for the pastoral life of the Church: including the essential need for theology and the church's preaching to be rooted in the biblical Word; the quest for holiness; the vital dialogue between Christianity and Judaism; and ecumenism. In the latter case, Pope Benedict notes, a study of the Word in common and the development of common translations between Catholics and Protestants are important means for striving for Christian unity.

Conclusion: The Future of Catholic Biblical Studies

In many ways, the future of Catholic biblical studies will depend on the same factors facing the Jewish, Protestant or Orthodox communities. Those aspiring to the study of Scripture will have to hone their expertise in the biblical languages, be steeped in the social and historical context of the biblical world, be skilled in the various historical, literary, and social scientific methodologies for analysing the biblical text. There is really no substitute for these fundamental disciplines of the biblical guild.

At the same time, those who aspire to biblical scholarship will benefit from the methodological reflections of past fifty years. No longer does it seem possible to assume that the historical critical method alone is the only 'objective' and scientifically approved approach to biblical interpretation. Biblical scholarship has now articulated an array of approaches that do not substitute for a historically grounded methodology but can complement it. In many instances, complementary approaches concentrate on the relationship of the text to the reader (as distinct from the historical focus on the background and context of the biblical writings) and leave a path open for the question of meaning in a way that is much more difficult for the historical critical method by itself. Pope Benedict XVI addresses this in his foreword to the first volume of his book on *Jesus of Nazareth:*

> The historical-critical method—let me repeat—is an indispensable tool, given the structure of Christian faith ... but it is important ... to recognize the limits of the historical-critical method itself ... It is a *historical* (italics original) method, and that means that it investigates the then-current context of events in which the texts originated. It attempts to identify and to understand the past—as it was in itself—with the greatest possible precision, in order then to find out what the author could have said and intended to say in the context of the mentality and events of the time. To the extent

> that it remains true to itself, the historical method not only has to investigate the biblical word as a thing of the past, but also has to let remain in the past. It can glimpse points of contact with the present and it can try to apply the biblical word to the present; the one thing it cannot do is make it into something present *today*—that would be overstepping its bounds. Its very precision in interpreting the reality of the past is both its strength and its limit.[5]

Third and finally, future Catholic biblical scholarship will need to exercise its work in the context of a living community of faith. Here is where the question of methodology, including recognition of both the essential nature and the limits of the historical critical approach meet. Those aspiring to be Catholic biblical interpreters will need to be at home both in the objective and religiously detached environment of biblical scholarship that prevails in many of the professional societies and is imposed in the 'religious studies' requirements of many colleges and universities, as well as prepared to address the contemporary meaning of the Bible as a sacred and normative text within a living community of faith. This means a much closer relationship between biblical exegesis and theological inquiry.

It has to be recognised that the welcome entrance of lay men and women into the ranks of Catholic biblical scholarship also brings a challenge to this view of the role of Catholic biblical scholarship. Whereas in the past the majority of biblical scholars were priests and religious most of whom had an extensive theological training prior to their specialising in biblical studies, more and more lay men and women begin their graduate work in Scripture with relatively sparse theological background. The Catholic biblical scholar of the future will need both theological and exegetical grounding. The interface of biblical exegesis and theological inquiry cannot be simply a matter of devotion or reverence for the biblical text but the capacity to articulate the theological dimensions of the bible and their relationship to the ongoing tradition of the Church. The goal, however, is not to create false harmony between the two nor to reduce the message of the Bible to a reinforcement of catechesis. Catholic biblical scholarship

---

5. *Jesus of Nazareth*, Volume I, xvi.

in the future, I believe, will require a deeper penetration both of the complexity of a pertinent biblical text or tradition and of the theological intuitions of the Church's teaching. Love of the biblical text may well lead to a 'hermeneutics of love' in approaching the potential problems raised by the Bible but it cannot mean blunting the use of historical-critical and other methods in exploring the meaning of the Bible in order to keep peace in the family of faith.

The biblical renewal that has swept through the Church in the past century can bring incredible richness and spiritual nourishment to people of faith. It has also, I believe, significantly changed expectations for the role of the biblical scholar who aspires to serve the Church.

14

History as Bulwark, Bridge and Bulldozer: *Dei Verbum* and Ecumenical, Biblical Endeavour

Alan Cadwallader

In 1664, the Reverend Dr John Luke, who would later (in 1685) be appointed to the Chair in Arabic at Cambridge University, rose to deliver a sermon before the board of the English Levant Company.[1] This was the ultimate test of prospective candidates for chaplaincy at one of the company's commercial centres at Constantinople, Smyrna and Aleppo. In spite of its length, he managed to secure the position. Luke's sermon stands out from the usual offerings into the competition for a chaplaincy in the eastern Mediterranean. The familiar fare relied on a healthy dose of morality combined with justifications of the business ventures of the company in the Ottoman Empire. One chaplain thirty years later, Edmund Chishull, for example, had pinned his sermon and his hopes on Psalm 107:23—'those that go down to the sea in ships to do business on the great waters'. Needless to say, the text provided the authorisation for the Levant Company's ventures; God even became 'the great Proprietor'.[2]

Luke however, whilst extolling the hallmark, protestant, exegetical principle of a 'plain' reading of Scripture, accented that history ought to be taken to deliver this 'plain meaning' of the text. The supplying history was to be found in early Christian texts closest to the time, the practices of Graeco-Roman culture and, perhaps most importantly, 'the poor reliques' of once famous and flourishing churches.[3] Already

---

1. For the little we know of the life and career of Luke, see my 'The Reverend Dr John Luke and the Churches of Chonai', in *JGRBS*, 48 (2008): 319–338, at 328–29.
2. Edmund Chishull, *Sermon Preached Before the Honourable Company of Merchants Trading to the Levant-seas at St Hellen's, January 16 being Sunday 1697/8* (London: S Manship, 1698), 4.
3. J Luke, *Sermon Preached before the Right Worshipfull Company of the Levant*

in Europe, word had begun to spread of the material remains of churches mentioned in the New Testament.[4] There may have been an initial valorisation of history over pilgrimage as a mark of distinction between Catholicism and Protestantism.[5] Luke certainly felt compelled briefly to mention catholic impiety and deception.[6] But he was more interested in the connection between ancient text and artifact.

Luke became part of a revolution in biblical interpretation that would take another three centuries to unfold. Even though his own journals of tours through Turkey remained unpublished,[7] they were excavated by the English Consul, Sir Paul Rycaut for a series of books published towards the end of the seventeenth century.[8] Most noticeably, these writings began to tear at the fabric of a mystical or prophetic reading of the letters to the seven churches of Asia in the Book of Revelation.[9] Such readings can still occasionally be found today. But contemporary scholarship generally reads Revelation within a first century context rather than as a trans-temporal overview that sees each named church as indicating a particular age in the church's development, almost always privileging the interpreter's own position as either penultimate or the ultimate one. History, the 'poor reliques' or material culture of history, had revolutionised biblical interpretation.

Merchants at St Olav's Hart-Street, Thursday Dec 15, 1664 (London: R Daniell, 1664), 14, 15, 24.

4. See James T Bent, *Early Voyages and Travels in the Levant 1. The Diary of Master Thomas Dallam 1599-1600 II Extracts from the Diaries of Dr. John Covel 1670-1679 with some account of the Levant Company of Turkey Merchants* (NY: Burt Franklin, 1968 repr). H Timberlake's *A True and Strange Discourse of the Trauailes of Two English pilgrims what admirable accidents befell them in their journey towards Ierusalem, Gaza, Grand Cayro, Alexandria and other places. Also what rare antiquities, monuments and notable memories (according with the ancient remembrances in the holy scriptures) they saw in Terra Sancta* (London: Thomas Archer). The journal went through eight editions from 1603 to 1631.
5. See Paris O'Donnell, 'Pilgrimage or "anti-pilgrimage"? Uses of mementoes and relics in English and Scottish narratives of travel to Jerusalem, 1596-1632', in *Studies in Travel Writing*, 13 (2009): 125–39.
6. Luke, *Sermon*, 7.
7. They are held in the British Library, Harl Ms 7021.
8. *The Present State of the Ottoman Empire* (1686), *Account of the Greek and Armenian Churches* (1679), *The History of the Turkish Empire* (London: John Starkey, 1680).
9. See, for example, that of Berengaudus of Ferrières (*PL* 17.770).

The rise of the historical critical method as the privileged method for biblical interpretation was however neither uniform nor unchallenged across the different churches. During the nineteenth century, 'history' was a highly contested arena, even if one of the epistemological foundations privileged in that century (along with science). The lines of conflict that were drawn in that century continue to operate today,[10] though the identity of the protagonists shifts both within and between confessional allegiances. The Anglican Richard Hutton, one-time editor of the London-based newspaper, *The Spectator*, wrote to his friend John Henry Newman, 'it is the most difficult of earthly problems to combine the religious spirit with the spirit of intellectual severity as to the objective conditions of belief.'[11]

Hutton was naming the disease that haunted religious life in that century as well as the assumptions about 'objective conditions'. The very method that much of Christian scholarship was embracing, whether enthusiastically or begrudgingly, that of historical criticism, was yet rendering suspect the very focus of its enquiry, the truth of biblical, even religious, foundations and transmission. For some, like the 'Cambridge Triumvirate' of Church of England Professors, Joseph Barber Lightfoot, Fenton JA Hort and Brooke Foss Westcott, this simply demanded a better harvest of the available historical materials and a better handling of the result. For them, history was the unequivocal arena for the display of God's providence and any difficulties in matching the two was either fuel for further research or, in the face of inadequate results, a resigned humility that left the foundation untrammeled.[12] Where history was turned against Providence, as was thought to be increasingly emanating from continental sources after the publication of Strauss' *Life of Christ* (1835), Lightfoot turned his mastery of detail into a methodical defence of Christian origins in the apostolic age,[13] and Westcott and

---

10. See Mark C Taylor, *About Religion: Economies of Faith in Virtual Culture* (Chicago: University of Chicago Press, 1999).
11. Hutton to Newman 20 February, 1872 (*The Letters and Diaries of John Henry Newman*, edited by Ian Ker et al [31 vols; Charlottesville, VA: InteLex Corp, 1995], Vol 26, 40). Hereafter *LDJHN*.
12. See, especially, Geoffrey R Treloar, *Lightfoot the Historian* (Tübingen: Mohr Siebeck, 1998), 63–92.
13. See Lightfoot's demolition of the tendentious speculations of antagonists to orthodox Christianity as manifest in the anonymous (=WR Cassels) work, *Supernatural Religion* in his *Essays on the Work entitled Supernatural Religion*

Hort prized back the accretions of later ages in a new edition of the Greek text of the New Testament.[14] All three were committed to the study of ancient texts but they were also persuaded that other historical artefacts, such as coins, inscriptions and art were critical informants of the history to be reconstructed.[15] Providence however was capable of a number of perspectives, including that of defending the received traditions of the church as providentially ordered. Westcott and Hort's *bête noir*, Dean John Burgon, vehemently denounced the new directions, considering that this loosened the sense of God's control of the history of the church.[16]

The Cambridge professors, by contrast, considered that the understanding of the church in its origins and development had been distorted through a series of accretions over time. The text of the Bible for example had received manifold adjustments in its transmission and translation over the centuries—including, famously, the various endings supplemented to Mark's gospel and the trinitarian formula in 1 John 5:7–8.[17] Similarly, the number of letters written by Ignatius of Antioch had multiplied far beyond the seven that Lightfoot demonstrated were authentic. History therefore became a crucial judgment of understandings that frequently carried the privileged label of the tradition of the church—when applied uncritically, a type of 'ecclesiastical terrorism', as Lightfoot ventured in an unusual extravagance.[18] History was an instrument of reform, which therefore

---

(London: Macmillan, 1889, second edition, 1893).
14. Brooke F Westcott and Fenton JA Hort, *The New Testament in the Original Greek* (London: Macmillan, 1881).
15. Lightfoot and Hort, for example, were responsible for the collation and translation of a number of the first inscriptions to come out of John Turtle Wood's excavations in Ephesus (1863 74) and a revision of most of the 200 that were eventually published. See John T Wood to Joseph B Lightfoot 7 February 1876 (Durham Dean and Chapter Library, Lightfoot Papers) and the list of assisting scholars in JT Woods, *Discoveries at Ephesus: including the site and remains of the great temple of Diana* (London / Boston: Longmans, Green and Todd / Osgood, 1877), xix.
16. See, for example, his *The Last Twelve Verses of the Gospel according to S. Mark vindicated against recent critical objectors* . . .(Oxford/London: J. Parker, 1871).
17. See my 'The Hermeneutical Potential of the Multiple Endings of Mark's Gospel', in *Colloquium* 43 (2011): 129–46.
18. See John B Lightfoot, *The Apostolic Fathers Pt II: S. Ignatius, S. Polycarp* (London: Macmillan, 1885), vii-viii.

placed the present (and its perceived needs) in direct connection with the past. The Bible, with its many and varied indications of the divine life and will incarnated into the past, especially in the person of Jesus Christ, was the ideal (though not the exclusive) focus for the historical task. These scholars were filled with what Westcott described as 'an absolute faith in language and so in Scripture'.[19] Indeed, Westcott was often cited as affirming that faults in grammar were the well-spring of heresy. However, there were differences even between the three. Lightfoot saw the discovery of history as tending towards a singular, fixed entity. Westcott however regarded this as simply the beginning which unlocked further variables to be entertained—in other words, after historical inquiry has done its requisite work, multiple meanings are then able to be adduced.[20]

Of course, this was not the only understanding of history. For John Henry Newman, even before his admission into the Roman Catholic Church, the historical critical method might as readily indicate flaws in the facticity of Scripture.[21] Newman was prepared to go further, arguing that Scripture was not homogenous, not uniformly inspired, indeed that there was a separation between the author of a text and the text itself: 'The great question . . . always is what did the sacred writer mean? Not, what does the bare letter say?' For Newman, the authority in matters of dispute therefore lay not in historical criticism (with its frequent preoccupation with authorial intent) but in the church: '. . . in order to solve them [ie matters of dispute], what does the Infallible Church say that the sacred writer meant.'[22] However, for Newman, the 'Infallible Church' was more to be defined by reference

---

19. Brooke F Westcott to Alexander Macmillan, 9 December, 1859 (British Library Add Ms 55092 [Macmillan Correspondence]), f.73.
20. Westcott is reported as delineating the difference between himself and Lightfoot as one of making a subject indefinite compared to making it definite: Francis K Aglianby, *The Life of Edward Henry Bickersteth Bishop & Poet* (London: Longmans, Green & Co 1907), 42.
21. See Tract 85: *Holy Scripture in its Relation to the Catholic Creed* (1838). Newman readily acknowledged that the Pentateuch was made up of several documents, that the Psalms were not all composed by David, even that the Vulgate was a mixed translation. Inspiration meant no more than preservation from errors of faith and morals not from faults. See Jaak Seynaeve, *Cardinal Newman's Doctrine on Holy Scripture, according to his published works and previously unedited manuscripts* (Louvain: Publications universitaires de Louvain, 1953), 88, 104.
22. Seynaeve, *Cardinal Newman's Doctrine on Holy Scripture*, 150.

to the whole church expressing itself through an encyclical than in the encyclical itself. His defence of the consultation of the laity in matters of doctrine,[23] aroused suspicions of heresy, if not of a hangover of his Anglican (read as 'protestant') past.[24]

Whatever the perspective or approach, at this point in development of the interpretation of Scripture, there was a basic controlling assumption even if its sources of guarantee were different. In Peter Lampe's succinct distillation, there was a 'Thomistic correspondence' between the reality and the language used to describe that reality: *ens intellectui concordat*, being accords with cognition.[25] Historical criticism was for some the means by which this might be demonstrated. Indeed, the first English Cardinal, Nicholas Wiseman, grounded his biblical writings in the 'grammatico-historical' method,[26] both for the polemical purposes of demonstrating Catholic respect for the inspired treasure of the Bible committed to the Church as against Protestantism and as demonstrating the validity of Church dogma as grounded in the Bible. Some Catholics were uneasy about Wiseman's accent, which sometimes gave too much ground to protestant shibboleths. For them, tradition or at least the church's teaching was the ground on which surety was to be found, even if the method was not thereby dismissed. Wiseman never allowed his biblical scholarship to stray from confessional lines, even producing a substantial defence of the authenticity of 1 John 5:7–8. But for him, there was also no question that the method yielded support for Church teaching.[27] In this sense, there was a marked parallel with the use of the method by leading Anglican and Protestant interpreters, though the purposes and results were vastly different and hardly encouragement for common tasks.

---

23. An article published in the magazine, *The Rambler*, July 1859.
24. The Bishop of Newport, TJ Brown, certainly raised Newman's argument as deserving the attention of Rome. See Newman to TJ Brown 17 November 1859, *LDJHN* Vol XIX, 239).
25. Peter Lampe, *New Testament Theology in a Secular World: A Constructivist Work in Philosophical Epistemology and Christian Apologetics* (London: T&T Clark, 2012), 6 *et passim*, citing from Aquinas, *Questiones disputatae de veritate* 1, art. 1–2.
26. Nicholas Wiseman, *The Real Presence of the Body and Blood of Our Lord Jesus Christ in the Blessed Eucharist, Proved from Scripture* (Dublin: James Duffy, 1836), 37.
27. See Timothy Larsen, *A People of One Book: The Bible and the Victorians* (Oxford: Oxford University Press, 2011), 43-65.

For the scholarly leaders of the Established Church of England, the battles over the method were largely resolved by the end of the nineteenth century. Less than forty years had passed since heresy charges had rewarded a number of clergymen for their promotion of critical approaches to Bible in the collection titled *Essays and Reviews* (1860).[28] One Anglican Bishop, John Colenso, had been excommunicated (in 1866) for impugning the accuracy of the Pentateuch.[29] Westcott, though he had disagreed with some of the conclusions of the volume, nevertheless had vehemently defended the right of scholars to explore the issues. He wrote a telling letter addressing what was, in his view, at stake 'I look on the assailants of the Essayists, from Bishops downwards, as likely to do more harm to the Church and the Truth than the Essayists. The only result of such wild clamour must be to make people believe that the voice of authority alone, and not of calm reason, can meet the theories of the Essayists.'[30] It is the fever of these times that likely lies behind Lightfoot's barb about 'ecclesiastical terrorism'.

By century's end, Westcott (by then a Bishop himself), recognized that the field of biblical studies had irrevocably changed. In a preparatory briefing on the 'Critical Study of Holy Scripture' for the Lambeth Conference of the bishops of the world-wide Anglican Communion,[31] Westcott systematically laid out a review of the century. He regarded three aspects as characteristic of the old attitude to the Bible:

> i) that the authority of the several books was equally in all cases placed beyond the range of historical enquiry

---

28. See Ieuan Ellis, *Seven Against Christ: A Study of 'Essays and Reviews'* (Leiden: Brill, 1980).
29. See Timothy Larsen, 'Bishop Colenso and his Critics: the Strange Emergence of Biblical Criticism in Victorian Britain', in *Scottish Journal of Theology*, 50 (1997): 433–58.
30. Brooke F Westcott to JF Wickenden 25 Feb 1861 (Arthur Westcott, *The Life and Letters of Brooke Foss Westcott* [2 vols; London: Macmillan, 1903] vol 1, 215).
31. 'Notes on the Critical Study of Holy Scripture' Lambeth Palace Library Ms 1401 ff 5–6. These notes have never had a public airing until now (and here the treatment of necessity must be condensed). The notes were marked as 'Strictly Confidential' either as a safeguard in preparation for the Lambeth Conference or out of apprehension that the notes were still too radical for popular consumption.

ii) that the current text was free from corruption to which other ancient texts are liable

iii) that the interpretation of the Bible was guarded by an authoritative tradition.

'Serious enquiry into the facts' he noted, 'showed that such assumptions were baseless.' By contrast he argued that it had been established beyond question:

i) that the composition, the history, the reception of the different Books of the Bible, offered problems of varied and grave difficulty which have not been finally solved in all cases

ii) that the current texts of the Scriptures show phenomena exactly like those of other ancient writings

iii) that traditional interpretations, even when right in spirit, often rest on unsubstantial foundations.

Having argued for the value of the several Books (disputes about the status of the 'apocryphal' or deutero-canonical books notwithstanding), *when each is placed in its historical environment*, he expressed the anticipation that the fresh study of the Bible, if not engineering the reunion of Christendom might at least bring together 'in spiritual fellowship men [sic] widely separated by confessional differences'.

John Henry Newman was far less sanguine. He had witnessed the vehement reaction to the attacks on foundations of biblical and church teaching that historical criticism was perceived to be fostering. These were not confined to the Roman Catholic Church, as evidenced by the far-from-singular attacks by John Burgon mentioned above.[32]

He had also witnessed the remarkable tenderness felt between members of various denominations in the decade-long work of revision of the English Bible, a work which he had been invited to join.[33] But he felt that 'never were the obstacles greater or

---

32. See further, Larsen, *People of One Book*, 247-76.
33. See my 'Star-cross'd lovers: John Henry Newman and the Revision of the Bible', in *Australian E Journal of Theology*, 19.3 (2012): 229–43.

stronger which divide' the 'various Christian communions'.³⁴ The Ultramontane influence on the Roman Catholic Church which he had quietly disdained in his own time,³⁵ certainly appeared to accent these divisions. In America, the parallel and support to the English work of revision never extended an invitation to Roman Catholic scholars on the tendentious grounds that the Authorised Version was not the Roman Catholic Bible and they would have no interest in it.³⁶ The Bible, or at least the ancient and modern translated Bible, lent support to Newman's lament.

They were felt even more particularly when the same influences reverberated upon the interpretation of the Bible in the 1893 *Providentissimus Deus*. The document did recognise the humanity of biblical authors and endorsed the importance of knowing the linguistic, material and cultural world of the text for interpretation. But Providence remained clearly harnessed to the congruency of historicity and the Bible against the so-called modernist heresies that would undermine the dogmatic affirmation of the inerrancy of Scripture. If the Scriptures sprung from God, then any suggestion of error therein was ultimately an attack upon God (and God's Church). Heresies of course need heretics and a range of Catholic biblical scholars from Marie-Joseph Lagrange OP to Alfred Loisy soon enough became impaled on the horns of the encyclical. But, just like the Church of England half a century earlier in the aftermath of the hot-blooded onslaught against Bishop Colenso and the 'Essayists', change was afoot. Obedient in its pursuit of biblical studies as endorsing Church teaching it may have been at first,³⁷ but the Pontifical Biblical

---

34. Newman to David Brown (Principal of the Free College, Scotland), 24 October, 1872 (*LDJHN* 26.178).
35. Newman was most uneasy about the moves to formalise papal infallibility by edict: JH Newman to Bp Ullathorne 28 Janary 1870 (in Wilfrid P Ward, *The Life of John Henry Cardinal Newman* [2 vols; London: Longmans, Green & Co, 1912], vol 2, 287–9).
36. Resolution of the American Bible Revision Committee, 30 November, 1872 (American Bible Revision Committee Minute Book in the American Bible Society Archives Box RG 86 0-3-6). The Dean of Westminster Abbey, Arthur Stanley had tried to change the mind of the Committee, to no avail: see AP Stanley to Philip Schaff May 30ᵗʰ 1871 (*Documentary History of the American Committee on Revision* [New York: Private Printing, 1885], 46).
37. Such as in its affirmation of the Mosaic authorship of the Pentateuch (1906), the single authorship of the Book of Isaiah (1908) and the historicity of Genesis 1–3

Commission by its very formation (in 1902) was an indication that the Bible had become such a contested arena that direct attention to developments was required.[38]

The momentum thereafter was probably inevitable, even if the polemical inheritance that Newman had bemoaned would take some shedding. Herein, a growing familiarity with, if not endorsement of, the range of methods embraced under the heading of historical criticism generated an ecumenical climate to achieve what the Bible itself had been unable to do. The method became the bridge for a community of scholarship across the various Christian communions. The bridge would not be an immovable steel fixture and other methods have since complemented, challenged and supplemented the historical method just as serious questions about the method itself, its afideist foundations and its often conflictual relationship with tradition, have in recent decades threatened the structure and those collaborating upon its principle tenets.

The usual succession of Vatican pronouncements that are cited as the tracking of the gradual acceptance of the historical-critical method are *Spiritus Paracletus* (1920), *Divino Afflante Spiritu* (1943), *Dei Verbum* (1965) *L'interprétation de la Bible dans l'Église* (1993), and *Verbum Domini* (2010),[39] though only *Dei Verbum* (*DV*) held the status of 'dogmatic constitution'. The document *The Interpretation of the Bible in the Church* (henceforth *IBE*) stated baldly, 'The historical-critical method is the indispensable method for the scientific study of the meaning of ancient texts . . . diachronic study remains indispensable for making known the historical dynamism which animates sacred Scripture.'[40] At least in continuity from that (and previous documents) *Verbum Domini* (*VD*) also acknowledged 'the benefits that historical-critical exegesis and other recently-developed methods of textual analysis have brought to the life of the Church'.[41]

(1909).
38. See Ronald D Witherup, *Scripture: Dei Verbum* (New York: Paulist Press, 2006), 8–9.
39. This last, a Post-synodal Apostolic Exhortation, included a series of other pronouncements on the word of God in the life of the Church. See *The Interpretation of the Bible in the Church* footnote 8. Online text prepared by Felix Just, SJ http://catholic-resources.org/ChurchDocs/PBC_Interp-FullText.htm (last accessed 30/5/2013).
40. *IBE* I.A, I.A.4.
41. 'Post-synodal Apostolic Exhortation *Verbum Domini* of the Holy Father Benedict

The ecumenical dimensions of these documents have likewise followed a gradual path of affirmation, at times even recognised within the documents. The 'Introduction' to *IBE* itself affirms that the progress of Biblical studies within the Catholic Church 'has greatly smoothed the path of ecumenical dialogue'.[42] *VD* credited *DV* with delivering 'great benefits' on the 'ecumenical plane' amongst a number of arenas. *VD* provided a demonstration of that ecumenism with an acknowledgement of the contributions of biblical reflections from leaders of other traditions, Orthodox and Jewish, at the Synod of Bishops for and from which *VD* arose.

The ecumenical hope was not expressly touted in though it did affirm 'cooperation with the separated brethren' in the production of 'suitable and correct' translations of sacred Scripture,[43] a venture soon realised with a French ecumenical version, beginning with the Epistle to the Romans in 1967.[44] Similarly *DV* held out no particular method for the interpretation of the Bible, even though it recommended liturgical, devotional and instructional settings for exposure to the Bible, especially highlighting the accompaniment of prayer.[45] It advised the preparation of accompanying explanations for the biblical texts, which, whilst intended for 'the children of the Church', would doubtless pay attention to 'literary forms' (the closest the document came to indicating an exegetical method), the intention of the sacred writer in 'his own time and culture' and the human language in which the words of God are expressed.[46] This incarnational view extended to the tradition and judgment of the Church. Indeed 'Sacred tradition and Sacred Scripture form one sacred deposit of the word of God' even

---

XVI to the Bishops, Clergy, Consecrated Persons and the Lay Faithful on the Word of God in the Life and Mission of the Church', 32. English text from http://www.vatican.va/holy_father/benedict_xvi/apost_exhortations/documents/hf_ben-xvi_exh_20100930_verbum-domini_en.html (last accessed 30/5/2013).

42. *IBE*, Introduction A.
43. *DV* 22. Another document of the Second Vatican Council, the decree *Unitatis Redintegratio*, did affirm the 'precious instrument' of the 'sacred Scripture' for dialogue directed towards the unity held out by 'the Saviour' (21). English text from http://www.vatican.va/archive/hist_counciols/ii_vatican_council/documents/vat-ii_decree_19641121_unitatis-redintegratio_en.html (last accessed 30/5/2013).
44. See Yves Congar, *My Journal of the Council* (Adelaide: ATF Theology, 2012), 795.
45. *DV* 25.
46. *DV* 12–13.

though, at the same time, tradition itself is living and developing.[47] As much as such sentiments can be traced back through Catholic documents, the influence of the document on Scripture, Tradition and traditions published by the Fourth World Conference of Faith and Order held in Montreal in 1963 has been noted.[48]

It was well-known at the time, and can be confirmed by a careful reading of the text, that *DV* was the product of certain compromises between conservative and more open forces within the Council.[49] Such forces continued to play themselves out even in the translations of the Dogmatic Constitution. There is no authorised English translation of it, and so the affirmation of a correspondence between the four Gospels and the words and deeds of Jesus became variously translated. The Latin reads *ita semper ut vera et sincera de Iesu nobiscum communicarent*.[50] The phrase *vera et sincera* was retained in its separate elements in French, German and Italian, though with the addition of an explanatory substantive.[51] The English however took it as a hendiadys, 'honest truth' being the outcome.[52] The point may be subtle but it illustrates that *DV* did not conclude debate about the Bible, its interpretation and its relation to revelation but became as much an incitement to debate as a mirror of it. The call by some to have an authorised translation itself witnesses to the debate, even in the effort to settle it.[53] Translation is interpretation (*traduttore traditore*?)[54] and

---

47. *DV* 8–10.
48. Jean-Marie-Roger Tillard, 'Rome and Ecumenism' Faith and Order Commission Essays (1995), III.3. http://www.oikoumene.org/en/resources/documents/wcc-commissions/faith-and-order-commission/xii-essays/rome-and-ecumenism (last accessed 30/5/2013).
49. See Robert Crotty, *Three Revolutions: Three Drastic Changes in Interpreting the Bible* (Adelaide: ATF Theology, 2012), 72–74.
50. *DV* 19.
51. Respectively, varies et sincères choses; Mitteilungen . . . wahr und ehrlich; cose vere e sincere. All these are taken from the official Vatican website: http://www.vatican.va/archive/hist_councils/ii_vatican_council (last accessed 30/5/2013).
52. Both the Abbott and Flannery translations opted for this rendering. So too did the Spanish.
53. The prefect of the Congregation for the Doctrine of the Faith, Archbishop William J Levada has called for an official translation for the fiftieth anniversary of *DV* in 2015.
54. 'Is the translator a traitor?'—an old Italian proverb. Compare the aphorism of Cardinal John Henry Newman, 'The translated Bible is the stronghold of heresy', quoted by Frederic William Farrar, *The Bible: Its Meaning and Supremacy*

the effort to nail down a translation reflects a wariness (or weariness) about ongoing debate and the variety of authentic options that such a debate implies. Political determinations are inescapable.[55]

The politics of the immediate aftermath of *DV* were unwittingly given a decisive direction by a publication in the field of biblical studies. Raymond Brown's two-volume commentary on the Gospel of John was 'an epoch-making publication that changed the very nature of the series',[56] and followed on the heels of the release of *DV* in 1965. Although the historical-critical method had not been explicitly named in *DV*, the allusive reference to one of its arms, form-criticism (see above), became an express endorsement because of his demonstration of its worth. And when this was followed in 1968 by his joint editorship (in the Catholic Triumvirate of Brown, Joseph Fitzmyer and Roland Murphy) of the *Jerome Biblical Commentary*—this time in express honouring of the terms of *DV*— the method gained the explicit and underscored approval of the Pontifical Biblical Commission (PBC) in its 1993 pronouncement, which expanded a theological justification of it by drawing a parallel with the Christological dogma of the incarnation, 'its character both human and divine'.[57] And even though the PBC acknowledged the burgeoning of new methods of biblical interpretation, most especially in the variety of literary critical methods, the preference of Brown remained evident. In his own words, advising caution in the use of narrative criticism, Brown affirmed, 'by its own self-understanding Christianity is too fundamentally based on what Jesus actually said and did to be cavalier about historicity'.[58]

The ecumenical reach of Brown's authorial and editorial work

(London/New York: Longmans, Green & Co, second edition, 1901), 199.
55. See Umberto Eco, *Mouse or Rat?: Translation as Negotiation* (London: Phoenix, 2003).
56. Francis J Moloney, 'The Gospel of John: The Legacy of Raymond E Brown and Beyond', in *Life in Abundance: Studies of John's Gospel in Tribute to Raymond E Brown, SS* edited by James R Donahue (Collegeville, MN: Liturgical Press, 2005), 19. Brown's two volumes on John's Gospel in the Anchor Bible series published in 1966 and 1971 remain classics in the field.
57. *IBE* Introduction B. Compare *DV* 13 where the warrant for such a move is to be found. This was a major accent in Raymond Brown's 'centrist' position. See Brown, *Biblical Exegesis and Church Doctrine* (New York: Paulist Press, 1985), 14-15.
58. Brown, *An Introduction to the New Testament* (New York: Doubleday, 1997), 27.

became an indication of the ecumenical potential of *DV*, as was noted in the new edition of the *JBC*.[59] There was little doubt that the common ground had been tilled for such fertile developments by the historical-critical method. Roman Catholic biblical scholarship was no longer serving its own constituency alone. It was gaining respect and leadership in biblical circles generally, 'catholic in the non-parochial sense of the word' as the triumvirate wrote.[60]

However, there were a number of shifts occurring in relation to the historical-critical method that were threatening not only the authority of the method itself but also its ecumenical dimensions. *DV* had asserted that sacred Scripture and sacred Tradition comprise one sacred deposit of the Word of God. Congar noted in his diary, when this was proposed, 'I think that very bad.'[61] The statement that the teaching office of the Church was not above the word of God but serves it[62] was welcomed in protestant circles but nervousness remained about the relation of Scripture and Tradition.[63] *DV* affirmed their 'close connection and communication' and affirmed that Sacred Tradition was to receive the same sense of loyalty and reverence as Scripture.[64] The language was deliberately designed to separate Tradition from the teaching office of the Church so that the latter received its certainty and revelation from it, knows the canon of Scripture from it rather than creating it. Hence, 'not every Catholic teaching can be proved directly from Scripture'. There were three tensions consequent upon this affirmation. Firstly, Scripture was capable of demonstrating certain commitments that were absent or muted in later Tradition (such as the ecclesial leadership of women) or of not demonstrating elements that were given substantial regulation in Tradition (such as the three-fold order of ministry). Raymond Brown's little book, *Priest and Bishop: Biblical Reflections* (1970) highlighted this latter tension with what at times seemed to be a tepid affirmation of the leading of the Spirit in the later Church to develop offices of ministry

---

59. 'Preface' in *The New Jerome Bible Commentary* edited by Raymond E Brown, Joseph A Fitzmyer and RE Murphy (London: Geoffrey Chapman, 1989), xx-xxi.
60. *NJBC* Preface, xx.
61. Congar, *My Journal*, 799.
62. *DV* 10.
63. See, for example, Steven Harmon, 'Dei Verbum §9 in Baptist perspective', in *Ecclesiology* 5 (2009): 299-321.
64. *DV* 9.

that were not sustained in Scripture itself. This indicates the second tension. *DV* itself combined the notion that Tradition could develop along with the notion of deposit. The static and the dynamic are however not easily reconciled.[65] Thirdly, given the affirmation of the connections between Scripture and Tradition, it followed that approaches to the Scripture were likewise to be applied to Tradition. That is, the historical-critical method could embrace Tradition as it had done so with any other ancient text. Indeed the method could be applied to the very texts that authorised its use.[66] The implications for the teaching authority of the Church—also bound to Scripture and Tradition in the *DV*—were manifest. Texts, *all* texts, were now being located within their historical particularities. As Helmut Koester wrote, 'Those who fear that the historical-critical method threatens their control over religious orientation and theological judgment of their constituencies are absolutely correct.'[67]

This has lead, in some quarters, to a revival of nineteenth century fears that the historical-critical method is not sustaining faith in the Bible as the word of God. On the one hand, this can lead to almost apologetic efforts to privilege the Gospels as history above other early Christian texts—the battle over the relationship between sayings in the Gospel of Thomas and the canonical gospels being a case in point.[68] On the other, the very method itself has come under sustained attack from protestant and Catholic scholars alike. Walter Wink's tract, *Manifesto for Biblical Studies*, published less than a

---

65. The efforts of Orm Rush to define tradition as 'a power at work in people's lives' whilst accenting the dynamic side of tradition, especially in its aspect of the *sensus fidei*, obscures the more static element that is also present in the documents. See his 'The Prophetic Office in the Church' in *When the Magisterium Intervenes* edited by Richard R Gaillardetz (Adelaide: ATF Theology, 2012), 102.
66. Witherup, *Scripture*, xv.
67. 'Epilogue: Current Issues in New Testament Scholarship' in *The Future of Early Christianity: Essays in Honor of Helmut Koester* edited by Birger A Pearson (Minneapolis, MN: Fortress Press, 1991), 474.
68. See the latest contribution of John P Meier, 'The Parable of the Wheat and the Weeds (Matthew 13:24–30): Is Thomas's Version (Logion 57) Independent?', in *Journal of Biblical Literature*, 131/4 (2012): 715-32, a further illustration of his privileging of the canonical Gospels above all other writings for the development of the history of Jesus, argued in his *A Marginal Jew: Rethinking the Historical Jesus Vol 1: The Roots of the Problem and the Person* (New York: Doubleday, 1991).

decade after *DV*,⁶⁹ noted the lack of faith perspective in the method itself and its limitations in assessing matters that can only be subject to a faith stance—such as the resurrection.⁷⁰ The recognition of the (necessarily) atheistic assumption of the method initially failed to gain significant Catholic attention. The PBC's 1993 paper, *IBE*, was more intent on noting the problematics of the atheistic foundations of a psychoanalytic-critical methodology for the Bible.⁷¹ Wink retained the method with its limitations, ensuring that it collaborated with other methods which also had their own limitations. But the death of Raymond Brown and rise of Luke Timothy Johnson, who has shown little reserve in criticising both Brown and the approach,⁷² has witnessed a substantial lowering in the status accorded to the historical-critical method.⁷³

Whilst this lowering of status has failed to take account of the Christian underpinning of Brown's own practice,⁷⁴ the relation of the method and the presuppositions of the practitioner have only recently begun to be examined. Brown had already demonstrated that his faith presuppositions could entertain later readings and developments of texts that, in the time the texts were written, would struggle to be supported. However, this neat classifying distinction is not always easy to sustain. When Brown was able to affirm that Joseph of Arimathea was a disciple but that the women who followed from Galilee could not be accorded this designation,⁷⁵ there was a suspicion that there had been a confusion of historical-critical method and church teaching.⁷⁶ After all, *IBE* reserved its most

---

69. It was republished with considerable editing of his own personal journey, as *The Bible in Human Transformation* (Philadelphia, PA: Fortress Press, 1973).
70. See the discussion in Martin C Albl, *Reason, Faith and Tradition: Explorations in Catholic Theology* (Winona, MN: St Mary Press, 2009), 325–29.
71. *IBE* D.3.
72. See Moloney's defence of Brown against Johnson's criticisms: 'Gospel of John', 19–20.
73. Witherup, *Scripture*, 101–4.
74. See Kevin Duffy, 'The Ecclesial Hermeneutic of Raymond E Brown', in *Heythrop Journal*, 39 (1998): 37–56.
75. Brown, *The Death of the Messiah*, 2 volumes (New York, NY: Doubleday, 1994), 2.1155–59, 1224–25.
76. See the criticism by Elaine Wainwright, who argues that the 'also a disciple of Jesus' of Matt 27:57 must have the women (27:56) as its antecedent: *Shall We Look for Another: A Feminist Re-Reading of the Matthean Jesus* (Maryknoll, NY:

trenchant reservations for feminist criticism. It is worth noting the tenor of the comments:

> Feminist exegesis, to the extent that it proceeds from a preconceived judgment, runs the risk of interpreting the biblical texts in a tendentious and thus debatable manner. To establish its positions it must often, for want of something better, have recourse to arguments *ex silentio*. As is well known, this type of argument is generally viewed with much reserve: It can never suffice to establish a conclusion on a solid basis. On the other hand, the attempt made on the basis of fleeting indications in the texts to reconstitute a historical situation which these same texts are considered to have been designed to hide—this does not correspond at all to the work of exegesis properly so called. It entails rejecting the content of the inspired texts in preference for a hypothetical construction, quite different in nature.[77]

The attempt to imply the sanctity of the historical-critical method by a demeaning of feminist approaches failed to recognise that all history is constructed. More dangerously it has lead to a magisterial silencing of religious women, notably Elizabeth Johnson, CSJ. It is pertinent to note at this point that other critical methods have begun to turn on more substantial limitations of the historical-critical method. History, the writing that is produced after the application of the historical-critical method, is not privileged as a value-free text. This is one of the foundation points of feminist criticism but it derives from developments in literary method that have highlighted that all writing is located in a particular time and reflects the values of particular groups. The provocative question 'Is history fiction?'[78]

Orbis, 1998), 108–9.
77. *IBE* E.2. It is worth noting that the final paragraph of the section on feminist criticism, which contains a finger-wagging admonition was expressly not endorsed by four members of the PBC, with four others abstaining from voting.
78. See Ann Curthoys and John Docker, *Is History Fiction?* (Sydney: UNSW Press, 2006).

highlights the state in which biblical scholarship finds itself fifty years after *DV*.

This is not a cause for lament, even though there have been some efforts within the Roman Catholic Church to seek alternatives to the historical-critical method in the approach to the sacred text. The more recent revival or dissemination of *lectio divina*, an accent on the spirituality of the biblical texts, the reclamation of patristic interpretation are but a few indications of a collapse of confidence in the method and its results and the effort (frequently heavily constructed)[79] to establish a more stable, permanent surety. For others, the material reality of the early basileia movement, however historical writing will constantly reframe it, remains as an on-going invitation to explore the text and artifact of the past, lest there be, as Cardinal Ratzinger warned, a retreat into gnosticism.[80] The sheer diversity of the resultant interpretations is not something to be bemoaned nor is it to warrant a flight into another monolithic frame, that in its transtemporality or attempted atemporality only re-invites a gnostic hegemony, not unlike the history-adrift prophetic/mystical interpretations of the Seven Churches of Revelation with which we began. Rather the acceptance of our own temporality and the contingency of our historical constructions, serviceable as they may be in any present moment, are themselves potently conducive to the ecumenical dimensions of both faith and the writing of history. The certainty of Thomistic correspondence may be gone, but, as Peter Lampe perceives of the present state of historiography, 'Epistemology drives us towards looking at each other at eye level, towards modesty about oneself, which provides a basis for tolerant behavior without condescension.'[81]

---

79. See my critical assessment of the 'Ancient Christian Commentary on Scripture' series, in 'The Fall, the Samaritan and the Wounded Man: An Example of Multiple Readings of Scripture (Lk 10:24–37)' in *Lost in Translation?: Anglicans, Controversy and the Bible,* edited by Scott Cowdell and Muriel Porter (Thornbury: Desbooks, 2004), 155–56.
80. 'On the 100th Anniversary of the Pontifical Biblical Commission: The Relationship between Magisterium and Exegetes' (2003). Text at http://www.vatican.va/roman_curia/congregations/cfaith/pcb_documents/rc_con_cfaith_doc_20030510_ratzinger-comm-bible_en.html (last accessed 31/5/2013).
81. Lampe, *New Testament Theology*, 157.

List of Contributors

Dianne Bergant, CSA is Carroll Stuhlmueller, CP Distinguished Professor of Biblical Studies at Catholic Theological Union in Chicago. She was President of the Catholic Biblical Association of America (2000-1) and has been an active member of the Chicago Catholic/Jewish Scholars Dialogue for the past thirty years. Besides a three volume commentary on the lectionary, she has written commentaries on Genesis, Job and Ecclesiastes, Lamentations, and the Song of Songs. She is currently working in the areas of biblical interpretation and biblical theology, particularly issues of peace, ecology and feminism.

Alan Cadwallader is Senior Lecturer in Biblical Studies at the Australian Catholic University (ACU), Canberra Campus. An Anglican priest, he has worked in ecumenical consortia for most of his teaching life and is particularly concerned at the interface between Bible and culture, past and present. He is editor of a number of recent publications: with Fr Michael Trainor, *'Colossae in Space and Time'* (Göttingen, 2011); *'Pieces of Ease and Grace'* (Adelaide, 2013) and *'Where the Wild Ox Roams'* (Festschrift for Norm Habel; Sheffield: 2013). He is currently working on a series of books related to material and textual history of the ancient site of Colossae.

Antony F Campbell SJ was doing his theology in France as Vatican II was ending. Studies took him to the Biblicum (Rome) for a licentiate, to Munich (Germany) for experience, and to Claremont (California) for a PhD. He has published widely, his publications sanctioned with a Doctor of Divinity from the then MCD. He taught Older Testament at Jesuit Theological College, within the United Faculty of Theology, until his retirement at the end of 2009.

Mark Benedict Coleridge was ordained a priest in 1974 for the Archdiocese of Melbourne. In 1984 he received the Licentiate in Sacred Scripture from the Pontifical Biblical Institute in Rome, and its doctorate in 1992 for his dissertation on the Infancy Narrative in Luke's Gospel. He returned to Melbourne in 1992 and held a range of theological appointments, including lecturing in New Testament at Catholic Theological College where he was subsequently appointed its Master. He later returned to Rome, working in the Holy See's Secretariat of State.

He was ordained to the episcopate in 2002 and served as auxiliary bishop of the Archdiocese of Melbourne from 2002 to 2006. In 2006 he was appointed Archbishop of Canberra and Goulburn, a position that he held until 2012, when he was appointed Archbishop of Brisbane.

In 2004, he was appointed a member of the Pontifical Council for Culture and Chair of the Roman Missal Editorial Committee of the International Committee for English in the Liturgy. He was subsequently named Chair of the International Commission for the Preparation of an English-language Lectionary. In 2011 he was appointed a member of the Pontifical Council for Social Communications.

Elizabeth Dowling RSM is a lecturer in the School of Theology, Australian Catholic University (ACU). After many years as a teacher in Secondary Schools, Elizabeth took up the opportunity to pursue theological studies and completed her doctorate in Biblical Studies in 2005. She has lectured in the area of Biblical Studies at ACU ever since. Elizabeth's main focus is on the Gospels, particularly the Gospel of Luke. She is the author of *Taking away the Pound: Women, Theology and the Parable of the Pounds in the Gospel of Luke* (London: T&T Clark International, 2007), as well as several articles on the Gospels.

Dale Launderville OSB is a member of St John Abbey in Collegeville, Minnesota, and a professor of theology at St John's University School of Theology and Seminary, St John's University and the College of St Benedict. He received his doctorate from the Catholic University of America. His most recent book is *Celibacy in the Ancient World* (Liturgical Press). He is a frequent contributor to the Faith Alive!

series distributed by Catholic News Service and published in many diocesan newspapers, including The Witness.

Peter Malone MSC studied at the Australian National University in Canberra for an Arts degree in History and at the Gregorian University in Rome for Theology. From 1972 he taught in the Yarra Theological Union, Old Testament Studies and Introduction to Theology. He also worked at the National Pastoral Institute and the Heart of Life Spirituality Centre in Melbourne, specialising in Media Studies as well as Australian Theology. He was awarded a Doctorate in Theology (*Honoris Causa*) in 2008 by the Melbourne College of Divinity. He edited Compass, a review of Topical Theology from 1971 to 1998. He was the first president of SIGNIS, the World Catholic Association for Communication (2001–2005). He writes and lectures on theology and cinema. His books include *Films and Sacraments, Mary and Film* and *Screen Jesus*.

Denis P Minns OP is a Dominican, presently living in Sydney. He has taught the history and theology of early Christianity in Melbourne, Sydney, and Oxford. He is the author of *Irenaeus: An Introduction* (T&T Clark, 2010) and (with Paul Parvis) of *Justin Martyr, Philosopher and Martyr, Apologies* (Oxford University Press, 2009). He has recently completed an English translation of Yves Congar, *Journal d'un théologien 1946–1956*, to be published by ATF Theology.

Francis J Moloney SDB, was born and bred in Melbourne. A Doctor of Philosophy from the University of Oxford in 1975, he has worked in Australia, Europe and the USA. From 1999–2005 he was the Professor of New Testament and the Dean of the School of Theology and Religious Studies at the Catholic University of America, Washington, DC, and from 2006–2011 the Provincial of the Salesians in Australia. He is currently a Senior Professorial Fellow at Australian Catholic University, the author of many studies, including commentaries on the Gospels of John and Mark. His most recent publications are *Love in the Gospel of John*, and *The Resurrection of the Messiah*.

Christopher J Monaghan CP studied at the Pontifical Biblical Institute in Rome and is President of Yarra Theological Union, a College of University of Divinity, where has been teaching New Testament since

1987. His publications include *A Source Critical Edition of the Gospels of Matthew and Luke in Greek and English*, Subsidia Biblica 40 (Rome: Gregorian and Biblical Press, 2010) and *A Friendly Guide to Paul* (Mulgrave: Garratt, 2014).

Mark O'Brien OP, is an Australian and an ordained member of the Dominican Order (Order of Preachers). He completed the License (Masters) in Biblical Studies at the Pontifical Biblical Institute in 1976 and a Doctorate in the University of Divinity (formerly the Melbourne College of Divinity) in 1987. He has held academic and administrative positions in the Dominican Order, the University of Divinity, and other institutions. He has published a number of books and articles on the Hebrew Bible/Old Testament. He is currently Associate Professor of Biblical Studies in the University of Divinity.

Gerald O'Collins SJ, was born in Melbourne, and took his PhD at the University of Cambridge and taught at the Gregorian University (Rome) 1973–2006, where he was also dean of the theology faculty (1985–91). Now adjunct professor of ACU and a research fellow of the University of Divinity, he has authored or co-authored sixty-two published books, which include *The Second Vatican Council on Other Religions* and *Rethinking Fundamental Theology* (both Oxford University Press), as well two volumes of his autobiography, *A Midlife Journey* and *On the Left Bank of the Tiber* (Connor Court).

Jerome Murphy-O'Connor OP died in Jerusalem on 11 November 2013 at the age of seventy-eight. He completed his doctorate at Fribourg University, Switzerland and was for many years Professor of New Testament studies at the École Biblique in Jerusalem. He was a specialist in Pauline studies. He received four honorary doctorates, from Villanova, Notre Dame, Graduate Theological Union Berkeley, and the National University of Ireland, as well as the Dominican Order's highest academic honour, Master of Sacred Theology.

John Owens SM is a Catholic priest of the Society of Mary. He holds a licentiate in philosophy from the Angelicum, Rome, and a doctorate in philosophy from the University of Munich. He is currently lecturer in philosophy at Good Shepherd College Auckland. His main research interests are in late twentieth-century philosophy in relation to the pre-modern philosophical tradition, and in the life-philosophy of Aristotle and its significance for metaphysics.

Donald Senior CP, was born in Philadelphia, he is a member of the Passionist Congregation and was ordained a priest in 1967. He received his doctorate in New Testament studies from the University of Louvain in Belgium in 1972, with advanced studies at Hebrew Union College in Cincinnati and Harvard University. He is a frequent lecturer and speaker throughout the United States and abroad, and serves on numerous boards and commissions. He has published extensively on biblical topics, with numerous books and articles for both scholarly and popular audiences. He is the general editor of the acclaimed *Catholic Study Bible* (Oxford University Press, revised edition 2006) and editor in chief of the journal, *The Bible Today*. He is past President of the Catholic Biblical Association of America (1997–1998) and of the Association of Theological Schools of the United States and Canada (2007–2009). He currently serves as the President of the Council of Religious Leaders of Metropolitan Chicago. In 2001, Pope John Paul II appointed him as a member of the Pontifical Biblical Commission and he was reappointed in 2006 by Pope Benedict XVI.

Justin Taylor SM is a Marist priest, born in New Zealand in 1943. He graduated Phd at the University of Cambridge in 1972. From 1988 to 2011, he taught at the École Biblique et Archéologique Française of Jerusalem in the fields of New Testament and Christian origins and was Vice-Director from 2007 to 2010. In 2006 he received the degree of Doctor of Divinity of the University of Cambridge. In 2011 he was given a Doctorate of Sacred Theology (*honoris causa*) by the Pontifical University of St Thomas (Angelicum), Rome. He is the author of several books and numerous articles.

Marie Turner obtained her doctorate from Flinders University in Adelaide, South Australia, and is a Senior Lecturer in Biblical Studies there. Her special research interests are in the wisdom literature of the Bible, in theologies of creation, and in ecological readings of biblical texts. She is currently writing an ecological commentary on the book of Ecclesiastes.

Biblical Index

Old Testament

Genesis
1:26	94
3:15	91, 92, 102
3:22–23	110
6:7	94
8:21	94
12:2	102
15:6	64
17:23	64
22:10	126

Exodus
7 – 12	63

Deuteronomy
9:3	98
13:3	98
21:18–21	98

1 Samuel
13:14	71

2 Samuel
1:25–26	94

1 Kings
13	94
22	94
22:23	94

Psalm
8	93
107:23	207
137:8–9	94

Ecclesiastes
1:4	106
3:9–22	xviii, 105, 112
3:9–13	107
3:11	xviii, 109, 110
3:14	xviii
3:18–22	109
3:18	104

Wisdom
11 –19	63

Isaiah
7:14	63
54:8	93
63:7 – 64:11	128
64:1	128
64:11	128

Jeremiah
28	94
28:2	94
28:15–17	94

Ezekiel
36 – 39	157
36:16–17a	156
36:18–28	156
36:23c–38	156, 157

37:1–14	156	3:18–21	34
38–39	156	16:12–15	33
		20:29	32
Hosea		20:30–31	32
3:1	94		
		Acts	
Micah		1:21–22	121
1:10	76	17	174
		17:22–31	174

New Testament

Matthew		Romans	
1:23	63	1:19–20	102, 104
21:1–22	144, 145	2:6–7	102
27L56	222	11:36	52
27:57	222	15:4	102
		16:25–26	4
Mark		16:26	10
1:9–11	125		
1:9	125	1 Corinthians	
1:10	128	8:6	51
1:10–11	126, 127,	10:11	64
1:11	128	11:23	xiv, 46, 58
1:15	39	11:2	46
6:7	121	15:3	xv, 46, 58
12:29–31	85		
		2 Corinthians	
Luke		3:3	44
24:44–48	84		
24:44	86	Galatians	
		1:9	46
John		4:21–31	64
1	168	5:16	81
1:3	102, 104	5:19–21	75
1:14	199		
1:18	168	Ephesians	
3:1–21	33	1:9	3, 4
3:1–2	34	3:4	4
3:2	25	3:9	4
3:3–5	34	6:19	5
3:6–10	34		
3:11–12	34	Philippians	
3:13–15	34	3:8	137, 138
3:16–17	34	4:9	46

Colossians
1:15 168
1:27 4
2:6 46
4:3 4

1 Thessalonians
2:13 46, 77
4:1 46

2 Thessalonians
2:15 46
3:6 46

2 Timothy
3:16–17 124

Hebrews
1:1–2 3
1:3 168
12:22 64

2 Peter
3:14–16 32

1 John
1:2–3 3
5:7–8 210, 212

2 John
12 43

Revelation
21:2 64
21:10 64

Citations from *Dei Verbum*

DV 1	3, 16, 89, 168	*DV* 13	15
DV 2	3, 4, 5, 6, 7, 13, 34, 168	*DV* 14	5, 6, 7, 14, 15, 102
DV 3	5, 91, 101, 103, 112	*DV* 15	4, 5, 7, 95, 97, 169
DV 4	3, 5, 6, 7, 9, 10, 11, 16, 186	*DV* 17	4, 5, 6
		DV 18	120
DV 5	10, 13	*DV* 19	123, 124
DV 6	5, 8, 16, 17, 89	*DV* 21	5, 20, 99
DV 7	3, 5, 11, 25, 26, 89	*DV* 22	136, 146
DV 8	10, 11, 14, 15, 39, 62, 89	*DV* 23	24, 29, 101, 127, 146
		DV 24	4, 19, 24, 170
DV 9	3, 24, 35, 80	*DV* 25	10, 137, 139, 170
DV 10	4, 11, 24, 25, 35, 37, 62, 89, 95, 96, 187	*DV* 26	4, 20
DV 11	11, 29, 104, 124, 169		
DV 12	25, 26, 29, 76, 78, 91, 96, 97, 101, 125, 136, 139, 169		

Index of Names and Subjects

A

Athanasius, 49.

B

Benedict XVI, Pope, viii, xii, xvi, xxiv, 25, 33, 55, 67, 69, 76–79, 82–85, 129, 130, 157, 175, 194, 197–199, 204, 217,

C

Canonical criticism, 67.
Cassian, John, 64.
Chalcedon, Council of, 27,
Church Tradition, xi, xii, xiv, xvi, xx, xxiii, xxv, 3, 10, 15, 20, 23, 24, 26, 29, 30, 34, 35, 36, 38, 49, 53, 55, 60, 62, 63, 66, 68, 70, 74, 96, 179, 185, 186, 187, 194, 199, 203, 205, 210, 212, 217.
Chrysostom, John, 42, 43, 45, 84.
Conciliar Church/documents, xii, 1, 2, 3, 11, 15, 16, 18, 19, 69, 70, 93, 113, 118, 194.
Context, xii, xiv, xvii, xx, 2, 18, 20, 26, 28, 30, 31, 71, 72, 77, 79, 84, 104, 111, 116, 139, 194, 200, 204, 205.
Creeds, Christian, 33.
Cultural criticism, 139, 140.

D

Dionysius, 9, 49.
Divino Afflante Spiritu (DAS), 20, 22, 23, 25, 26, 33, 39, 72, 116, 119, 131, 135, 194, 196, 198.
Divine economy, 4.
Divine revelation, vii, ix, xi, 2, 5, 6, 8, 9, 11, 13, 14, 16, 18, 19, 28, 29, 30, 31, 41, 61, 69, 70, 89, 91, 135, 179, 181, 188, 198.

E

Eucharist/Eucharistic, 8, 12, 20, 45, 50, 92, 99, 100, 195, 212.
Economy of revelation, 5, 6, 8.
Economy of salvation, xviii.
Ecumenism, 89, 203, 217, 218.

F

Feminist criticism, 223.
Form criticism, xvii, xix, 20, 26, 93, 97, 113, 114, 136, 219.

H

Historical criticism, 65, 67, 136, 138, 147, 179, 209, 211, 212, 214, 216,

I

Instruction Concerning the Historical Truth of the Gospels, 119, 120, 131, 135, 136, 195.
Interpretation, viii, xi, xii, xvi, xx, xxiii, xxv, 1, 2, 20, 22, 24–31, 34, 36, 37, 38, 42, 47, 55–58, 62, 63–68, 70–74, 76–78, 80, 81, 85, 91,

92, 97, 105, 106, 117, 123, 126, 127, 128, 131, 135–147, 154, 157, 159, 161, 176, 179, 182, 183, 186–189, 191, 196–200, 202–204, 208, 209, 212, 214, 215, 217, 218, 219, 224.
Irenaeus, of Lyon, xiv, 44, 46, 47, 48, 91, 150, 151.
Islam, vii, 42.

J
John XXIII, Pope, 18, 61.
John Paul II, Pope, xxii, 4, 8, 16, 25, 78, 111, 131, 142, 174, 175, 196.
Judaism, vii, 34, 42, 103, 196, 203.

K
Koran, vii.

L
Lagrange, Marie-Joseph, OP, 21, 80, 115, 119, 129, 193, 215.
Literary criticism, 26, 33, 138, 139, 180, 202.

M
Magisterium, the, xv, 4, 15, 24, 25, 33, 34, 61, 62, 63, 77, 180, 187, 203, 223, 224.

N
Narrative criticism, 65.
Newman, John Henry, 209, 211, 212, 214, 216, 218.
Nicaea, Council of 27, 49.
Nyssa, Gregory, 48, 64.

P
Paschal mystery, 4, 5, 9, 120.
Patristic period, xiv, xv, 25, 26, 27, 34, 41–54, 64, 66, 80, 92, 161, 201, 224.
Paul VI, Pope, 17, 19, 61, 88, 100, 128, 129, 155, 171, 196,
Paul, the Apostle, xiv, 4, 14, 27, 29, 32, 38, 45, 46, 52, 58, 64, 82, 102, 168, 173, 174, 175, 182.
Pius X, Pope, 15, 21, 113, 119, 155,
Pius XI, Pope, 115, 119, 166,
Pius XII, Pope, viii, 20, 22, 23, 65, 72, 116, 119, 135, 166, 174, 188, 194, 198,
Pre-conciliar period, 25.
Proof text, 24.
Providentissumus Deus (PD), 20, 21, 22, 23, 24, 33, 116, 131.
Pontifical Biblical Commission, the, xii, xx, xxiv, 1, 21, 25, 33, 67, 72, 78, 81, 83, 85, 115, 116, 118, 119, 128, 130, 132, 135, 136, 141, 142, 179, 194, 195, 196, 198, 202, 216, 219, 222.
Pontifical Biblical Institute, 21, 22, 39, 115.
Post-conciliar Church, xi, 11, 23, 76, 136, 164.
Post-modern criticism, 30

R
Ratzinger, Joseph, xvi, 6, 14, 19, 25, 36, 37, 38, 41, 42, 69, 70, 77, 119, 181, 196, 198, 224.
Redaction criticism, 20
Reformers, xv, xx, 27, 59, 60, 64.
Revelation, vii, viii, ix, xii, xiii, xv, xxiv, 2–18, 19, 24, 28–31, 34, 38, 39, 41, 43, 54, 55, 57, 60, 61, 63, 84, 85, 103, 110, 118, 124, 168, 181, 186, 194, 198, 199, 203, 218, 220.

S

Sacred action, 8
Sacred authors, 21, 71, 72, 73, 79, 93, 96, 169, 211, 217.
Sacred books, xxi.
Sacred Page, xiii, 19, 23, 25, 31, 36, 37, 39.
Sacred Scriptures, xvi, xxi, xxi, 10, 11, 21, 32, 36, 41, 61, 77, 78, 80, 83, 84, 95, 96, 117, 136, 149, 151, 196, 217, 218, 220.
Sacred Text, 26, 74, 124, 125, 162, 169, 179, 196, 200, 204, 205, 211, 220, 224.
Sacred tradition, 58, 61, 220.
Scripture and Tradition, vii, xiii, xiv, xv, xvi, xxiii, xxv, 20, 24, 35, 37, 41, 42, 55, 58, 59–64, 66, 89, 95, 194, 218, 221.
Self revelation, xii, xxiv, 2, 3, 5, 6, 8, 9, 11, 12, 14, 15, 16, 17, 18, 58, 61.
Sola Scriptura, xiv, xv, xx, 42, 60, 89,
Source criticism, 20

T

Text tradition, 154.
Textual criticism, 20, 156.
The Interpretation of the Bible in the Church, 25, 30, 33, 128, 131, 179, 196, 202, 216, 222.
Trent, Council of, xv, 42, 50, 58, 60, 88, 89, 95, 100, 118, 159, 160.

V

Verbum Domini (VD), 77, 78, 80–85, 197–203, 216, 217.

W

Word, of God, ix, xv, xvi, xviii, 2, 7, 12, 19–25, 32, 37, 46, 63, 74, 77, 78, 82, 83, 88, 93, 95, 99, 100, 102, 139, 149, 150, 152, 158, 163, 165, 166, 170, 173, 177, 194, 199, 203, 216, 218, 220.

Lightning Source UK Ltd.
Milton Keynes UK
UKHW012009150822
407336UK00001B/317